WILDLY STROLLING ALONG

BEN & LARRY POUNDS

WILDLY STROLLING ALONG

Father-Son Nature Adventures on Tennessee's Cumberland Trail

BEN & LARRY POUNDS

ORIGINAL CARTOONS BY BEN POUNDS

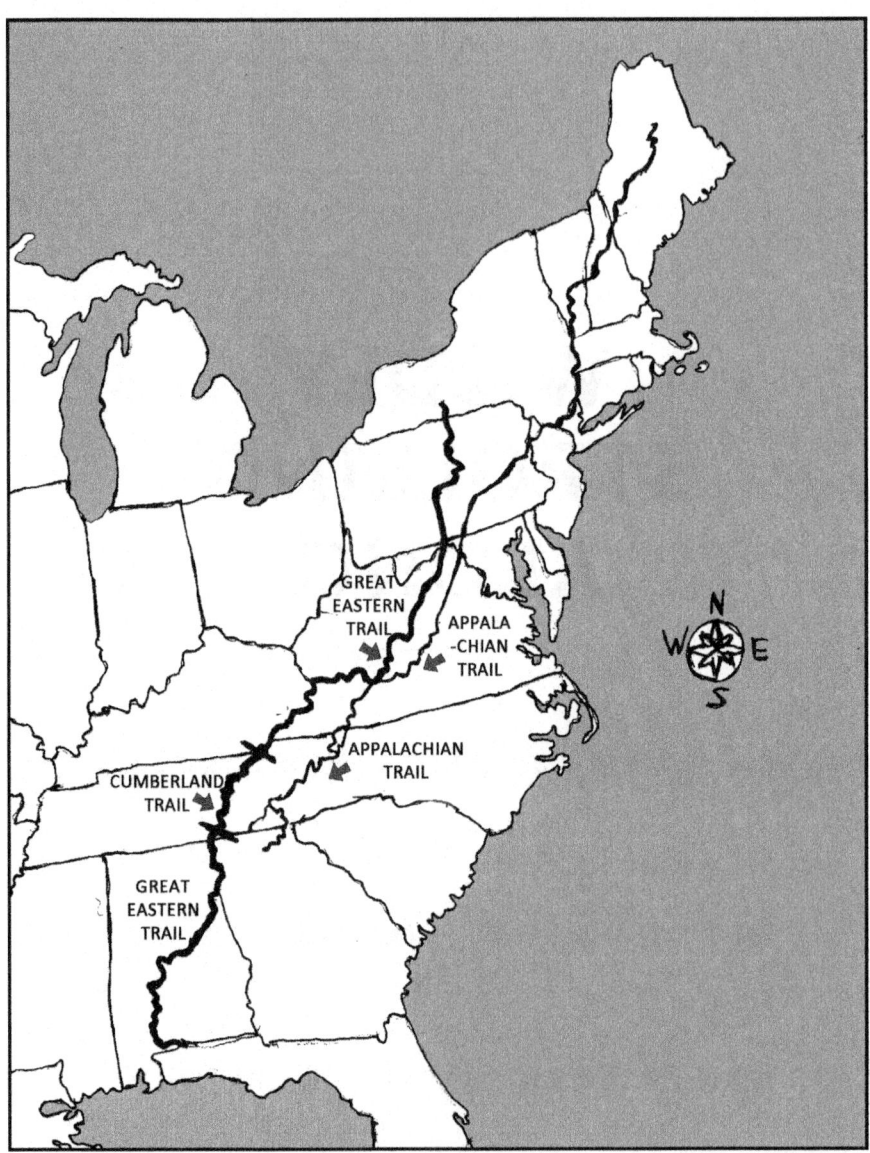

Map 1: The thin line is the Appalachian Trail (AT), and the thicker one the Great Eastern Trail (GET), with Cumberland Trail (CT) in brackets. This map is based on a 2013 map by the Great Eastern Trail Association, visible at greateasterntrail.net. Much of the GET route displayed here is speculative rather than complete.

WILDLY STROLLING ALONG

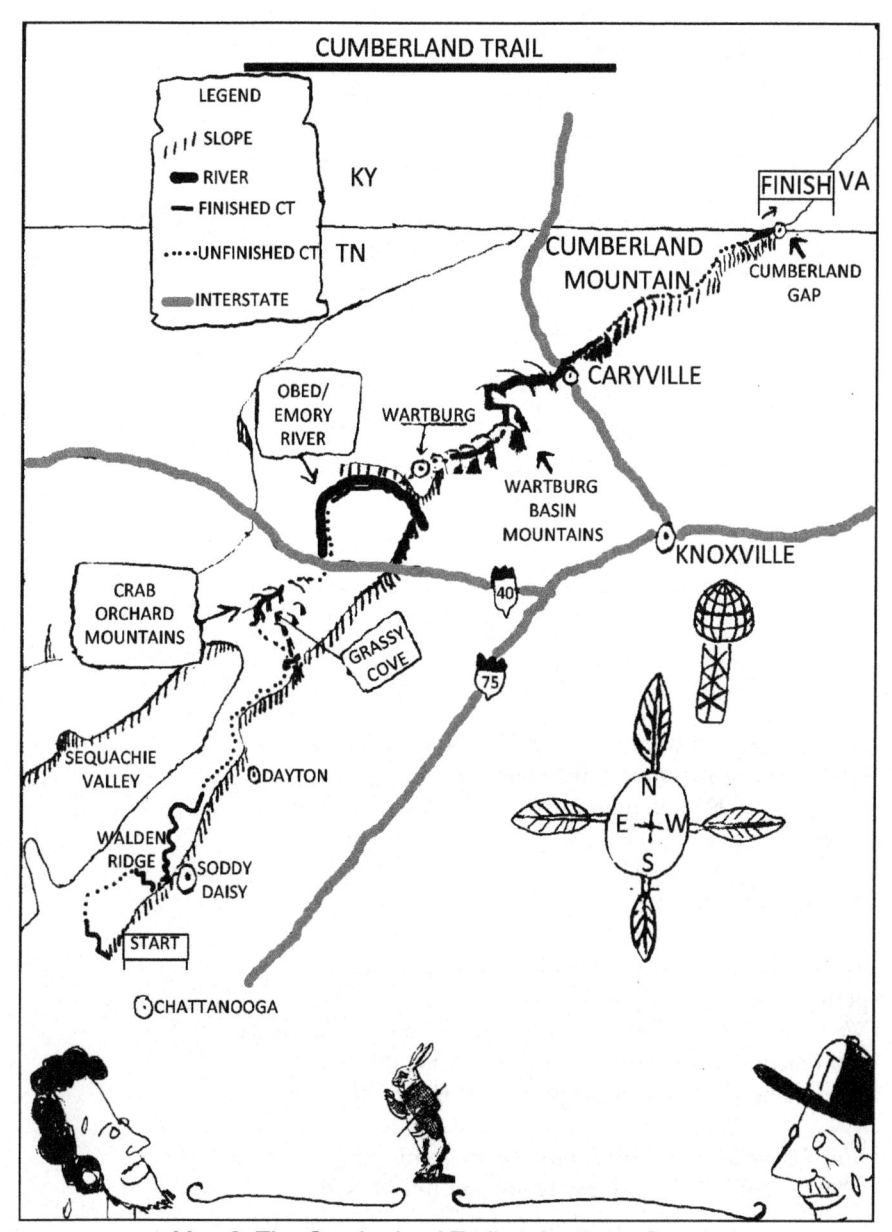

Map 2: The Cumberland Trail at the time of our trek.

BEN & LARRY POUNDS

Wildly Strolling Along: Father-Son Nature Adventures on Tennessee's Cumberland Trail.
©Copyright 2015 Ben Pounds and Zombie Salamander Press.

All Rights Reserved.
No part of this book may be reproduced, scanned, or distributed in any printed or electronic form without permission.
We have tried to recreate some conversations and incidents from memory. Some names and identifying details have been changed to protect the privacy of individuals.

Blue Highways: A Journey into America copyright October 1999 by William Least-Heat Moon and Bill McKibben.

Pilgrim at Tinker Creek copyright Harper Collins 2013.

Although we have tried to ensure that this book is accurate, we welcome corrections. Please send them to incumberland@AOL.com.

WILDLY STROLLING ALONG

Dedicated to all the people who have made the Cumberland Trail a reality. May many enjoy it in years to come.

ACKNOWLEDGMENTS

Wow, we got lots of help! In particular, many people read parts of various drafts. Since we didn't keep records of all this, we apologize to anyone left out here. In particular we would like to thank John Byrd, Paul Durr, Bob Fulcher, Cindy Jones, Catherine Reid, Judith Roitman, Elizabeth Roitman and Daniel Stevenson, for their comments and corrections. Russ Manning deserves particular attention as someone who not only reviewed the book but also by way of his earlier book, *The Historic Cumberland Plateau*, gave us much of the historical information we've used.

We give special thanks to the writing workshop groups led by Pam Strickland and Don Williams whose members gave helpful feedback on drafts of this book.

We would also like to mention Yvonne Rogers, Ben Pounds's lover who tirelessly edited and gave suggestions for much of what follows. Her father Lewis Rogers helped us with the design and the conversion to an ebook. All errors here are our own and not those of the abovementioned people.

PROLOGUE: GIVE ME SHELTER

They knew it was time for a hunting trip. Cold weather and hunger would come soon. From the valley they climbed up a path. At the base of a three-story house-sized sandstone cliff, they found a familiar cleft that had been used by many generations of their ancestors. They would return, after the day's hunting, to this natural rock overhang that blocked the chilling wind and snow. For the night it was their house, a rockhouse, as we call it today.

If we go back 12,000 years they might have hurled spears at mastodons. Into historic times, elk and bison might have been their game, and they would have used bows and arrows.

Before the Native Americans arrived, plants had adapted to rockhouses. A few wind-blown seeds landed in them. Some of these seeds survived the relative darkness and rocky soil.

The hunters would have noticed these seeds' descendants. One such plant is the Cumberland Sandwort with its delicate white flowers. As the hunters huddled for warmth by firelight on the rockhouse's sandy floor, they might have noticed the filmy fern, a plant that grows far back in the dark rockhouse recesses. It gets little light for photosynthesis, but the recesses protect it from freezing.

Many years after the hunters, moonshiners would use the rockhouse. The ruins of their distilling operations mixed with the artifacts of the hunting party in the sand.

Among the many people who have passed through the rock houses and rock splendor of the Cumberland Plateau, we can count ourselves, a team of father and son. We did not hunt for meat. We hunted for rare plants, salamanders, traces of history and more. We hunted for kinship with each other and the greater world.

So come with us to the Cumberland Plateau along the Cumberland Trail. Join our nature hunt. Listen for a roaring waterfall. Take your place among those who have found refuge under the roofs of rockhouses.

CONTENTS
→ ←

1.	**Rattlesnake!**	
	Prentice Cooper State Forest	1
2.	**Non-football Rivalries**	
	(Real or Perhaps Only Apparent)	11
3.	**In Which the Ticks Laugh at Us**	
	Snoop Rock Loop	15

Interlude 1: Walden Ridge   29

4.	**We're Off!**	
	Prentice Cooper State Forest	32
5.	**Rain, Trial on the Trail**	
	North Chickamauga Creek	46
6.	**Get Soddy!**	
	Explorations in Soddy-Daisy	54
7.	**Noticers**	
	Little Soddy Creek	62
8.	**Be a Frog**	
	Big Soddy and Board Camp Creeks	72
9.	**To Get Wet or not to Get Wet**	
	Possum Creek	88
10.	**Ben's Bridge (Well, Ben Helped)**	
	Rock Creek	95
11.	**Won't you Take me to Monkey Town?**	
	Dayton, Our First Stay-town	103
12.	**Those Crazy Americans**	
	Laurel-Snow State Natural Area	112

Interlude 2: Crab Orchard Mountains   124

13.	**Wildly Strolling Along**	
	Brady Mountain	128
14.	**A Place for Everything**	
	Black Mountain	136
15.	**In which Ben Ignores an Aerial Yellowjacket Nest**	
	Piney River	143

Interlude 3: Obed River   153

16.	**Finding Nemo Bridge**	
	Lower Obed River	154
17.	**Notice Or Else!**	
	Daddy's Creek and Obed River	166
18.	**A Town in Spite of Everything**	
	Wartburg, Trail Town	173

Interlude 4: Wartburg Basin Mountains   179

19.	**Log and Coal Country**	
	Lawson Mtn. Part 1	180
20.	**Land of Gnats and Rattlesnakes**	
	Lawson Mountain Part 2	183
21.	**Desire**	
	Arch Mountain	190
22.	**Pigs and Blood Blisters**	
	Frozen Head	196
23.	**Return to Devil's Breakfast Table**	
	Daddy's Creek Area	204
24.	**Here there be Dragons and Ghosts**	
	Caryville, Stay Town	211
25.	**Creation**	
	Big Bruce Ridge Eastward	216

Interlude 5: Cumberland Mountain   225

26.	**Hiking with the Devil**	
	Cumberland Mountain East of I-75	227
27.	**Hot Tang**	
	Cumberland Mountain Part 2	236
28.	**Names for Everything**	
	Anderson and Cross Mountain Section	245
29.	**Historic Cumberland Gap**	
	Cumberland Gap, Stay Town	259
30.	**The Wild Frontier**	
	Final Hike in Cumberland Mountain Region	265

Epilogue *,!   274

RATTLESNAKE!

→ 1 ←

Prentice Cooper State Forest (Tues. March 20)
Rehearsal Hike: Tower Drive to Indian Rock House

BEN: This is the story of tectonic plates shifting, miners mining, salamanders crawling and plants dropping seeds. It's also the story of two guys looking for a new adventure. One of them is an older, wrinkled man who has seen much of the world but is eager to explore the details of it. The other, his son, is a young man who wants to find his place in the world's vastness.

Leaves thrashed. Something darted across our path, although it matched the leaves too closely for me to figure out what it was. Then, the shape coiled and rattled, revealing itself to be a snake. The timber rattler moved nothing but its tail, making a fire-alarm buzz. I jumped back. I did not want to be stranded here, swollen and yelping in pain, looking at the trail through a haze. Perhaps a snake bite would make me too weak to move. Without a way back to the truck, there was a slight chance I could have died.

The snake's dull-colored scales had disguised it, making it look like just another part of the forest floor until it moved. Camouflage helps rattlers hide from predators and ambush small critters unaware. Many hikers pass timber rattlers without noticing them.

Maybe the snake had felt vibrations from my boots or Dad's trail-running sneakers as they hit the ground. Maybe it had detected us with its infrared-sensing pits on either side of its head. Now though, it hid its face while shaking its tail. The loud but shy snake was like a rebellious teenage boy, booming loud music from speakers in his room and shouting "Leave me alone!"

Some people ignore the rattling's message. For them, timber rattlers have two ready answers: hollow fangs with venom. Sometimes a rattler injects no venom at all. Other times, rattlers use painful amounts.

We were in Prentice Cooper State Forest, on a side branch of Tennessee's Cumberland Trail (CT). It was a practice hike on which we could test ourselves, our bright-orange big-pocketed vests and our voice recorders, each about the size of a Swiss Army knife.

Two months later in May we would start hiking the main Cumberland Trail which runs along Tennessee's Cumberland Plateau from Chattanooga to the Kentucky-Virginia border. Several sections of the trail are incomplete.

Dad, an environmental consultant, had offered to do a rare plant survey of the Cumberland Trail. Searching for plants was his passion, not just his job. He wanted to inspect the whole trail, from the lowest gorges and crashing rivers to the highest mountains and cliffs, before old age could stop him.

He wanted to encourage others to explore the CT too. So he asked me to come along and write about it. He had been planning a book about the CT since at least when I was in high school and brought it up whenever we hiked on the pieces that were open back then.

"I'd love for you to help me," he would often say as we climbed back in his truck. Then as now, he would never go outside without a baseball or knit cap to cover his bald head.

How not to do camouflage. Idea by Larry, drawn by Ben.
Song lyrics adapted from Disney's Winnie the Pooh movie.

By the time I graduated college with a creative writing degree, hiking in Tennessee didn't excite me. Compared to the rest of the world's extremes, my home state seemed like a childhood sandbox: full of memories but limited. I wanted to leave my parents and explore exotic places. I could go anywhere from Italy to Colombia, just so long as I traveled before growing old or becoming paralyzed in a job that would limit me. I rarely make up my mind. My mind prefers to make things up as it goes along.

In my time after college, I traveled as far away as Columbia, South Carolina, not Colombia in South America, before settling in Asheville, picking grapes for the Biltmore Estate. Then, the grape season ended, forcing me back in with my parents who now lived in Loudon, Tennessee. Independence from my parents would have to wait.

I could still explore. The Cumberland Trail offered a perfect chance. It ran through remote country into strange and wonderful places. I might have seen East Tennessee before, but I hadn't seen all of it. I could dig deeper into the sandbox, discover its every grain, watch ants crawl through it and puzzle about the children who had dug into the sand and made it their own.

The snake stayed coiled. Its buzzing became a constant background noise like a refrigerator. Somehow being in front of the snake for as long as we had made me less scared of it. I pointed my camera at the snake. The video looked terrible. The tail hardly looked like it was moving. I had to inch closer to get the head in the video.

"Stay back!" Dad shouted, frightened. It was the first time he'd yelled at me since my toddler days, back when his head still had stringy hair, at least in the back. Generally, he never raised his voice.

I stepped away, scared of the snake and embarrassed about forgetting to be scared. Following Dad's orders felt like admitting that I could not take care of myself, even if those orders involved obvious things like avoiding a bite from a venomous pit-viper.

Why's it Called Cumberland?

BEN: English explorer Thomas Walker named the Cumberland River after William "The Butcher" Augustus, Duke of Cumberland. As noted by Russ Manning in his book *The Historic Cumberland Plateau,* William Augustus was infamous for his lack of mercy toward Scottish rebels. *BBC Historical Magazine* put him on their "Ten Worst Britons" list. Still, the name has stuck to the Plateau. The trail was named after the Plateau which was named after the river.

I wondered if my 67-year-old father and my 24-year-old self could spend 24 hours a day for a whole month working as a team to hike the CT. After moving back, I'd often avoided him except during dinner. I loved Dad but wanted to be free of him.

The snake slithered off the trail. Dad scanned the ground and stopped to record the Latin names of violets, blooming sedges and honeysuckles into his voice recorder. It was Mid-March, hardly time for rattlesnakes. Tennessee's timber rattlers spend the winter curled up in cozy dens under rocks. In the past they came out in April. This year's March was hotter than usual though. If it was hot enough for me to feel like chugging down most of the water in my bottle, it was hot enough for a rattlesnake to come out of its den.

Now that Earth is warming, other animals are changing habits too. For example, fire ants and armadillos have spread north. No one would make a disaster movie about these nuisances though. *The Day After Tomorrow: Month-Earlier Rattlesnakes* would never get produced. "Giant wave drowns city" sells more tickets than "more ants."

Indian Rockhouse was roomier and taller than other rockhouses we had passed that day. Charred logs marked a camping spot underneath it.

Below the overhanging roof of rock, the soil was sandy. The sand was once part of the rock before crumbling. The rock was once sand until it got pressed and hardened. The cycle continues today. Rock, solid and seemingly unchanging, becomes sand, which flows and blows easily. Things that look stable, like a cliff or a travel plan, can become fleeting. Things that look fleeting, like sand or a journey full of setbacks, can become stable.

We had come to the Indian Rockhouse side trail as a rehearsal to test ourselves and our equipment. I knew about rehearsals from acting in plays. Some rehearsals showed the production to be a rock, stable and needing little change. Others revealed it to be sand, hard to pull together. Today's rehearsal had been sandy. The rattlesnake showed that anything could happen to us, even on day hikes.

We already knew that we loved hiking and loved the CT before we started our month of walking along its open sections. Still, we expected a physical and mental challenge that would mix our love with harsher emotions. We did not know if heat, snakes, ticks, long uphill hikes or Dad's collapsible left knee would stop us.

Something rustled again. It was a branch that moved when I stepped on it. After experiencing one rattlesnake, though, I imagined rattlers everywhere.

We took a different route to get back to our truck than the way we had come. Dad was curious about it.

"I always prefer making a loop," he said. "It helps me see more places." I agreed.

We walked down a dirt ATV road. A kiosk held a map behind a plastic cover. "It looks like we're going twice the distance we would have gone if we'd gone back the way we came," said Dad. Our feet felt sore.

I speed-walked to beat the darkness. Dad jogged behind me.

"Just a light jog to change the pace," he said. It seemed crazy that jogging would be less tiring than walking, but I could try. I jogged. My feet and legs did not feel as tired now. I was working different muscles. So, I jogged, speed-walked and slow-walked down.

Night came as we walked on a paved road. I thought of the cold cans of Fresca back at the truck.

"You know how children are always asking, '"Are we almost there?"' said Dad with a chuckle.

I was twenty-four, hardly the age to be asking, "Are we almost there?" Also, Dad had already said it. So instead I said, "Okay, I think we're close now," even though I knew we were not close. I chanted, "We're close! We're close!" over and over to make myself believe it. It was probably more annoying than asking "Are we almost there?" but Dad said nothing.

Ferns and Fern Allies

LARRY: Ferns and fern allies lack flowers. Many of them don't look like ferns, but they all have spores for reproduction.

Learning ferns and their allies makes a good starting place for learning to identify our wild plants. This is because they are a distinctive group, and there are only 94 species, which divide easily into dissimilar smaller groups in Tennessee. If you get a chance, go to one of Dr. Pat Cox's talks on Tennessee ferns. She shows pictures of all 94 in her presentations. Fern allies are species that are not ferns but reproduce in a manner similar to ferns (see Chapter 5). Beginners can reduce the possible choices for the ferns they find to a few species by looking at drawings or photos. Beyond that, they will need to learn basic botany skills by using keys or descriptions found in books. A lightweight fern guide with drawings, such as *A Field Guide to the Ferns* in the Peterson Field Guide Series, is helpful. Our website has a list of ferns and fern allies that we saw while hiking the CT.

At last we found Dad's red Toyota Tacoma. We arrived at our home in Loudon after ten, a bedtime that Dad had kept strictly in the past. I usually stayed up later but was tired enough to plop into bed after reaching home. It was not the way that we had planned for the day to go.

We would be hiking about 200 miles with about 180 actually the main CT, averaging eight miles a day to experience the entire existing portion of the main trail. Seven of our 25 days of hiking would be backpacking days. Neither of us had done much backpacking, so we did not know how it would feel. After a single day's hike, our sore feet told us that we weren't physically ready to go that far yet, even without backpacks. It had been a sand kind of day.

To me, backpacking seemed like the only proper way to experience a backpacking trail. Dad, however, worried that the weight would distract from nature observations. Also, he had gotten a kidney stone out of a previous backpacking trip on the Cumberland Trail. On that trip, we hiked around lost and thirsty while searching for a shelter.

LARRY: Actually there was very little time spent lost off the trail, but we were uncertain of the route at times as the trail was poorly maintained. Our big problem was carrying too little water.

BEN: Dad eagerly sat down at his computer desk, near the microscope, specimens and plant books in his home office. He typed a chart of hikes, miles, stopping points, ending points and places to sleep. A few pieces were backpacking. Backpacking would provide a chance for more detailed exploration because we could set up camp and wander. Most of the time, we

Herps

BEN: You can find my list of herps on www.benandlarryincumberland.com as well. My lists are less authoritative than Dad's lists of plants. *Herpeton* is a Greek word meaning "creeping thing." It was applied to reptiles and amphibians both. Later scientists separated them into reptiles, scaled creatures that hatched from shelled-eggs, and amphibians, smooth animals that hatched from soft jelly-like clusters of eggs. People who study reptiles, amphibians or both are still called *herpetologists*. It's an old fashioned distinction, given that reptiles may be related more closely to birds. "Herps" is our informal word for both reptiles and amphibians.

would be car shuttling between trailheads and staying in motels. In some cases, he even plotted for us to go down one side of a hill on one day and down the other side of the hill on the next day. This strategy reduced the amount of hill climbing. Staying in towns and driving to trailheads would allow us to take our time without worrying about the weight on our backs.

He handed me the schedule. I did not have much to say about it. The chart looked like names, numbers and safety precautions, not my idea of an adventure. Behind those names and numbers though was Dad's yearning to inspect and dissect what the trail had to offer. He wanted to make sure he had time to climb down into ditches, up steep hillsides and through thick muddy swamps, hoping to find endangered plants. He still saw it as a long-distance hike but with plenty of time to explore. I would be following him through all of it.

I showed Dad my description of a section we hiked before our month-long CT trek. In a vain attempt to sound cool and independent, I had written it as though he hadn't been on the hike. "Maybe you should tell what it's like hiking with your dad," he said. Exactly what I had tried not to do. I decided to go along with his advice, anyway.

Young timber rattlers stay near their mothers for days. Some people, like my father, see that time as a period of parental care, as he says in Chapter 26 of this book. Others, like my high school mentor John Byrd, mentioned here in Chapter 10, disagree. Regardless, the mother snake keeps the young snakes protected.

My hiking on the Cumberland Trail and wandering through towns nearby taught me many eclectic facts which appear on these pages, from the sex life of ferns to the fate of a burning fireworks store to scenes from my father's memory. Everywhere, I saw stories of living organisms, either consciously or unconsciously struggling to find niches. They were stories of evolution. As a young man struggling to find his own trail to follow, these stories began to fascinate me.

Yet there's more to evolution than struggling for oneself. Long ago, we evolved the ability to love, an ability which has served us well. This book is the story of Dad's love for plants, scientific investigation and hiking. It's the story of my growing love for historic small-towns, crawling salamanders and grand views. It's also the story of my sometimes-strained but ultimately powerful love for my father and his for me.

We are father and son, boomer and millennial, scientist and writer. This is the Cumberland Trail's story. It's also ours.

The BLTs are exaggerated versions of us that will pop in from time to time.

Sources and Suggested Reading

Rattlesnakes:
Barish, Robert A. *Snake Bites.* February 2009. http://www.merckmanuals.com/home/injuries_and_poisoning/bites_and_stings/snake_bites.html (accessed April 19, 2013).

Behler, John L., and F. Wayne King. *The Audubon Society Field Guide to North American Reptiles and Amphibians.* New York: Chanticleer Press Inc., 1979.

Glenn, J.L., R.C. Straight, and T.B. Wolt. "Regional variation in the presence of canebrake toxin in Crotalus horridus venom." *Comparative Biochemistry and Physiology Part C: Pharmacology, Toxicology and Endocrinology 107*, no. 3 (March 1994): 337-346.

Minnesota Department of Natural Resources. "Snakes." *Minnesota Department of Natural Resources.* 2013. http://www.dnr.state.mn.us/livingwith_wildlife/snakes/index.html (accessed April 3, 2013).

New York State Department of Environmental Conservation. *Timber Rattlesnake Fact Sheet.* 2013. http://www.dec.ny.gov/animals/7147.html (accessed April 3, 2013).

Saint Louis Zoo. *Timber Rattlesnake.* 2013. http://www.stlzoo.org/animals/abouttheanimals/reptiles/snakes/timberrattlesnake/. (accessed April 3, 2013).

Trott, John. *The Virginia Naturalist.* Kerney: Morris Publishing, 2006.

Global Warming and Ants:
Morrison, Loyd W., Michael D. Korzukhin, and Sanford D. Porter. "Predicted range expansion of the invasive fire ant Solenopsis invicta, in the eastern United States based on the VEMAP Global Warming Scenario." United States Department of Agriculture Agricultural Research Service. 2005. http://afrsweb.usda.gov/sp2UserFiles/Place/66151015/publications/Morrison_et_al-2005(M-3988).pdf (accessed April 3, 2013).

The CT:
Brill, David. *Cumberland Odyssey: A Journey in Pictures and Words along Tennessee's Cumberland Trail and Plateau.* Johnson City, Tennessee: Mountain Trail Press, 2010.

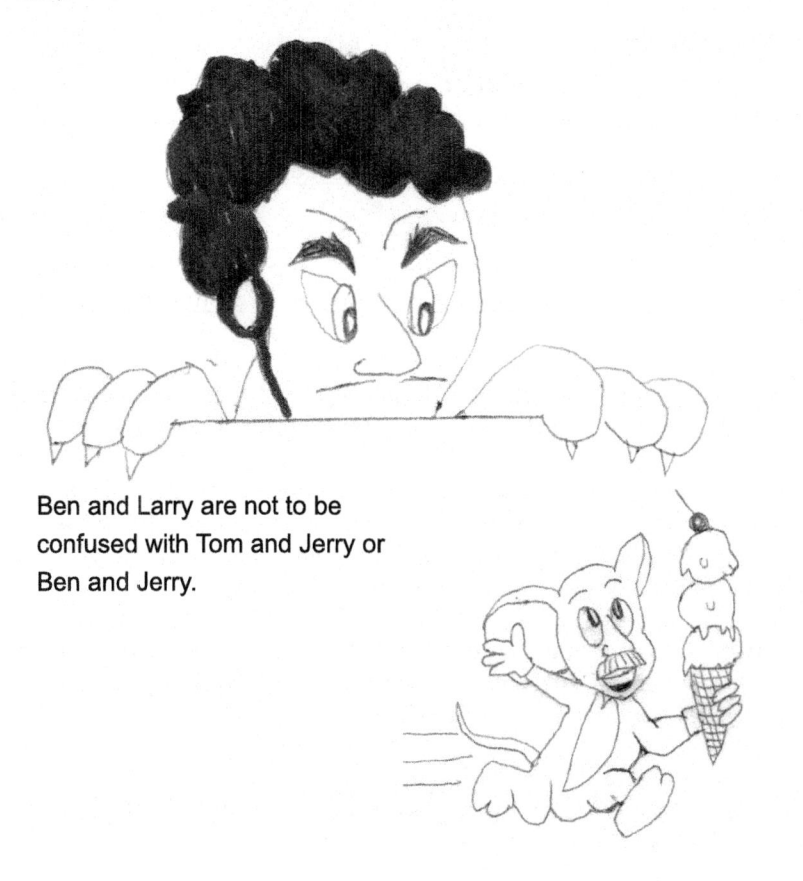

Ben and Larry are not to be confused with Tom and Jerry or Ben and Jerry.

Cumberland Trail Conference. *CTC's Guide to Hiking the Justin P. Wilson Cumberland Trail with Maps/Guides.* www.cumberlandtrail.org. (accessed July 19, 2012).

Manning, Russ. *The Historic Cumberland Plateau: An Explorer's Guide*, Second Edition. Knoxville: University of Tennessee Press, 1999.

Rock Houses and Early Hunter-Gatherers:
Benton, Ben. "Cumberland Plateau Art Reveal's Native Peoples' Lives." *Chattanooga Times Free Press.* July 15, 2013. Accessed September 24, 2013. http://www.timesfreepress.com/news/2013/jul/15/historys-rock-stars/

Tennessee State Museum. "First Tennesseans: What Happened to the Mastodons?" *Tennessee 4 Me.* http://www.tn4me.org/article.cfm/era_id/1/major_id/28/minor_id/86/a_id/285. (accessed September 24, 2014).

Herps (Particularly the Term):
Goin, Coleman J. and Goin, Olive B. *Introduction to Herpetology.* San Francisco: W. H. Fremand and Company, 1962.

Zug, George R. *Herpetology: An Introduction to Biology of Amphibians and Reptiles.* San Diego: Academic Press, 1993

NON-FOOTBALL RIVALRIES: REAL OR PERHAPS ONLY APPARENT

→ 2 ←

LARRY: I grew up in the big city of Cincinnati, but some of the steep hills around my home were still wild during my childhood. So, I had a large forest to explore. At that time, my favorite wild critters were salamanders and mammals.

The wilder regions of Appalachia, including the Cumberland Plateau, were about 100 miles away. By my early twenties, I made regular visits there to hike and study.

I tried a brief experiment in living off the land in Red River Gorge on the Cumberland Plateau in Kentucky. My preparation had included study of edible plants and, for safety, poisonous ones as well. Wild plants in general and rare ones in particular began to fascinate me. This fascination led me to a doctorate in plant ecology and work as a freelance field botanist centered in East Tennessee.

Often for my work, I explore project sites to check for plants on lists for protection. This is often a legal requirement for my employer. For this work I need to be correct with the rare plant identifications, and I seldom have enough time to be sure I haven't overlooked a rare plant. Few things could be more miserable than a hopeless search for rare plants in a weedy briar patch full of ticks and with the temperature over 90. Yet few things could be better than going on a treasure hunt for plants that I find fascinating in the outdoors that I love.

As I have grown older, I get less paying work, especially in the winter. I found myself sucked into an addiction to Sudoku and later Kenken puzzles. I still need new challenges. I wanted to explore and encourage others to do the same. The Appalachian Trail was something of a cliché, not to mention that it would be a struggle for someone like me with a bad knee. However, hiking the existing parts of the Cumberland Trail and writing a book about it seemed both doable and unique. My son Ben, a young creative writing major, could help with it, especially the writing part. The sooner we got working on the project the better. I might not be in hiking condition by the time the trail was finished.

Some potential problems:

A. I have mixed feelings about backpacking, preferring the freedom you have without the weight.

B. I don't sleep well on the ground.

C. My left knee gets tired and tries to give way. I haven't let it yet, but 180 miles may give it a good shot of coming to the ground.

BUT I STILL THINK I CAN MAKE IT. I REALLY WANT TO.

List of potential problems by Larry, dramatized here by Larry Toon.

➔Cumberland Plateau vs. Blue Ridge←

Most East Tennesseans live in the lower country called the Ridge and Valley. This area includes Knoxville and Chattanooga. Many people in the Ridge and Valley enjoy leaving it for recreation in the wilds. They either go east into the Blue Ridge, which includes the Great Smoky Mountains National Park or, less often, west to the underdog Cumberland Plateau. The choice between the two is one of Tennessee's great non-football rivalries. We root for the underdog but love both wild areas.

The Cumberland Plateau can compete on parks. It has more, though smaller, National Parks (Obed Scenic River, Big South Fork, Cumberland Gap and Signal Mountain), some exceptional state parks (Frozen Head, Pickett and Fall Creek Falls) and several state natural areas. The Cumberland Trail State

Park itself is a uniquely linear state park, long and skinny, with a few bulges.

The Cumberland Plateau is a place of rock arches, rockhouses, deep gorges, cliff-top overlooks and high waterfalls. This rock splendor is on display as you hike the Cumberland Trail (CT) along the Plateau's eastern side.

A wide variety of plants and animals live on the Plateau. The biodiversity of the Plateau rivals the famous biodiversity of the Blue Ridge. Here you will read particularly about the array of flowering plants and the crawling, slithering or hopping "herps" i.e. reptiles and amphibians.

→CT vs. AT←

The Appalachian Trail, or AT, is America's most famous long-distance trail. We hope the CT will one day rival its fame in Tennessee.

The CT is a work in progress, still needing many hard-working volunteers. It has gaps where the trail has not yet been built. The completion date has recently been moved up to 2018. The CT will form the Tennessee part of the Great Eastern Trail which will parallel the AT and run from Alabama to New York.

→CTC Maps vs. Our Maps←

We are not the first people to write about the Cumberland Trail or make maps of it. The Cumberland Trail Conference (CTC) has a great website (www.cumberlandtrail.org) with lovely trail maps and accurate trail descriptions. Yet there is no real rivalry, as we set out to put our book in a different niche. Our maps are for fun and to illustrate the book. The CTC's maps are more precise than ours and are a big help for hike planning. Eventually, the CTC will publish a trail guide you can tote. We encourage you to buy it when available. This book is not a trail guide. It spotlights natural history and memoir.

Physiographic Provinces

LARRY: The Cumberland Plateau, the Ridge and Valley and the Blue Ridge are examples of physiographic provinces. These are areas of similar land surfaces and outcropping rock layers which provide various habitats for life. People use these provinces as a guide for which plants and animals they are likely to find. The CT runs almost entirely on the Cumberland Plateau Physiographic Province.

Speaking of maps, check out Map 2: Cumberland Trail, at the beginning of this book to get an overview of the trek.

Sources and Suggested Reading

The Cumberland Name:
BBC News. "Worst" Historical Britons List. December 27, 2005. http://news.bbc.co.uk/2/hi/uk_news/4561624.stm (accessed March 29, 2005).

Trevathan, Kim. *Cold hearted River: A Canoe Odyssey Down the Cumberland.* Knoxville: University of Tennessee Press, 2006.

The Cumberland Trail:
Cumberland Trail Conference. *CTC's Guide To Hiking the Justin P. Wilson Cumberland Trail with Maps/Guides.* http://www.cumberlandtrail.org (accessed July 19, 2012).

Other Suggested Books:
Bryson, Bill. *A Walk in the Woods: Rediscovering America on the Appalachian Trail.* New York: Broadway Books, 1998.

IN WHICH THE TICKS LAUGH AT US

→ 3 ←

Our Back Yard (Tuesday and Wednesday, May 1, 2)
Prentice Cooper State Forest (Saturday and Sunday, May 5, 6)
Dress Rehearsal before the Big Trek, Snoop Rock Loop and Other Preparations

LARRY: I trained by strapping on a weighted backpack and walking about two miles in our neighborhood, up to the top of a hill at the end of our street. It felt comfortable, even though backpacking is not usually my thing. Soon, Ben was joining me with his backpack.

BEN: We needed to find backpacking supplies before we left on our rehearsal backpacking trip, which would take us on a side trail to the main CT. At a sporting goods store, we saw bags of freeze-dried food. We could hardly find anything vegetarian. Even the macaroni and cheese had bacon bits.

Dad won't eat any meat besides seafood. He'd raised me to have the same diet as him. During my time in college, though, I'd experimented with gateway meats, like North Carolina style pulled pork. My lack of food inhibitions didn't matter though. I'd still be hiking with Dad. We would have to improvise our own travel meals.

Vegetarian food aside, the store seemed to have everything a hiker could want. We could prepare for every emergency and comfort by stocking up on everything.

[Panel 1: "I'M PREPARED! RATTLESNAKE ANTIVENOM... BUG REPELLENT,"]

[Panel 2: "SHARK REPELLENT"]

[Panel 3: "KRYPTONITE FOR RABID SUPERMEN..."]

You can pack everything...

[Large panel: "Maybe the Kryptonite was a mistake."]

...but then you'll have to carry everything.

Or we could go light, as advised by Pacific Crest hiker and hiking accessory entrepreneur Ray Jardine. Dad checked his book *Trail Life* out of a library. It was full of great advice, and I wanted to follow all of it. Dad had read further into the book than I had, however.

"Ray Jardine is a little crazy," said Dad. "He recommends hunting rattlesnakes for food by throwing rocks at them."

I wouldn't have minded eating rattlesnakes but Dad, being a piso-lacto-ova-vegetarian, did not care to eat them.

> HIKER AND ENTREPENEUR RAY JARDINE WROTE THAT THROWING ROCKS IS A GOOD WAY TO KILL RATTLESNAKES.
>
> DINNER!
>
> UM...SINCE I'M VEGETERIAN...CAN'T YOU FIND A TOFU SNAKE OR SOMETHING?

LARRY: Ben is a kidder. It is *illegal* to harm animals or plants in a Tennessee state park. It is important for all of us to conserve the minerals, artifacts, plants and animals of the Cumberland Trail. I like Jardine's light-weight and sometimes light-expense approach to backpacking, but replacing our clunker backpacks with modern light-weight ones would have been a major expense. Also, with regard to Ray Jardine's advice about rattlesnakes, he includes the disclaimer that he is, "not recommending anything."

BEN: In the year before our trek, I worked at Walmart on the night shift, a job that Dad had persuaded me to keep.

"It may not be your dream job," he had said, "but it'll get you money for now."

We wanted a light tent. None of the tents at Walmart had anything on the label indicating weight. While shoving cereal boxes onto shelves, I remembered the scale in produce. It was hard not to remember it. Months before that night, I'd cut my nose on it while cleaning.

So, the morning after my shift, I went to the sporting goods section, took each tent to the store's produce side and weighed each one on my archnemesis, the banana scale, while workers on the morning crew stared at me. I wrote down each tent's weight, but, as usual, put off making a decision. In the end, we did not have to make up our minds about a lightweight tent. My sister gave us one as a present.

At another outdoor supply store, we saw thin sleeping bag liners, intended for insulating regular sleeping bags.

"We could use these instead of sleeping bags," I said. "They'd be much lighter." Dad agreed. In May and June we did not need to lug around thick sleeping bags designed for chilly nights, or so we thought.

→Dress Rehearsal Before the Big Trek←
Tuesday, Wednesday, May 1, 2

After struggling to understand the setup directions, we pitched our new tent in the back yard. Then, we strapped on our backpacks with our sleeping bags and carried them 50 feet from the house to the tent.

"Is there a reason we're doing this?" I asked Dad.

"Mostly for symbolism," he said, with a smile that turned up his mustache's edges.

We crawled in and sprawled onto our pads to reward ourselves.

"Dad," I asked, "Are you planning on staying in here for the night?"

"No, I have to get a good rest for tomorrow."

I, however, had quit my job at Walmart to prepare and did not need a good rest. Unlike Dad, I loved sleeping on the ground. So, I went back inside, watched an HBO documentary on the Beatles, showered, finished reading *Scott Pilgrim's Precious Little Life*, brushed my teeth and went camping, with a pair of shorts wrapped in a sweaty t-shirt for a pillow. Even without leaving Loudon, sleeping outside and listening to neighborhood dogs, insects and frogs felt better than sleeping inside.

The heat kept me on top of my sleeping bag liner as I sweated my way to sleep. If early May was this warm, June would be an oven.

Later, I woke to find the air cool, slid into my sleeping bag liner and wondered about the Plateau's weather. The liner was enough for now. I slept, dreaming about white-tailed deer having sex in the sleeping bag next to me and a fellow in another sleeping bag saying, "Yeah... that sometimes happens."

→Rehearsal Backpack, Snoop Rock Loop←
Saturday, May 5

One shoulder felt sorer than the other. The pack strap did not seem to fit around my shoulder any other way. So, I wobbled forward.

In front of me were trees and more trees. I did not feel prepared to think or write about the trees, they just were. So instead, I thought about the last time an outdoor experience had inspired me to write.

Days before the hike, I had stretched out on our lawn and stared up at the blue sky, my curly head resting on the grass. Wispy clouds drifted. Birds fluttered and sang. An airplane flew above the birds. My stress faded, leaving me at peace.

Nature is not peaceful. Songbirds' songs are often territorial warnings. No matter how sweetly a bird sings, his message is likely, "Yo! Get off my lawn!" By lying on the ground, I risked being nibbled by fire ants. The people in the airplane sat ready to be somewhere else and probably worried about their own lives. My sense of peace did not come from the world around me being at peace. It came from the universe's vastness. The sky seemed to continue forever. I was small and so were my problems by comparison.

Now, in the woods, trees blocked my view of the sky. Seedlings sprouted, young skinny trees grew and older trees stood with wide trunks. Logs, long past death, crumbled into soil. The trees lived lives of struggle. Branches stretched out in different directions, each aiming to grab sunlight and block other plants from getting it. Their roots grew into soil that had bits of dead trees corpses in it, including the trees' rotting relatives. It was tree cannibalism.

"To help people contemplate the true nature of the body, we have human skeletons in the assembly hall," said Ajahn Chah, a Buddhist monk from Thailand whose writings I had studied in a college course, "because when one doesn't understand death, life is very confusing." Here, all the stages of life and death showed themselves. Once again, I felt small in a happy way, knowing that my life was surrounded by many other lives, including the lives of trees. It did

Ben Toon states the obvious.

not matter that one shoulder felt more tired than the other.

Dad took off his backpack and placed it behind a tree. I threw down my backpack next to his. I sat at a nearby overlook and looked out at the grand view of the sky, valley, river and rolling hills, framed by a leaning tree. Dad moseyed carefully to the overlook, looking at plants along the way and heading back to the trail after a quick glance at the drop-off.

LARRY: Unfortunately, many interesting plants grow on cliff tops, so I do have to visit them. I like cliff tops, except for my fears and the accompanying uncomfortable feelings in my lower belly.

BEN: I saw the forest as a place to think about big things like life, death and my place in the universe. I kept my brown eyes straight ahead and sometimes up. Dad saw the forest as a place to search for plants and other curiosities. He kept his head down and scanned the ground from side to side with his hazel eyes.

Mountain laurel bushes at the end of their flowering period rained petals that decorated plants below. Hemlock trees with thumbnail-length needles grew above them. We found the campsite near a trickling stream. Dad took off his backpack and collapsed against a tree. I found another tree and did the same.

After resting, Dad tried a few wobbly methods of standing before finally getting on his feet. Now that we could set our backpacks aside, we explored. I waded in the stream, as I'd done as a child on family camping trips and as a teenager before leaving Tennessee for college in North Carolina. Dad wandered along the bank and grabbed a small animal.

"This is a red eft, the juvenile stage of the red-spotted newt," he said, pointing to the salamander in his hand. "It's red to warn predators of its poison."

He loved having someone to whom he could explain his knowledge. He'd been the one who first taught me how to read and work math problems. For the moment, I did not mind listening.

Dad had suggested counting the species of herps, meaning reptiles and amphibians, we found. Searching for herps appealed to me, as it gave me a naturalist treasure hunt of my own, not to mention a reason to wade other than old times' sake. Ready to find more squirming salamanders, I passed Dad and stepped into an inch-deep pool.

To my bare feet, some rocks felt rough, others smooth and others slimy with algae. A crayfish swam away, possibly frightened by my strange-to-a-crayfish feet. Something painful jabbed my toe. Imagining a snake's fangs, I lifted my foot. It was nothing but prickly-edged holly leaf. The cut was small and would not stop me from wading further. It was nothing compared to a produce scale.

For dinner, we'd brought Ramen Noodles or as Dad called them "Raymon noodles." As a recent college grad, I was the local expert on Ramen.

Because Dad wanted to focus on exploring and didn't care for firebuilding, we set a small isobutene-propane burner on a rock. I placed a pot of filtered stream water on the burner.

"It's hot enough. I think we can use it now," I said, pouring some of it into my cup.

"Is that what you're supposed to do?" said Dad.

"No, but it's the way I always do it." Still, given that Dad had never had Ramen before, I owed him Ramen Noodles done right.

I lit another match. Somehow the flame stayed lit this time, and the water boiled. I held the pot with a sock and poured the boiling water. It overflowed, out of my cup of noodles and onto hemlock needles on the forest floor. To avoid having my noodles too watery, I poured some of the water from my chili-lime shrimp noodles into Dad's cheddar cheese noodles, giving them a

Salamanders

BEN: The book *The Amphibians of Tennessee* mentions twenty-five known salamander species on the Cumberland Plateau and its escarpment. While not as high a number as the Blue Ridge Mountains' forty-two salamanders, it's still tied for second place out of eight in most salamander species for a region in Tennessee. For comparison, only three native salamander species live in the United Kingdom. On the CT, I would learn salamanders' true variety and grow to love them for it.

Salamanders (order *caudata*) have a lizard-like shape with four legs and a tail. Some people, especially the ones who use them for fishing bait, call them spring lizards. Unlike true lizards, salamanders never have claws or even toenails; whereas true lizards have rough and scaly skin, salamander skin is soft and damp. The skin absorbs water from which the salamander breathes, although some also have lungs or gills. True lizards often lie in the sun like other reptiles, but if a salamander did that for too long, she would suffocate.

Most salamanders live in damp places like logs, caves, pools, under rocks and in streams. These hidden homes have made salamanders easy for many people to ignore. For me though, their hiddenness makes finding them even more appealing. The species in this book are just a few of the many shapes, sizes and colors that our toenail-lacking friends can take.

spicier flavor.

"How long are you supposed to wait?" asked Dad.

"It depends on how much you care," I said, digging into my half-cooked noodles. "If you want to know the official way to make them, look at the lid."

Dad stared at my tall curly-haired face, intrigued that a self-proclaimed Ramen expert didn't care about getting the noodles perfect.

We added some tuna to the noodles for protein.

"These are good," said Dad, "A little salty but good." Feeling flattered that he liked something as dear to my heart as Ramen, I boiled water for another cup of noodles and lifted the pot by the bail with my bare hand.

"Yow!" I screamed. A pale narrow line burned on my finger where I had touched the bail.

It was the most trouble I had ever had making Ramen in my entire life. Before now, I'd been worried about Dad's left knee, but Dad, with his logical mind inside that bald, reddish, wrinkled head could avoid getting hurt. With my luck at being injured by mundane things, I would end our trek by choking on trail mix.

The songbird sounds of day changed into the frog, cricket and owl sounds of night. By the light of my solar flashlight, I climbed down the bank to bathe.

I stripped off my clothes, stood in a three-inch-deep pool, splashed cold water on myself and threw ticks off my knee and neck for a few minutes. I was done. Not quite. Two ticks clung to my crotch. I picked them off and dropped them into the stream. *Okay*, I thought, *maybe I'm done now.* No, there was yet another tick sucking on my leg. After pulling her off, I figured she was the last. No, they were everywhere: on my ankles, my elbow, the small of my back, the tangles of my curly mess of hair and my scraggly excuse for a beard. *I'll never finish*, I groaned to myself, but after a while, it was hard to be frustrated about spending hours in a forest stream. Whippoorwill calls filled the woods. Then, human-sounding voices that weren't Dad's started talking. They might see me naked in ankle-deep water yanking ticks off myself, but it didn't seem right to stop now. Every last tick had to drown.

Then, Dad's unmistakable Southern-Ohio voice shouted "Ben!" Still covered in ticks, I ran out of the water, shoved on my clothes and trotted to the campsite.

"Did you think I got bit by a snake?" I asked.

"No," said Dad in a quiet voice that sounded nothing like the desperate one from minutes ago. "You were just gone a long time. Did you hear the coyotes?"

"I don't know," I said, "What do they sound like?"

"They started out howling and then kept going with yipping, like they were having a conversation with each other."

The voices had been coyotes. They would have been as naked as I was.

It was another hot night. With his head on a bath sponge for a pillow, Dad fidgeted. He scratched and reached for ticks in the dark. Soon he found himself yanking at ticks that weren't even there.

↦Rehearsal Backpack, Snoop Rock Loop↤
Sunday, May 6

We ate oatmeal for breakfast in our Ramen cups.

"I'm sorry if I hit you during the night," I said. "I'm just not used to sleeping this close."

"You only hit me twice," he said with no hint of irony. "The ticks were what kept me from sleeping."

Dad ducked under a limbo limb with his clunky backpack. I laughed but knew I would have to try to duck under it after he finished.

We walked on a natural sandstone arch and stopped to eat trail mix. My face itched. A tick nefariously nestled near my eyelid. She had almost perfect strategy. It was a place that I could never have spotted her with my eyes. My fingers found her though and threw her off the arch.

"We really can't see the arch from here on top," said Dad. He pointed to a slope covered in leaves and said, "I guess that's the best route down." He slipped as he walked. "Maybe we'll have to slide," he said, as though it was the only logical solution. He sat down, slid and slinked through the swishing leaves on the steep hill. I followed, until we reached the arch's bottom. The sun's bright light shined through its grand rock shape.

Back on the trail, Dad stopped at a plant. With field glass in hand and the knees of his pants in the dirt, he examined the leaves. An intense look yielded to a slight, fascinated smile that lit his sweaty face. The plant was rare, and he wanted a good look at it.

"This proves I'm still looking for things," said Dad. "The backpack's not keeping me from looking, even when we're dead tired."

Like a demonic PEZ dispenser cornucopia, the trail kept throwing me tick after tick. Two ticks crawled on my arm. Two more hitched a ride on my ankle.

I flicked a few off. Then, I put one on my finger and forced her to pose for a picture.

"Ticks are a marvel of evolution," I told Dad as we hiked. "You can't crush them. You can't even see them half the time. Does it ever worry you that we're just getting rid of the more obvious ones? Will we cause them to evolve into super-ticks that are even smaller and harder to destroy?"

"No," said Dad. "We are not their main prey since people are scarce out here. Other mammals can't remove ticks as easily as we can. Humans don't have much effect on them." His logic comforted me.

While we were setting out, the *Knoxville News Sentinel* ran the headline "Ticks, Diseases they Carry on Rise This Year in Tenn."

"It's nuts. I'm scared to go outside," said one woman in Cleveland, Tennessee quoted in the article. Another woman said that she was considering moving because of the ticks. It was easy for me to laugh off these people as sobbing, screaming idiots, worried about tiny arachnids that they could easily just pull off of themselves.

Still, with the rise in ticks came a rise in diseases spread by ticks. The Tennessee Department of Health reported a 553 percent rise in Rocky Mountain spotted fever, a disease carried by brown dog ticks. It can lead to headache, fever and possibly death. Lyme disease reports also rose in Tennessee. Most ticks do not carry disease, but don't allow them to remain attached for more than a day. You don't want tick diseases.

Tick paranoia can lead to insanity. I had to remind myself that the natural moles on my skin weren't ticks and should not be ripped from my flesh.

Two deer leaped up the hillside.

"It's easier for animals to use the trails than to bushwhack," said Dad. "It takes less energy for them." The ticks were probably here for the deer and other beasts who frequently used the path rather than us.

At Snooper's Rock, I looked out at the Tennessee River as it wound through the gorge. Motorboats made tiny white lines in the river as they drove. From up here, all the trees looked green and alive, without a hint of cannibalism. It was a place for looking, breathing and feeling small in a good way.

It was also a splendid place for throwing ticks off the ledge and

Animals on Trails

LARRY: Some hikers feel that they don't see animals because they stay on trails, and the animals avoid the trails. In my work, I've spent much of my time off trails. I see more animals on trails than off. I believe animals use our trails and their own to save energy. Hikers can be quieter on trails thus giving less warning as they approach the forest critters.

imagining them falling to their deaths. In reality, ticks are too light to be bothered by falling. I might as well have tried taking a tick's picture without her permission in order to make her feel humiliated. Not like I would do that or anything (see this chapter's page at www.benandlarryincumberland.com for a picture taken by me of a tick in order to make her feel humiliated).

If a tick could have laughed at my silly human notions as she fell off of Snoop Rock, she would have. Maybe I was reading too much into their behavior. They just wanted to eat. Still, I found it hard to tell myself that ticks didn't enjoy harassing us. They had all the ironic timing of Bugs Bunny or

A Few Notes on Limestone and Many More on Sandstone

LARRY: Some plants prefer limestone soils. Others prefer sandstone. Limestone was rare enough that every time we encountered limestone on the CT, we were excited to see the special plants that lived in it. We found limestone on slopes and in valleys but never on the CT's highest areas. Caves and sinkholes, which we discuss later, can form in limestone.

By contrast, sandstone occupies the heights. Miles and miles of sandstone cliffs run along the Cumberland Plateau. Sandstone is a hard rock that caps the plateau, slowing erosion. It formed from ancient sand and gravel deposits that were pressed into rock. Rock with a significant amount of gravel mixed with sand is called conglomerate. If the rock has little gravel with the sand, it is called sandstone. As is customary, we will call both types of rock sandstone unless the distinction between the two is important. The plateau's many scenic features come from the eroding and cracking of sandstone.

Streams cut through the sandstone cap to make cliffy gorges. House-sized boulders sometimes break off from the gorges' cliffs, landing in the streams. Sandstone cliffs' bases tend to erode, undercutting the cliff. The undercuts are places to shelter, called rockhouses. With their differing levels of shade and wetness, rockhouses are unique habitats for plants and animals. People, including Native Americans, have also lived in them. You will find that the sandy floors of almost all rock houses have been dug up in the search for artifacts.

If rockhouses are back-to-back on opposite sides of a narrow ridge, they may erode into each other, leaving a natural arch or, if the opening is small, a window. We saw such a window on Cumberland Mountain.

Droopy Poodle, showing up exactly when we thought we were through with them.

When we got back to our truck, what seemed like millions of ticks still covered us. We could not wait to shower and drown the little blood-suckers in the toilet. Right now, throwing them out the truck windows was all we could do.

Dad's detailed, calculating mind wanted to figure out a cheap but decent motel in which we could stay in between our first set of hikes. He also wanted one with Wi-Fi. So we searched as we rode back.

At first, I had opposed having Wi-Fi, even after approving our staying in motels. Wi-Fi allows me to be elsewhere. It is my enemy when trying to

---

The natural arch we saw on the rehearsal backpack formed in a different way. An enlarged vertical crack intersected the back of a rockhouse to form the arch. Another type of scenic sandstone feature is the mushroom rock, a big stone on a narrow pedestal. The Devil's Breakfast Table is a large mushroom rock near the CT. You can see more rock mushrooms along the CT at Frozen Head State Park and near the trail's start in Prentice Cooper State Forest.

Flowing water crosses the extensive cliff system, creating waterfalls and cascades. In order to be a waterfall, the water must do a free fall through the air. A steep descent along a rock face is called a cascade. We encountered many waterfalls and some cascades during our trek.

Large vertical cracks may open perpendicular to a cliff face. When they have sloping floors, these cracks can be handy to use as passages to get down the cliffs. So, they are called stone doors. The CT uses stone doors to drop down from Black Mountain and for a descent near the Mowbray Pike Trailhead.

Sandstone cliff-tops often have little or no soil covering, making life difficult for trees. Thus, the trees are few and stunted. This produces an open habitat with lots of sunshine. So, on cliff tops we have another special habitat for plants formed from sandstone.

An iron compound can form dark red or brown bands in sandstone. Sometimes the bands form nearly perfect rectangles. This compound is hematite. Other sandstones show patterns, indicating they were formed from sand dunes.

observe or write about a particular place. Dad, however, used the internet for quick glances at e-mail and the University of Tennessee Herbarium website. He wanted to do the same during our trek. The internet could be useful for research. Still, I would have to control my internet use. I couldn't be looking up the egg-being with a Fu-Manchu mustache that fought Wonder Woman unless it related to the trail.

We stopped at Hometown Inn in Soddy-Daisy. A young clerk sat behind a Plexiglas shield.

"Why does a place called the Hometown Inn have a Plexiglas shield?" asked Dad after we left the building.

Dayton's Deluxe Holiday Inn had counters that looked like pink marble, a lobby restaurant and no weekly rate. "I'll consider it," said Dad in a polite voice.

Just when it looked hopeless, I spotted a sign:

Scottish Inn
Weekly rates
Free Wi-Fi.

It also had no marble and no Plexiglas. The clerk was a friendly woman in what looked to be her thirties. She was from India, which surprised me. I had thought the towns on and near the Cumberland Plateau were isolated places with little influence from immigrants or foreigners. Later, I would learn how wrong that assumption was.

"Are you here for work?" she asked.

"We're going hiking," said Dad.

"I don't know that word. I don't speak much English," she said.

"Do you know walking? Walking in the mountains?" He motioned up to the Plateau, making a walking person sign with two fingers. She nodded.

Back at home, Dad sprayed every shirt, pair of pants, shorts or underwear we planned on taking with us with toxic permethrin fumes. He dried them on the porch and then sprayed my white Camry and his red Tacoma, leaving the doors open so that we wouldn't later breathe the pent-up poisons. I got a whiff of it from walking by the car which made me worry, though not enough to protest. I was ready for an end to the ticks.

After all our preparations and rehearsals, we began to feel ready. We had seen many ways things could go wrong. Now we could make them go right. It was as Alice of Wonderland said, "After such a fall as this, I shall think nothing of tumbling downstairs."

Sources and Suggested Reading

Ray Jardine:
Jardine, Ray. *Trail Life: Ray Jardine's Lightweight Backpacking: 25,000-Miles Worth of Trail-Tested Know-How.* Arizona City, AZ: Adventure Lore Press, 2009

Bird Songs:
Cornell Laboratory of Ornithology. "All About Birds: Why Birds Sing." Accessed September 18, 2013. http:// www.birds.cornell.edu/AllAboutBirds/studying/birdsongs/whysing.

Salamander Diversity:
Bryson, Bill. *A Walk in the Woods: Rediscovering America on the Appalachian Trail.* New York: Broadway Books, 1998.

Niemiller, Matthew et al. *The Amphibians of Tennessee.* Knoxville: University of Tennessee Press, 2011.

Ticks:
Associated Press. "Tick-Carried Disease Spreading in Tenn." *Knoxville News Sentinel.* May 21, 2012. http://www.knoxnews.com/news/2012/may/21/tick-carried-disease-spreading-in-tenn/ (accessed September 17, 2013).

Martin, Marian. "Ticks, Diseases they Carry on Rise." *Knoxville News Sentinel.* May 4, 2012.

Geology:
Brill, David. *Cumberland Odyssey: A Journey in Pictures and Words along Tennessee's Cumberland Trail and Plateau.* Johnson City, Tennessee: Mountain Trail Press, 2010.

Luther, Edward T. *Our Restless Earth: The Geologic Regions of Tennessee.* Knoxville: University of Tennessee Press, 1977.

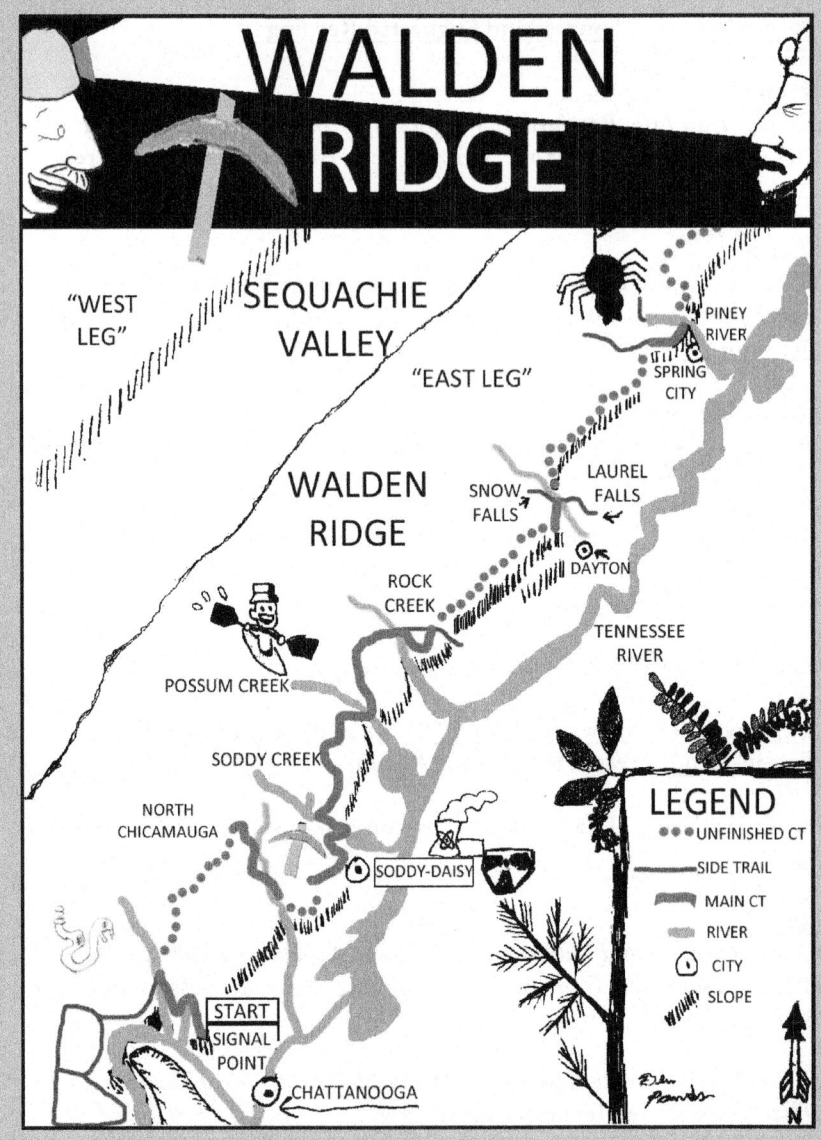

Map 3: Walden Ridge

Interlude 1
Walden Ridge: The Eastern "Leg"

BY LARRY

➔ ←

WALDEN RIDGE DESCRIPTION

In this book, we divide the CT's land into different regions: Walden Ridge (discussed here), Crab Orchard Mountains, Obed-Catoosa, Wartburg Basin Mountains and Cumberland Mountain. (See Map 2). We will have an interlude describing each region. The Cumberland Plateau has two legs when you look at it on a map. (See Map 3). A wide western leg and narrower eastern leg called Walden Ridge make up the southern half of the Plateau. The land between these legs is the Sequatchie Valley. I-40, about ten miles north of the split between the legs, crosses the Plateau like a belt. Confusingly, some people use Walden Ridge as the name for the eastern edge of the Plateau all the way from the Tennessee River gorge to Caryville. We won't use Walden Ridge that way. For our purposes, Walden Ridge is below the belt and the crotch, south of Hinch Mountain and Spring City. It was named after the hunter Elisha Walden who explored the area.

When viewed from places to the east, like Chattanooga, Walden Ridge appears to be a tall wall topped with rocks and an occasional home with a view. Indeed, the plateau-top on Walden Ridge is fairly level at around 2,000 feet. However, a few streams make breaks in the wall while flowing out of the Plateau. They cut gorges up to a thousand feet deep. The CT trends north from Signal Point to Piney River along the east side of Walden Ridge. It climbs in and out of several gorges, crossing many streams. From the Piney River, the CT turns west across the Walden Ridge leg to the Plateau's crotch at Brady Mountain. There, it enters the Crab Orchard Mountain region of the trail.

THE WALDEN RIDGE TREK

At the time of our trek, about 60 miles of existing main CT were open on Walden Ridge. Besides the main CT, there are many miles of side trails, including our rehearsal hikes in Prentice-Cooper State Forest (Chapters 1 and 3) and most of our hiking in Laurel Snow (Chapter 11). As of 2015, the main trail consists of five unconnected fragments: (1) Signal Mtn. toward TN 27, (2) North Chickamauga, (3) the Three Gorges, (4) Laurel-Snow and (5) Piney River. A new piece of trail covers part of the gap between the Three Gorges and Laurel-Snow in the Graysville Resource Management Area near Roaring Creek.

THE HUNT FOR RARE PLANTS ON THE WALDEN RIDGE CT

I was pleased to see mountain skullcap (*Scutellaria montana*) several times along the CT on Walden Ridge. It is lovely.

For the two years before our CT trek, I participated in the May mountain skullcap monitoring project for TVA. Monitoring involves counting plants at various locations to see how those populations are doing over time. TVA surveys the land in the Chattanooga area along Chickamauga Lake, which is east of Walden Ridge and thus east of the CT. TVA is particularly interested in mountain skullcap because the Federal Endangered Species Act protects it.

Recent monitoring of a skullcap population on TVA land found damaged habitat. An adjacent homeowner had cleared trees on the TVA land to improve his view of the lake. In the process of cutting down the trees, people trampled on the land, damaging the skullcaps' habitat. The deforestation also deprived the skullcaps of shade and opened the door to invasive plants that TVA is now trying to contain. Hopefully, the population will recover from this attack on their habitat.

For my dissertation at the University of Tennessee, I created a computer model to study the vulnerability of plants to extinction. I focused on the effect of spatial arrangement on populations and their likelihood of going extinct. The skullcap's arrangement of populations has negatives and positives for allowing persistence. On the negative side, mountain skullcap occurs only within about twenty miles of Chattanooga, a very small total range for a species. On a positive note, numerous well-scattered populations of the plant grow in that range. Many mountain skullcap populations thrive on protected public land, though as we saw with the tree clearing above, this protection is not perfect. Still, I think authorities should consider removing this species from the Endangered Species List. However, it should only be removed from the list if there is no reason to expect its extinction in the foreseeable future.

I encountered a new plant for me on Walden Ridge, mountain bush-honeysuckle (*Diervilla sessilifolia var. rivularis*), a life list addition. I don't actually have a written-down list of plants that I have seen in my life, but I do have one in my mind. Many times before, I had seen its close relative, northern bush-honeysuckle. We saw both on Walden Ridge. The square cross-section of mountain bush-honeysuckle's stems easily separates the species from the round-stemmed northern bush-honeysuckle. Both are on the rare plant list for Tennessee.

I saw the state-listed yellow jessamine (*Gelsemium sempervirens*) over-topping and showing signs of dominating the other plants on Walden Ridge. This plant may be spreading northward with a warming climate. I have observed it growing rather weed-like along I-75 in northern Georgia. I think its protected status should be debated because it is spreading quickly in such a weedy manner.

See our website www.benandlarryincumberland.com for my Walden Ridge CT Rare Plants List.

WE'RE OFF!

→ 4 ←

Prentice Cooper State Forest (Saturday, May 12)
Hike 1: Signal Mountain Overlook to TN 27
5 miles

BEN: We drove past the Spaceship House, a fancy round, white residence on stilts that looked like a flying saucer. A father created it for his son in 1973.

We were in a well-off Chattanooga suburb with houses I could never dream of affording, not the kind of place I expected the CT to begin. The neighborhood was called Signal Mountain. Our trek would begin at Signal Point.

Union troops during the Civil War occupied a narrow area that included Signal Point. They signaled from the mountain with flags and torches. Confederates had surrounded the area, keeping the Union soldiers deprived of supplies. The starving Union soldiers plundered area gardens for food. According to General Ulysses S. Grant, "This was about the time that mules were living on chicken tongues and fence rails."

It was hard for me to think about suffering soldiers when passing the upscale houses of modern-day Signal Mountain, especially when one of them looked like a UFO. Instead, the Spaceship House reminded me of a crazy childhood obsession.

Extraterrestrials loved quiet misty places, so naturally, if a place was misty and quiet, they would come. One misty Saturday morning, I had walked to my elementary school's playground and looked on a flat field for their craft. As if I could pick up signals, my senses told me that it was the right moment for them to land and come out in their bulky robotic space suits.

Hours passed. Dad drove up to the playground.

"If they haven't shown up by now, they're probably not coming," he said, in a polite, sympathetic voice. Many other parents would have yelled at me or laughed. I sobbed but soon agreed and rode back with him.

———•—•———

At Signal Point, a stone wall guarded visitors from falling into the gorge. I wanted to stare down at the Tennessee River as the starving Union soldiers had done. I did, for about a second.

"Are you ready?" Dad asked in a slow, quiet dramatic voice. He had his hands in his pockets and a wide-eyed smile on his face, looking as eager as a child waiting to open a Christmas stocking. It was the world beyond Signal Mountain that he wanted to discover.

"Yes," I said with a sigh. We were not here for a view that people could reach by car. A sign labeled "Cumberland Trail" pointed into the forest's green depths, promising a wild and unseen world beyond Signal Mountain. We were on our way to Cumberland Gap, stoked to experience everything along the way.

As if to continue the theme of alien invaders, English ivy from a yard crept along the forest floor and tangled in trees, sprawling out in the area beyond the suburb. It snatched space to grow away from native plants.

LARRY: We side with the native forest plants, but the ivy vines are doing just what they have evolved to do.

BEN: As we walked down, a group of young, spandex-clad women joined us. I couldn't flirt with them though. It seemed too awkward around Dad. He handled the young women's questions about our project and the various organizations they could contact about volunteering on the CT.

A wooden suspension bridge, about as tall of two of me, hung above a gurgling stream. I thought about jumping in order to hear the bridge squeak. Dad's footsteps creaked behind me, giving me second thoughts about my jump.

I strode ahead of Dad and the young women, up a rocky slope and over fallen logs. Dad followed, even when what I had confused for the CT fizzled into nothing. People from the nearby neighborhood had made their own, unofficial paths, making it easy to get lost.

"I think this is the wrong way," said Dad. "We haven't seen a blaze for a long time." A white spray-painted blaze on a rock led us back to the CT.

Dad searched the sandstone outcrops for plants. Sometimes he would lie down on the ground and put his field glass up to a single leaf. Differences between species could be small. He wanted to know for sure.

Bells rang the hour from nearby buildings, reminding us that we were still close to Chattanooga, like birdsong marking territory for birds.

Dead stumps and logs around us sported black scars. New plant growth sprouted green among the burnt. The forest looked like a tended garden

Ben Toon hears the bells.

with few leaves on the ground. Flames had killed shrubs and burned leaves from the forest floor.

"I figure there was a fire here about five years ago," said Dad. I envied his guessing ability. Possibly I could have learned how to identify the age of a burned forest from him if I had dedicated more of my mind to it, instead of all the trivia from Wikipedia that occupied space there.

At an overlook, the Plateau's green slope fell into a deep gorge eroded by the Tennessee River. The river split at tear-drop-shaped Williams Island, made from the river's gathered silt.

The group of young women in exercise spandex looked out at the view. They'd arrived here while we'd been lost. Dad stayed back from the cliff edge. I sat a little further out on the bare rock near the other hikers, not wanting to turn down an opportunity to be close to women in skintight clothes, even if flirting did feel wrong near Dad.

Because the spot was near Chattanooga, other hikers came here often. A sweaty, middle-aged trail runner in shorts soon joined us at the overlook.

"Are you sure you won't lose anything?" Dad asked me as he sat on fallen pine needles

"Yeah, I'm sure," I said, glancing back at Dad. "The wind's blowing the other way." I turned back around to feel it on my face. My statement probably wouldn't change Dad's mind though. Once I got worried, few things could stop me from worrying. Maybe Dad was the same way.

I took out my water bottle, washed an apple I'd packed for lunch and splashed water onto my hands.

"I would save the water for drinking if I were you," said Dad in a matter-of-fact voice.

"We're paranoid about different things," I said.

LARRY: We were using the word paranoid loosely and colloquially.

BEN: Dad ate quickly and hiked ahead. I nibbled at my food, stayed back with the other hikers, looked at the view and enjoyed being separate from Dad for a minute.

Hikers shouted and waved at a speck of a person on the gorge's other side. Chimes sounded across the gorge from a cluster of resort-like buildings.

"Isn't that an old-peoples' home?" said a young hiker with a pony-tail. "Wait that came out wrong, I meant a retirement home. A place where old people go to die," she said, laughing.

One black and two light-brown birds circled below us. I asked the resting trail-runner in shorts if he knew what the birds were.

"That's a turkey buzzard," he said, pointing at the black one, "and those two are…brown hawks. I don't know. I'm not an ornithologist." The word "ornithologist" stumbled off his tongue in an amused way.

Dad wasn't one either. Still, my instinct to ask for names had come from many hikes with him, starting when I was roughly two years old and he pointed out devil's walking stick near my preschool. Without him, more things stayed nameless.

The vulture reminded me of a Cherokee story about how high and low places had formed, as recorded by the anthropologist James Mooney. I've paraphrased it here.

In the beginning, animals lived in a world above the sky. All land was underwater. A beetle dived down and brought up a heap of mud. Someone then stretched the mud and attached it to the sky with four cords to keep it above the water. Mooney doesn't say who it was. Perhaps no one remembers, given that all of this happened long ago.

The animals sent the Great Buzzard, father of all today's vultures, to

CT Birding for Non-Birders

LARRY: I'm a lapsed birder. So here's some basic stuff for us non-birders.

Soaring Birds

The many overlooks along the CT are great places to see soaring birds. Soaring is a type of flight with little flapping of the wings. It uses vertical winds called thermals. The sun generates thermals by heating the ground, which in turn heats the air near the ground. The hotter air is relatively light, so it floats upward.

Our two vultures, the black vulture and the turkey vulture, are the most common soaring birds. The black vulture soars with wings straight-out while the turkey vulture makes a shallow "V" with its wings. The black vulture has white patches, near the wing tips. The turkey vulture lacks these patches. Occasionally, I have stumbled onto vulture so-called "nests" on rock ledges. The nest is basic: one or two large eggs and nothing more. Black vultures have become more common in Tennessee in recent years, perhaps a sign of climate change. In the past, it was a more southern bird.

The bald eagle, the national bird, likes big lakes. Look for it at CT overlooks with views of lakes. Mature birds have white tails and heads.

I have never seen a golden eagle, our other soaring eagle. Tennessee Wildlife Resources Agency has captured them on motion-activated cameras at deer carcasses on the Plateau during the winter (Morgan Simmons in *The News Sentinel*, "Biologists Set Sights on an Elusive Predator," 3/11/2012).

Another soaring bird, the raven, is a rare find on the Cumberland Plateau but more common in the Great Smoky Mountains. It is like a crow

see if the land had dried yet. He got tired and started flapping his wings low against the ground. When he slapped the Earth by accident, he made valleys. When he lifted his wings, he made mountains.

Later, the land dried. Cherokee stories go on to describe the first man hitting the first woman with a fish and telling her to multiply.

Fish slapping aside, the story describes East Tennessee's bumpy land well, especially the Cumberland Plateau and its gorges. Geologists believe the Plateau was once underwater. Then, it became a marshy swamp. After a collision between plates, it rose, turning into a plateau. Rivers, like the Tennessee, whittled gorges into it.

Some people look down into the valley from the Plateau and think of an intelligent designer making a beautiful world for us. Others see plates moved

....

but a bit larger with a deeper voice. You will also see various hawks soaring from lookout points.

Night Singers

While camped along the CT, you may hear the question, "Who cooks for youoo?" This is the medium-sized barred owl, length 18-22 inches according to Peterson's guide. Our two other frequent owls are the larger (20-23 inches) great horned owl which is big enough to capture skunks and cats and the smaller (8-10 inches) eastern screech owl, which makes an eerie wail rather than a screech.

Another night singer with a famous song is the well-camouflaged whip-poor-will. I've been lucky enough to spot whippoorwills nesting on the ground on two occasions.

Forest Flushers

You may startle some birds into flight from the forest floor as you hike nearby. The biggest is the turkey, which has become much more common in recent years after reintroduction. Expect to see the ground scratched up by turkeys where they have moved the leaves to find food. The ruffed grouse may startle you when it flushes because it will often wait to fly until you are very close.

The woodcock has a shore bird's bill, making it an odd bird to see in forests. Its relatives live on shores rather than in forests. It uses its long bill to extract worms from moist bottom areas. The woodcock is famous for its plummeting courtship flights in the spring. It flies high up and then dives.

....

by forces deep within the Earth. Still others see a giant, tired vulture flapping around in fear about the bumpy mess he made.

The women in exercise spandex headed back. It was time to catch up with Dad. I followed the trail, which left the Tennessee River Gorge to run above Suck Creek Gorge.

Caught up with Dad now, I asked about his fear of heights.

"It hasn't gotten any worse," said Dad, "but I give into it more now. I'm happy to sit way back, because I know I feel better when I do that. That's

If only they had sent a hummingbird.

Vulture Parenting

BEN: Vulture mothers lay two large eggs (see Dad's "Birding for Non-birders" box) and hide them in decaying logs, stumps, deserted buildings, rock ledges or under thick brush. Mother and father turkey vultures take turns incubating their eggs. Once the eggs hatch, mothers brood their children at night. Both parents regurgitate food for their young.

part of aging. You decide 'Who cares?' You don't try to hide anything. You just do what feels good."

"My own philosophy is the opposite: I always need to do better," I said.

"I can live comfortably with my fear of heights," said Dad.

A fence lizard ran through the leaves. Dad spotted a chipmunk.

"So, one herp, one mammal," said Dad. "Not major pickings, but we've got miles to go. In the book, I'll have to mention that before our trek I have seen elk and bobcat in the trail area. Also coyotes."

"I've never seen coyotes in the wild." It was true, even though I'd heard that they lived in East Tennessee near my own Loudon home.

"You will," said Dad, sounding certain, like he could summon them magically.

"Have you ever failed to make curfew and had people impound your car?" I asked. Our parking place at Signal Mountain had a parking curfew time.

"No, and if everything works out, it looks like we won't have a problem," said Dad.

By definition, no one has problems when everything works out. Arguing with a man who could judge the age of a burnt spot seemed pointless though.

"What they really don't want is people drinking and fornicating in the park," Dad added.

Now that we were farther away from Chattanooga's suburbs, the forest was full of native rhododendron bushes with dark green leaves but none of the tangling and strangling English ivy.

A tree trunk bent at a near-right angle.

"Didn't people tie trunks down so they'd grow bent?" I asked. "A teacher told me that on a field trip."

"There's a whole book by Don and Diane Wells about how Indians did

The Suck Sucked

BEN: Suck Creek was named after a whirlpool, descriptively called "the Suck," near the point where the creek entered the Tennessee River. A Cherokee story describes people living in an underwater house below the Suck and reaching through the roof to pull travelers down. Thanks to a hydroelectric dam, the Suck no longer sucks.

it," said Dad, looking up at a tree. "I suppose there might be some truth to it, but almost every tree you see bent in an odd direction is that way because another tree fell on it."

On another field trip, back in my Middle School days, Dad had been a chaperon. Often back then I felt embarrassed to be near my parents. On this particular field trip though, I wanted to show off my awesome scientist Dad. I was ready for him to share plant facts like he had always done on hikes with me.

Dad stopped at some bright flowers. "These are fire pinks," he said, holding their stems. "They're red, but their petals look like they were cut by pinking scissors." He looked to see if anyone was listening. Most students had moved on.

"Oh look," said one, "there's a squirrel."

"You can see squirrels in town," I said.

"You can see flowers in town too," the kid said.

Back in the present, my hands brushed through shrubs and grass. Then, something pierced my hand.

"That's needle-grass," said Dad.

A bulging red rock balanced on a narrower stem of rock about as tall as three of me. It looked like a statue of a mushroom. People call it Mushroom Rock. The rock somehow stays balanced.

A mother, father and young girl came down towards us, hiking from the other direction. "Can I go on top of the rock?" asked the girl.

"No," said the mother, in a polite voice, not angry, but amused as Dad had been the time I had waited for aliens.

A toad squirmed in my hand after I picked it up, and a white liquid oozed from it. I didn't care. I'd held plenty of toads before, and they'd all done it. Somehow the white liquid just made them cuter. You can have your kittens and bunnies. For me, toads, with their roly-poly bodies, round eyes and silly hopping, are the cutest animals in all creation.

"There are two kinds of true toads around here," said Dad, "Fowler's and American. Take a picture of its parotoid glands and figure it out from there."

"Sure," I said, pretending to understand.

"Do you know where parotoid glands are?"

"Not really." Just because I found toads cute didn't mean I knew squat about them.

"Get a good close-up photo of the head," said Dad, eager to teach me about toad identification.

When I was a child, Dad had taught me how to read. He'd later tutored me in math. Out here he was ready to teach me the forest like no one else could.

We drove to our Dayton motel. Both of us felt too tired to explore the town. Instead we looked at our reference books, including one on frogs and toads.

The parotoid gland is a big bulge behind the eye. Toads use the gland to spew an irritating fluid onto anyone that disturbs them. Feel free to pick up

A Needle Sewing Seeds

Needle-grass (*Piptochaetium avenaceum*)

LARRY: Spotting needle-grass on the Signal Mountain portion of the CT should be easy when the needles are present on the grass. It grows in woodland openings on top of the Plateau and likes recently burned areas. The needles are striking and attaching, striking in their appearance and attaching in the sense that they attach to your clothes. The needle, which is about two and a half inches long, is the grass's seed. If you stray from the path when the seeds are ready to disperse, the grass may find you before you find it.

Pick a needle from the grass and touch both ends. Oddly, the sharp end of the needle is not the end that sticks out from the plant. This arrangement would seem to make attachment to clothes or fur trickier. Still, the grass did well at dispersing seeds on our clothes.

At the base of the needles are structures called awns that can twist and are hygroscopic. Hygroscopic means water absorbing. As the awns absorb water, they untwist, and as they dry, they re-twist. According to some authorities, the twisting and untwisting with different moisture levels helps the seed drill into the ground. Others, like the late University of Tennessee plant ecologist and grass specialist Hal De Selm, are skeptical of this mechanism's effectiveness for seed sowing.

Someone could make a horror movie about people swallowing needle-grass seeds which then drill into their intestines. Veterinarians deal with something like this horror when grazing animals have the bad judgment to munch needle-grass. Needle seeds are a problem when swallowed. The problem may or may not be aggravated by twisting awns.

toads though. The fluid is harmless unless you rub it in your eyes or pick your nose, in which case it will burn. Back when I was younger and picked up toads, I just assumed they were peeing themselves out of fear. The toad was an American Toad *Anaxyrus americanus* because its crest above the eye did not touch the parotoid gland.

Like a plant routinely opening and closing its flowers, Dad had a rhythm to his life. He woke up at 6:00 AM and got in bed at 10:00 PM. Regardless of where he was at 10:00 PM, he would turn into a pumpkin, like Cinderella's carriage, becoming unable to do anything but sleep. We would hike together. So I shut down my computer and tried to sleep.

American Toad (*Anaxyrus americanus*)

BEN: Anaxyrus means "king" or "chief." When threatened, American toads often inflate themselves and stretch out their back legs to make themselves look bigger.

Along with Fowler's toads, American toads are the only true toads in Tennessee. You can find an American toad just about anywhere in East Tennessee, though they prefer sandy soil with leaves in which they can bury.

A mother American toad can lay up to 20,000 eggs. She lays them in a pair of long strands while her usually-smaller mate sits locked on top of her, dropping sperm into them. This position, called amplexus, can last for long periods of time.

Like other tadpoles, American toad tadpoles get no help from parents. They do, however, swim in dense schools with each other. Crayfish, diving beetles and birds eat American toad tadpoles, but the tadpoles are toxic to some predators. After 6 to eight weeks, the tadpoles grow legs and become adult toads, hopping on the land.

For an emerging toad, the land is a wonderland with new and different sights, sounds, things to eat and dangers. While before they fed on algae and dead fish, now they eat earthworms and insects and absorb water through a patch of skin. While before they feared giant water bugs and crayfish, as adults they fear skunks, snakes and opossums. When ready, they may travel more than a half-mile to breed. They call out to potential mates with a high pitched trill. Males also make a chirping sound when one male accidentally tries to mate with another male.

The day had worn out both of us, and we would need all the energy we could get for the next day, another day for stretching out into new territory. Like the girl who wanted to climb onto the mushroom rock, we were curious.

Sources and Suggested Reading

General:
Cumberland Trail Conference. *CTC's Guide to Hiking the Justin P. Wilson Cumberland Trail with Maps/Guides*. www.cumberlandtrail.org. (accessed July 19, 2012).

Manning, Russ. *The Historic Cumberland Plateau: An Explorer's Guide, Second Edition*. Knoxville: University of Tennessee Press, 1999.

Signal Point:
Sakowski, Carolyn. *Touring the East Tennessee Backroads: Second Edition*. Winston-Salem: John F. Blair, 2007.

Livingood, James W. *Sequatchie: A Story of the Southern Cumberlands*. Knoxville: University of Tennessee Press, 1974.

Space House:
Cheema, Sushil. "'Spaceship House' to be Auctioned in Tennessee." Wall Street Journal, December 15, 2008. Accessed September 24, 2014. http://blogs.wsj.com/developments/2008/12/15/spaceship-house-to-be-auctioned-intennessee/.

Geology:
Brill, David. *Cumberland Odyssey: A Journey in Pictures and Words along Tennessee's Cumberland Trail and Plateau*. Johnson City, Tennessee: Mountain Trail Press, 2010.

Luther, Edward T. *Our Restless Earth: The Geologic Regions of Tennessee*. Knoxville: University of Tennessee Press, 1977.

Cherokee Creation Myth:
Livingood, James W. *Sequatchie: A Story of the Southern Cumberlands*. Knoxville: University of Tennessee Press, 1974.

Mooney, James. "Myths, Cherokee." In *A Documentary History of Religious Life in America: To 1877. Third Edition*. Edited by Edwin Scott Gausted and Mark A. Noll. 21-22. Grand Rapids: Wm. B. Erdman's Publishing Co. 2003.

Originally published in James Mooney, trans., "Myths of the Cherokees" *Nineteenth Annual Report of the Bureau of American Ethnology 1897-1898*, (Washington: Government Printing Office 1900).

Birds:
Bull, John and Ferrand, John Jr. *National Audubon Society Field Guide to North American Birds: Eastern Region.* New York, New York: Alfred A. Knopf Inc., 1977.

Simmons, Morgan. "Golden Eagles Coming Back in East Tennessee." *Knoxville News Sentinel.* March 11, 2012. Accessed September 24, 2013. http://www.knoxnews.com/news/2012/mar/11/golden-eagles-coming-back-in-easttennessee/?print=1.

Simmons, Morgan. "Biologists set sights on an Elusive Predator." *Knoxville News Sentinel.* March 11, 2012.

Vultures:
Rollack, Chloë E., Karen Weibe, Martin J. Stoffel, and C. Stuart Houston. "Turkey Vulture Breeding Behavior Studied with Trail Cameras." Journal of Raptor Research 47, no. 2 (2012): 153-60. Accessed September 25, 2014. http://www.bioone.org/doi/full/10.3356/JRR-12-40.1.
   This article details the nesting, mating and parenting behavior of turkey vultures. It's my source for the fact that the parents take turns.

Haskins, Stacey D., Kelly, David G. and Weir, Ron D. "Trace element Analysis of Turkey Vulture (Cathartes aura) Feathers." Journal of Radioanalytical and Nuclear Chemistry 275, no. 2. (2013): 1331 -1339. Accessed September 25, 2014. http://link.springer.com/article/10.1007/s10967-012-1910-z/fulltext.html.
   Scholarly source confirming that turkey vultures defend themselves and their young by projectile vomiting. I observed similar behavior among black vultures during my time at the Clinch River Raptor Center.

Williams Island:
Jolley, Harmon. *Exploring Chattanooga's Islands: Williams Island.* January 7, 2003. http://www.chattanoogan.com/ 2003/1/7/30916/Exploring-Chattanoogas-Islands--.aspx (accessed February 27, 2013).

Rozema, Viki. *Footsteps of the Cherokees: A Guide to the Eastern Homelands of the Cherokee Nation.* Winston-Salem: John F. Blair, 2007.

Bent Trees:

Wells, Don and Wells, Diane. *Mystery of the Trees*. Jasper: Mountain Stewards Publishing Co, 2011.
    Please note that neither my father nor I find this book's arguments convincing. It's good if you want an opposing point of view to ours.

Toads:

Behler, John L., and F. Wayne King. *The Audubon Society Field Guide to North American Reptiles and Amphibians.* New York: Chanticleer Press Inc., 1979.

Dorcas, Mike and Gibbons, Whit. *Frogs & Toads of the Southeast.* Athens: University of Georgia Press, 2008.

Niemiller, Matthew L, and Graham R. Reynolds. "American Toad." In *The Amphibians of Tennessee*, by Mathew L. Niemiller et al., 253-256. Knoxville: University of Tennessee Press, 2011.

RAIN, TRIAL ON THE TRAIL

→ 5 ←

North Chickamauga Creek State Natural Area (Sunday, May 13)
Hike 2: Bark Camp Creek Road to Montlake Road
8 miles

BEN: With too little water, a seed cannot grow. Too much water can drown a seed, stopping it from getting oxygen from the soil. Rain can be a gentle tap or a frightening force. Life thrives between the states of drought and flood.

    Dad woke me up at six. I stumbled out of bed and slouched like a gargoyle while eating my cereal. Rain poured outside, but we did not wait.

    Rain pounded on my head as we left my white Camry. I looked down at the gravel road we would walk on to the trail while pulling on my hood-strings, trying to keep my head dry. I wore easy-to-soak jeans, as did Dad. Neither of us had water-resistant pants. I knew I would hate this day.

    I had wanted a challenge. I should have been happy to get my beard full of drops, my face poured-on and my socks turned to wash rags. I should have been shouting into my voice recorder, "This is awesome!" I should have been telling Dad "Your plants are going to get unlimited drink refills today! Woo-hoo!" Yet I was not happy to be wet and hear thunder mocking my steps. I felt as miserable as any of my non-outdoorsy friends would have felt. It was like William Least-Heat Moon had said in his book *Blue Highways*: "There are two kinds of adventurers: Those who go truly hoping to find adventure and those who go secretly hoping they won't." Up until now, my preference had been a secret even to me, at least with regard to this kind of adventure.

The rain lightened, even stopping at times. Fog varied as well. Sometimes it was thick and covered any view of the valley below. Sometimes it lifted, highlighting curving trees' shapes.

I found myself on a long wooden ramp. It seemed like a perfect place for me to slip and break my neck. I was happy to be scared. Being scared was a lovely distraction from being soggy. Excited by the possibility of falling down the ramp, I took pictures from many angles while walking down. I could not help but think that Dad, who climbed down the ramp ahead of me, must have been terrified.

Neither of us slipped. The ramp had a sturdy rail and was safer than any ramp-less trail leading down that same hill might have been.

"So were you scared of that ramp?" I asked Dad.

"No."

It seemed like a role reversal for us, with me as the one scared of falling and Dad as the one who was not scared. Perhaps it wasn't though. After all, it was a ramp, not a drop-off, so Dad's fear of heights did not play a part. Meanwhile, I was doing my typical writer's thing of looking for danger in order to get a good story, even when there was no danger to be found. I might just as well reduce my own house to its dangers: "Kitchens are death traps with all of their knives, Cuisinart blades, flammables, hot stoves and toxic dish soap." Or I could write a danger obsessed version of *Walden*: "Man! Log cabins sure are full of splinters! I could get infected!"

Yet an account of dangers misses the world's beauty, including the beauty of rain. When wet, rhododendrons' bark turned a brighter shade of red. Waterfalls ran down curving sandstone walls which were usually dry.

Ferns took on different hues of green than on sunny days. Water made them shine. They depend on a wet ground to continue their life cycle. Fern sperm could not swim to fern eggs without a damp ground.

Rain has other benefits for hikers. No bugs flew into my eyes or ears. My face did not catch a single spider web. Possibly, the storm had wrecked them.

In spite of anything good I can say about it, rain tends to get people wet. So, we walked faster than the day before. We tripped on wet roots and rocks. We slid on slippery leaves. No matter how clumsy the wet trail made us, we chose not to slow down.

Falling drops made rings in a wide, rocky stream. Slippery rocks were the only way we could cross. Getting wetter was not the worst thing that could happen to us, given how wet we already were. So we climbed over big, small, skinny and fat rocks, wading at times.

We stopped at a rockhouse for lunch and shelter, as other visitors to the area had done before us, including hunter-gatherers who would not have worn orange vests with huge back pockets for keeping trail mix and peanut butter sandwiches on pita bread. The desire for shelter was what mattered to us at the moment, and that would have mattered to anyone.

The rockhouse offered a shelter from the wet wandering on the trail, just as my family had offered me a shelter from my own drifting. We sat on boulders over the sand floor as water dripped from the overhanging ledge, veiling the entrance. With no sunlight, we could only drip dry. Sand stuck to our pants. Still, it was better than no shelter.

Ben Tries to Explain Fern Sex

BEN: Ferns rely on both wetness and dryness. They release spores in dry weather. A spore begins to grow when it hits a moist spot. It grows cell-by-cell into a heart-shaped gametophyte which works as a fern's sperm and egg machine. Some fern allies, plants similar to ferns, have separate gametophytes for producing sperms and eggs.

On the fern gametophyte, microscopic ball-shaped male organs and tube-shaped female organs grow. The sperm won't go anywhere without water, however. When water hits the male part, the thin-skinned male organ bursts open, and the corkscrew-shaped fern-sperm swim free. They use little hair-like organs to kick themselves through the water. Female tubes churn out chemicals to attract these sperm.

Most of the time a gametophyte just has sex with itself. If there is enough rain though, sperm can swim further away and sometimes reach other gametophytes and other female tubes. After the sperm joins with the egg, the tube closes. The fertilized egg gets food from the gametophyte and produces leaves to start making its own food while its roots dig into the ground. It is a baby fern.

If fern sex sounds confusing, it's probably because ferns are very distant relatives to humans, adapted to a different life from ours. They live on sunlight, not Ramen.

We left the rockhouse, crossing a stream at a flat spot between two waterfalls. The crossing undid any effects that drying under the rockhouse might have had.

The trail followed an old mining road past places where miners had cut into the rock. Coal formed here from plants that grew in swamps millions of years ago. Near an old mine, I spotted a fossil of one of these plants on a sandstone cliff. It was a bumpy pattern that weaved across the red and gray sandstone. The ruins of a coal

Rockhouses and Lions among Ants

LARRY: Rockhouses, with their varying water and light, form distinct habitats for plants and animals. The light can vary from slightly reduced at the front to near absence at the back. No rain falls inside the rock house other than the occasional windblown drop. Water dripping off the cliff faces makes lines in the sandy soil as the drops splash at the openings to rockhouses. Behind the drip lines, the ground may be dry since there is no rain, but it can also be wet. Water can flow into the rockhouse from a stream or through cracks.

BEN: On the trail, we saw many rockhouses. Rock tripe decorated the sandstone rock faces like peeling wallpaper. Mud dauber wasps built their tube-shaped nests along the sandstone walls like miniature broken-off sets of organ pipes.

In one rockhouse, the sand on the floor had small inverted cone-shaped dents pointing into the ground. "Those are antlion traps," said Dad.

Antlions are neither ants nor lions. They are insects that hunt ants. Thousands of antlion species live around the world. In their larval, or baby, state, antlions have long hooks sticking out from their heads. They dig small pits in the sand and wait for insects, especially ants, to fall into them. The ant may try to escape but often slips back down in the falling sand that the antlion throws at it, in a scene straight out of *Return of the Jedi*. When the ant reaches the pit's bottom, the antlion stabs it with one of its hooks. After giving the ant a good dose of venom and digestive enzymes, the antlion sucks out the ant's juices through grooves in its hooks.

Some people find antlions creepy. Other people, especially farmers, find them helpful. After all, they eat animals that could be pests for our crops.

They grow up and leave the sand. As adults, they have mouths, long wings, long bodies and club-like antennae.

tipple, or device for loading coal onto trucks, stood by the road. Only some posts made of cinder blocks remained of it.

A smoke smell filled the forest, reminding me of a barbecue and making me think of grilled salmon or possibly soy burgers, our typical grilled foods at home. I wondered how a fire could start in the rain.

By the time we got down to the trail head, the rain stopped. Two friendly rangers for the Cumberland Trail State Park, the younger Antony Jones and the older, white-bearded Jim Manson, stood in the parking lot. They were kind enough to answer some questions.

They had seen my white Camry at the barricade where we started our hike. Antony warned me that the sleeping bag liner was too obvious in the back seat. Usually I wouldn't worry about getting robbed so far outside of a city, but he had a point. This was the most popular part of the Cumberland Trail according to them, due to its closeness to Chattanooga.

"The month of April this year, we've had over eleven-thousand visitors just here," said Antony. Thieves could thrive around here like ticks thrived on deer paths. Antony mentioned with a laugh that some people were dumb enough to leave jewelry visible in their cars for thieves to find.

We asked about the smoke smell and the charred stumps. According to the rangers, forest fires raged across the Walden Ridge two years ago, leaving the burned trees we had seen the day before. Dad's estimate had been off by three years. That year, 2010, was a year of fire. By November sixteenth of that year, the state reported

Firepower

LARRY: The young trees growing under a forest's canopy give an indication of the forest's future. Young oaks do not grow well in oak forests unless there are occasional fires. We are seeing oak forests with few young oaks growing under the canopy. With the control of wild fires by people has come a concern for the oak forests which currently dominate much of the Plateau. With less fire, other species dominate. White pines do well starting out in shade, giving them an advantage over oaks in the absence of fire. I don't know if the arsonists did us a favor. Fire ecology is complex. The effect of a forest fire depends on how it burns, in particular how hot it burns.

The warming climate appears to be increasing forest fires in the western US but probably not on the Plateau. On the other hand, forest fires might change global climate by putting particles into the atmosphere. Stay tuned as researchers with super-computers try to figure it all out.

a total of 20,872 acres burned. The same news report claimed that fires started by arsonists accounted for about twelve thousand of those burned acres that year.

Fires have lit up Tennessee for centuries. Lightning sparked many. Humans lit others. The Cherokee lit fires so that the then-thriving elk and bison had places to graze. European farmers burned the forest floor as they had back in Europe. Sparks from steam trains set tree plantations on fire. Some of Tennessee's living things, like oak trees, thrive thanks to fire because it clears open space for young oaks to get sufficient light. The flames of this particular 2010 fire spread to a coal mine entrance. "When the forest fire came," said Antony Jones, "it caught that hole on fire, and it smolders continuously until it burns itself out."

On a sunny day, you will see the smoke come out of it. We get a lot of reports on that," said Antony Jones, leaning against his truck.

"It's going to rain for the next few days," he said. "It'll be gradual though, so the Possum Creek won't flood." So, we would be able to do our next hike. We would just be wet.

We didn't feel as tired this time, even though it was almost as long of a hike as the day before. What we felt was wet. So, I was happy to be at a motel with warm showers. The light was dim, designed for flipping channels on a remote control, not

One I'd Rather not Pull

Sword or Mariana Maiden Fern (*Macrothelypteris torresia*)

LARRY: An attractive fern has recently turned up in Tennessee. People first spotted it in the Chattanooga area. I found it in 2010 about 50 miles north of there on the Oak Ridge Reservation. Later, an Oak Ridge resident showed me a fern specimen from her yard; again, it was the new fern.

If you check the range map for this fern on the University of Tennessee Herbarium website, you will see only four TN counties (Nov. 2013). I was negligent and didn't get a specimen from Oak Ridge into the herbarium, so Anderson, Oak Ridge's County, doesn't show up on the map. I suspect the fern is already in many more counties.

Sword Fern caught my eye on this second day on the CT. I never saw it again as we hiked north, but if the climate continues to warm you may well see it in your yard. It is originally from tropical Asia and Africa.

To recognize this fern look for a robust fern, perhaps 4 feet long by 3 feet wide, that looks like ferns put together to make a bigger fern (compound). See the picture on our website. Technically, it is bipinnate to tripinnate, repeatedly divided.

checking a plant book for threatened species. Still, compared to being outside in the rain, the room was a resort.

Sources and Suggested Reading

My Quotation:
Heat Moon, William Least. Blue Highways: A Journey into America. Boston: Little, Brown and Company, 1983.

Ferns:
"A Brief Introduction to Ferns." *American Fern Society.* Accessed October 3, 2014. http://amerfernsoc.org/ lernfrnl.html.
    This page is a good place for beginners to learn about ferns and their reproductive methods.

Cobb, Boughton. *A Field Guide to the Ferns and Their Related Families.* Boston: Houghton Mifflin Company 1963.
    While a bit old, this book was my introduction to fern sex.

    There are some other ferns you might confuse with it. Cinnamon fern fronds (leaves) may be as long but are not nearly as wide. Bracken fern may be as wide but not as long. So, you could call sword fern the biggest fern in our area in the sense of area measure of each leaf. Also, some wood ferns, a group of related ferns, are generally similar in shape but have loose scales near their leaf bases.

    I hope this fern can become part of our plant communities without disrupting them. Often, exotic plants arrive without the insects that control them in their homeland. Without the appetites of such insects acting on this fern, we could have a problem. English ivy, Nepal grass and plenty of other plants have become a threat to Tennessee's native plants. Often, I pull these bullies from the ground to slow their spread and displacement of our natives.

    I have yet to pull this exotic fern out of the ground as I often do to other exotics. They are beautiful. However, I may regret letting them produce spores if they start pushing out our natives.

Moran, Robert C. *A Natural History of Ferns.* Portland: Timber Press 2004.
This book goes into much more detail than I've done about the mechanics of ferns' reproduction, as well as some of the exceptions to the typical method.

Antlions:
Fetin, Arnold and Casas, Jérôme. "Efficiency of Antlion Trap Construction." *The Journal of Experimental Biology*, 209 no. 18 (2006): 3510-3519. doi: 10.1242/jeb.02401.

Milius, Susan. 2014. "Ant Lions Hunt Despite Sealed Lips." *Science News*, July 12: 4-5.

Swanson, Mark. *Antlion Pit: A Doodlebug Anthology.* Edited by Mark Swanson. 2012. http://www.antlionpit.com (accessed April 11, 2013).
This is not a particularly scholarly source, but is a good starting point for learning about antlions.

Fire:
Tennessee Government. *Marion County Man Charged with Arson.* November 16, 2010. https://news.tn.gov/node/6349 (accessed February 27, 2013).

Hallenbeck, Kathy H. "Fire." In *Encyclopedia of Appalachia*, by Rudy Abramson and Jean Haskell, 120-122. Knoxville: University of Tennessee Press, 2006.

GET SODDY

↳ 6 ↲

Exploring Soddy-Daisy

BEN: When looking at sky, streams, mountains, valleys, trees and birds, it can be easy to assume that humans have not disturbed the natural world. However, if you look closer, you can often see mounds of shoveled earth, blasted rock faces and remnants of stone walls. You might smell the smoke from an abandoned mine that caught fire. The people who dug into the land for mining years ago had their own stories, which are often hidden in small towns along the Plateau's edge.

    On the way back from our first few hikes, we passed through Soddy-Daisy. Businesses in it, both local and franchise, cluster along Dayton Pike. The drive down Dayton Pike shows hints of Soddy-Daisy's past. For a stretch within the town, the clusters of businesses disappear and forest grows on both sides of the road, interrupted by houses and "Evacuation Route" signs for the nearby Sequoyah Nuclear Plant. Then, the more cluttered part of town starts up again. The break has a logical explanation. Soddy and Daisy were once two different towns. Both were company towns for coal mining.

    Soddy's name could be from Tsati, meaning "sipping place," in Cherokee, an apt name for the creeks now called the Big Soddy and the Little Soddy, though less so during the coal mining era, when much of the stream was full of coal dust. Another theory states that it was named after William Soder's Trading Post, which Welsh immigrants nicknamed "Soddy."

    The old mines that the CT passes near Soddy Creek were leased to a group of these Welshmen. Wales has many coal mines. So, it was logical for Welsh people to come to Tennessee to run the mines near Soddy. They left a good enough impression that the Chattanooga Times wrote of Welsh people in 1930:

"If a Welshman is not pleased with any person or institution, he rarely or never undertakes the work of reform with a bomb or an automatic. He had no taste for gore. In other words, the average Welshman makes a good American citizen."

"The Welshman may, like the German, enjoy a modicum of lager once in a while, but he loves his home. Had all others been as restrained in their indulgence as the Welshman, sentiment against the liquor traffic would never have become as strong in this country."

In other words, the Welsh were great for not being drunken terrorists. Back when I worked at Walmart, a white haired coworker told me, "You know what I like about you? You don't wear piercings." I was amused but not flattered. Possibly the Welsh felt the same way.

The Soddy Mining Company had mined for coal along the present-day Cumberland Trail, and I wanted to learn more. I searched online from our motel room for directions to Soddy-Daisy's library, only to find that the closest thing Soddy-Daisy had to a library was Soddy Bible & Church Supplies. Dad dropped me off there and headed to a coin laundry.

Fluffy, yellow baby chicks peeped from inside the store. Though I'd hardly expected to see chicks for sale here, it shouldn't have surprised me. Plenty of book stores these days have added coffee shops in order to survive. This one happened to prefer poultry. *Veggie Tales* toys sat on shelves, along with Bibles and books about local legends and ghost stories.

"We're not open for business yet," said a smiling woman at the counter,

Coal

BEN: Giant ferns and other plants grew in lush swamps, millions of years before the dinosaurs, on land that is now the Cumberland Plateau. Back then, it was a flat place where seagull-sized dragonfly-like insects flew. Coal formed when sandstone pressed on the plants' remains, a process of turning plants to rock that for the most part happened only once in Earth's history. It might happen again to the northern peat bogs if global warming doesn't cause them to rot first.

In 2011, 42% of our electricity in the U.S. came from coal according to the U.S. Energy Information Administration. All of that power came thanks to forests of extinct plants.

"but you can look around."

"I'm looking for books about Soddy-Daisy's history," I said.

"These are the best we have," she said, pointing to a set of big white books labeled *The Good Old Days Volume I*, *The Good Old Days Volume II* and *The Good Old Days Volume III* by Steve L. Smith.

"They're read only," she said. "We've sold all the other copies we had."

According to the documents preserved in *The Good Old Days*, at one point as many as 800 people may have worked in Soddy's mining operations. To serve the growing Chattanooga steel industry, coal had to be dug up, washed and converted to coke in industrial ovens.

Mining involved many different steps in order to get coal ready to use and sell. Six days a week, miners walked in darkness from company houses to the coal washing plant. Soddy Creek ran by the plant, polluted with coal dust. Rails came down the mountain carrying ore. Miners hopped in empty cars and rode up to the mine. With a loud shrill noise, the rail ran along the waters of Soddy Creek, which were much clearer above the washer. Further up on the Plateau, at 7:00 AM, miners jumped off their cars at the operations hub where a blacksmith pounded, sharpening tools. From there, the miners rode on to work in the deep mines.

Certain things about the work changed over the years. Electric lights replaced oil lamps. Machines replaced shovels and picks.

In the early days, mules the size of ponies pulled the cars in and out of some mines. According to Steve L. Smith's books, the mules would not go into the mine unless each of them had one eye covered by a rag. Mules using the depth perception of two eyes might have seen the tunnel's depth and feared

....

During Europe's Middle Ages, coal was the solution to an energy crisis that involved running out of wood. Even back then, people worried about the health effects of burning coal. Today, people fear breathing asthma-inducing soot and sulfur. Other problems with coal include a warming climate from carbon dioxide and disturbance from strip mining.

Coal is a limited resource that can never re-form during our lifetime. There still are seams of coal, but the easiest seams to use are gone. Mountain top removal is a way to get at the less accessible coal, but its consequences are controversial. It takes mountains apart, creating new landscapes.

....

going far underground. Since early humans had no reason to breed giant cave salamanders or moles, these pony-mules were the available animals for use.

Could've happened but didn't.

Mules learned from experience how to jump out of mine carts' way. They got Sunday off to graze in a field.

The company did not have to put rags over miners' eyes to get them to come. Unlike mules, people can put aside instincts and fears in order to earn a living. Miners worked for long, hard hours. Their bosses paid them by the amount of coal they mined, not by the hour. They never left the mines during the work day, not even for lunch. They ate sandwiches, fried chicken and pies in darkness and grime.

When it was time to leave, miners lit fuses and blasted further into the ground to prepare for the next day. Then, they rode down to the washhouse and tried to get themselves clean.

Hungry mules clopped down the mountain to their barn to be fed. They needed no prodding.

The Soddy mines were among the safest in the country for their time according to Smith's research. Still, people got crushed by falling rocks, run over by coal cars, electrocuted by frayed wires and scalded in boiler rooms. Company records and personal accounts reproduced in *The Good Old Days* mention these and other stories that explain just how bad the old days could be.

Because people depended on the company for work, the company figured it could shove its fingers into every aspect of its workers' lives to get a profit. They charged rent on company houses and set prices on clothes and equipment at company stores. At times, the company paid company scrip rather than money.

At Right: Ben Toon enjoys the good ol' days. Miners did not leave the mines for lunch.

"ANYONE GOT HAND SANITIZER?"

Workers organized unions and went on strikes several times. The company responded to these strikes by threatening to use convict labor, which they did use for the coke oven work though not the mines. They built a road leading to the mines from a prison for that reason.

People in and near Soddy probably preferred working for the Soddy Coal Company and later the Durham Coal & Iron Co. to no work at all, which was what hit them in 1929. The Company collapsed like a mine ceiling cave-in. It was not the end of mining in the Soddy area though. As deep mining became less common, companies stripped the surface. Strip mining was often non-union and required fewer people. It was also harsher to the environment, changing the land more than deep mines did. All along the Cumberland Trail run hill side benches cut during the strip mining days: a torn-apart hillside, called a "highwall" on one side and a pile of shoveled up rock and soil or "overburden" on the other side of the bench. Little Soddy Creek itself changed route thanks to one of these strip mines.

These days there's not enough coal left to be worth mining in the Soddy area. Soddy married the nearby town of Daisy in 1969. Instead of coal, the combined city now has a nuclear power economy based on the nearby Sequoyah Plant.

A few old mines are safety hazards now. In the old days, the Number 7 Mine tunneled deep into the mountain with a long air shaft. It was a marvel of engineering. In more recent times, concerned parents rediscovered the shaft near an elementary school and worried that their children would fall into it. It's paved over now.

Dad came in and told me to hurry.

My history with coal was different from the experiences of miners.

When my sister Jessie and I were little, my Dad eagerly taught us the name of every pebble we found in our back yard and elsewhere. He especially liked showing us the black yet shiny nuggets of coal, left over from old piles of furnace coal. By the time of my childhood in the 1990s, no one used a coal furnace. Still, Dad told us it was the same material that fueled the Bull Run Steam Plant on the edge of town. Early on, coal was one rock of many that I wanted to collect. I'd added it to a rock collection that included a souvenir geode and random pieces of gravel. What I loved was not the coal itself but the act of finding it lodged in the earth like a buried treasure.

As an older, more cynical child though, I justified my digging by looking for coal exclusively. If I could find enough, I reasoned, I could sell it. I looked near school, near our house, anywhere, just to find more. Little chunks were everywhere. I'd be rich!

The coal had come to Oak Ridge in freight trains from the Plateau. There was no natural coal under Oak Ridge's soil, as Dad was keen to tell me. "There's not enough to be worth much," he said. Other kids at school made fun of my obsession. At first, I shrugged them off.

The sum total of coal that I found over the course of weeks filled a shopping bag. It was hardly a day's work for a real miner. Real miners would have rolled their eyes at me for even thinking my plan was possible. With eyes as disappointed as a miner who'd spent his last company scrip, I dumped out the bag in our back yard.

At the Sandwich Shoppe, country music played on speakers. Paintings for sale hung above us as we sat down. The one right above us was a colorful abstract expressionist piece called "Time Zones," done in splatters of bright blue and green. The woman serving us had a nose stud and a brown ponytail. My veggie sub was good, if sweeter than expected, with both honey wheat bread and honey mustard dressing. I got a monster-sized piece of red velvet 3-layer cake for desert and put it between two Styrofoam plates to take home.

We were now on the Daisy side of the town. The Tabler-Clendys Coal Company had named the town of Daisy after the daughter of the company's vice-president. Naming company towns after family or acquaintances was common in those days. In *Night Comes to the Cumberlands*, Harry Caudill mentions a Kentucky coal baron who named his company and town Dalna after his girlfriend. He later renamed his company Elsie after falling in love with another woman.

"Is there anything you want to do before we leave?" asked Dad.

"I'd just like to check out Poe's Tavern," I said.

Long before the Soddy or Tabler-Clendys companies came, Hasten Poe, a War of 1812 veteran, ran a tavern where travelers could sleep. Soddy-Daisy's website says that the tavern also served as the county's first courthouse, without mentioning whether it was still open as a tavern at that time. I imagined someone coming in and trying to order beer or a room in the middle of a trial.

According to a *Chattanooga Times Free Press* article 1,900 Cherokee stayed at Poe's Tavern along their forced journey to Oklahoma. Later it became a hospital for both sides during the Civil War. The city's website mentioned a project to rebuild it in a park near the original site. I had to see it. I wanted to see how people sheltered while traveling between the time of rockhouses and the time of motels.

The tavern was a log cabin that smelled of fresh cut wood. It was one and a half stories tall and smaller across than our room at the Scottish Inn. Maybe the 1,900 Cherokee had stayed there at different times. Maybe they'd slept on top of each other. This tavern showed me what the past was really like back when many people settled for far less on the frontier. Even a roof was a luxury.

No one had cared to rebuild the Soddy mines or mule barn. After all, they'd been unromantic, grimy businesses. It was better that nature reclaimed them. On the trail though, we would see what had become of their ruins.

Sources and Suggested Reading

Soddy's Name and the Joining of Soddy and Daisy:
City of Soddy-Daisy, Tennessee. "About." Accessed September 23, 2013. http://soddy-daisy.org/about .

Coal in General:
Bell, Augusta Grove. *Circling Windrock Mountain: Two Hundred Years in Appalachia.* Knoxville: University of Tennessee Press, 1999.

Brill, David. *Cumberland Odyssey: A Journey in Pictures and Words along Tennessee's Cumberland Trail and Plateau.* Johnson City, Tennessee: Mountain Trail Press, 2010.

Lienhard, John H. *How Invention Begins.* New York: Oxford University Press, 2006.

U.S. Energy Administration. "Electricity in the United States." Last Updated February 7, 2013. http://www.eia.gov/energyexplained/index.cfm?page=electricity_in_the_united_states .

Caudil, Harry M. *Night Comes to the Cumberlands.* Boston: Little, Brown and Company, 1963.

Life in the Mining Town of Soddy:
Smith, Steve L. *The Good Old Days: A Short History of Soddy, Daisy and Montlake.* Soddy-Daisy: S. Smith, 1991.

Smith, Steve L. *The Good Old Days: A Short History of Soddy, Daisy, and Montlake, Part 2.* Soddy-Daisy: S. Smith, 1994.

Smith, Steve L. *The Good Old Days: A Short History of Soddy, Daisy, and Montlake, Part III.* Cleveland, TN: Derek Press & Penman Publishers, 2003.

Schroeder, Jim. "Little Soddy Mining Brochure." Cumberland Trail.org. Accessed September 24, 2014. http:// cumberlandtrail.org/website/wp-content/uploads/2014/05/LITTLE-SODDY-MINING-BROCHURE-2.pdf.

Schroeder, Jim. "A Walk in History." Cumberlandtrail.org. May 10, 2014. Accessed September 24, 2014. http:// cumberlandtrail.org/website/maps-and-guides/trail-segments/three-gorges/soddy-creek-gorge-section-1/a-walk-in-history/.

Schroeder, Jim. "Mining History Synopsis of the Little Soddy Creek Valley on the Cumberland Trail." Cumberlandtrail.org. May 30, 2012. Accessed September 24, 2014. http://cumberlandtrail.org/website/wp-content/ uploads/2014/05/Mining-History-Synopsis1.pdf.

Poe's Tavern:
Cooper, Clint. "Poe's Tavern Re-Creation to Anchor New 2-Acre Park in Soddy-Daisy, TN." *Chattanooga Times-Free Press.* June 25, 2011. Accessed September 23, 2013. http://www.timesfreepress.com/news/2011/jun/25/poes-tavern-re-creation-anchor-new-2-acre-park-sod/.

NOTICERS

→ 7 ←

Little Soddy Creek (Monday, May 14)
Hike 3: Mowbray Pike to Hotwater Rd. and Mining History Loop
About 4.5 miles

BEN: At the motel, The Weather Channel gave soft news stories that had nothing to do with the weather. I brought my raincoat just in case.

As we left the trailhead, power lines buzzed above us in the cool air. They hung from tower to tower like vines from tree to tree. Trees and vines nearby took energy from the sun, a giant nuclear fusion reactor. The wires took their energy from a much nearer nuclear fission reactor.

Deep in the valley's fog, the cooling towers of Sequoyah Nuclear Plant released steam. The Tennessee Valley Authority (TVA) named the power plant after Sequoyah (c. 1770-1843) a Cherokee silversmith and soldier who created a written alphabet for the Cherokee language. He had no opinion on nuclear energy. No one had discovered it yet.

We walked sideways through a narrow stone door, a crack in the rock that people call "Fat Man's Squeeze." It felt tight and intimate like a sandstone hug and kept us cool in its shade. I half-sat and put my hands against the wall in

Translation: "What?" Sequoyah had no opinion on nuclear energy.

order to climb through it. Dad did the same, twisting his baseball cap sideways like an early 1990s pop star.

The stone door widened. Dad peered at leaves and seeds in a small hole in a cliff. "How do you think these got here?" said Dad. "Is there a crack in the rock letting this material creep down or is it animal-deposited?"

"I don't know, but did you see the salamander?" I said.

It clung on the rock wall, hard to miss, black with green splotches like splattered paint.

"Great spotting!" said Dad, amazed as he stared at it. "That's a green salamander. Maybe you notice different things than I do."

Dad could never stop noticing and wondering about small things. On our beach vacations, he would look at coastal plain grasses with the obsessive stare of a teenage boy peering at bikini babes. Unlike Dad, I had a habit of getting lost in my own thoughts. Yet when I kept myself in the present, I could be just as much of a noticer as he was.

The dictionary does not count "noticer" as a word. We already have a word for noticer: "Human." All of us notice different things.

Green salamanders hide in dark and narrow cracks most of the time. People rarely see them out in the open. Maybe today's cool air and mist made this one feel like coming out.

According to Joe Mitchell and Whit Gibbons' book *Salamanders of the Southeast*, some scientists believe that green salamanders evolved to hide behind tree bark first and adapted to live in rock cracks later as humans chopped down more trees.

A green salamander mother attaches her eggs with mucous and hides them from predators in bark or rock cracks. She stays with the eggs, protecting the surviving ones like a watchful hen but gobbling up miscarriages like a hen eating a delicious omelet.

Baby green salamanders hatch after two or three months. According to Brian T. Miller and R. Graham Reynolds' book *The Amphibians of Tennessee*,

Green salamander mothering.

green salamander hatchlings often spend two or three weeks with their mothers before crawling out of the crack. Unlike some other salamanders, the children never live in the water. Once they grow up, they live alone.

Male green salamanders defend their crevices from other green salamanders by biting and flipping the invaders.

Muscadine vines, which had not yet grown grapes, tangled in the trees around us.

"Box turtle," said Dad, pointing to one. A dome, called a carapace, with bright yellow marks protected it. It hid its head and legs, waiting for us to leave. A box turtle is box-like because the shell can open and shut. The plastron, or

A Grape for Foraging

Feature Plant: Muscadine Grape (*Vitis rotundifolia*)

LARRY: Muscadines are the only thoroughly edible wild grapes in the southeastern US. They grow as large as store-bought grapes and larger than any of our other wild ones. You can peel them or take them whole and spit out the tough skins, but the best way to eat muscadines is to break them open and suck out the insides.

Finding the muscadine vine is easy. It is a common plant. However, finding fruit is not as easy. Like many forest plants, the vines wait to fruit until there is extra light and thus more energy for producing fruit. This can happen when a tree falls nearby, opening a hole in the leafy canopy that allows more light to reach the vines below. Some other vines grow high up into the forest canopy to get light, but muscadines don't go as high. Thus, before fruiting, muscadines may wait many years for a tree to fall.

Some fun facts follow:

1. For the botanist, berries are fleshy fruits with small seeds inside. So, all grapes are berries.

2. Muscadine is fun to say. It also has two other names which are fun: bullace and scupper-nong. The scupper-nong grape is a variety of muscadine with greenish mature fruit while typical muscadines are black or bronze when ripe.

3. There are hundreds of cultivated forms of muscadine, many used in wine making.

Good luck with your grape foraging!

underside of the shell, has two hinged lobes which can close like drawbridges to protect the turtle's head and feet. In times of danger, sleep or hard weather, box turtles stay closed.

"Baby box turtle," said Dad, pointing to another one. His shell was as wide as my thumb was long.

I used to survey box turtles for a group called the Clinch River Environmental Studies Organization (CRESO) in Oak Ridge. From that experience, I knew how to figure out a few things about the turtle in front of me, including how to sex them. Like other males, he had an indentation on his underside which would one day help him mount a female.

Box turtles can cool off in streams, munch mushrooms under trees or crawl under tall grass and thorny shrubs in search of insects. In the summer they rarely leave the shade unless it rains.

Some days during my time surveying turtles, a non-biologist turtle lover in parachute pants would bring his shaggy reddish dogs along to sniff for them. The dogs ran back to us with turtles in their mouths. The turtles, with their hard shells, remained unharmed. On other days, we found them either with our eyes or using radio tags. We focused on areas near logging and development, including a place near a Boeing factory, where the forest yielded to the red clay that developers had unearthed. From what I saw, turtles tended to leave the disturbed areas for less-disturbed ones. The end result was more turtles to share the food in the remaining area. An adult box turtle's shell can withstand fangs, beaks and talons. Still, it is no match for a car's weight or the crushing blade of a lawnmower. Turtle evolution plods while technology puts its foot on the accelerator and races down the freeway.

A closed shell might feel familiar and comforting. Or it might be a nervous place where a turtle imagines the dangers lurking outside. Close your eyes and imagine being encased in a closed shell. Perhaps a turtle would feel like you do now.

A career in wildlife biology was not my goal. I was dabbling at CRESO like I continued to dabble in many things. I crawled slowly in various directions but never rushed into any of them. When scary thoughts of the future came up, I hid from them, like a turtle. Yet I stood on a highway, the worst place for a turtle to be. Time sped forward, regardless of my wishes.

We walked up onto a mound of dirt. On the nearby slope we saw a rock outcropping called a high wall. In between was a deep ditch. Strip miners had torn this land many years ago.

"I don't think this mound is too interesting," said Dad, "but it looks like there are some cool things down in the ditch." He ran down the steep side, swinging from trees to tree, alternating his left hand and right hand like a square dance move. I followed. For all his fear of cliffs, Dad had no problem with steep slopes. Sometimes he came across as an easily-worried and careful old man, but when he set his mind toward searching for specimens, nothing could stop him. Fellow naturalist David Nestor called him a "kickass botanist." Now I saw it.

Water had gathered in the ditch's bottom. Ferns and green-branching lycopods grew from the wet ground. Back when the Plateau was a low swamp, similar but taller relatives had grown here and formed the coal.

"This is climbing fern," said Dad, pointing to a plant with climbing cords that expanded into small, hand-like leaves.

A fern had become a vine like many other types of plants that evolved into support stealing climbers. Other fern relatives had evolved into shrubs or trees. Evolution, both Darwinian and personal, can take many paths that are, for lack of a better word, creative. What comforts me is the variety of niches that organisms, including me, can fill. The green salamanders may have made new homes for themselves in rocks when logging threatened their habitat in the trees. A Cherokee silversmith became an alphabet creator when he saw the need for a written language. Dad had chosen a path that let him hunt for treasures in nature. Sometimes evolution favors the freaks and alternate path-takers. Someday I would notice a path for myself. It just hadn't happened yet.

As we scrambled out of the ditch, Dad pointed to a green spiny stock.

"This is devil's walking stick. It's the sort of thing that you might grab onto" Dad said, acting out grabbing the main stem without touching it, "and man would it hurt!"

"Each of these things," he said, holding what looked like a branch with many leaves, "is actually a leaf. When fall comes, this is what falls off."

At least the devil finds devil's walking stick handy.

"This is a rattlesnake plantain," said Dad, pointing to a stalk of small flowers growing out of a circle of dark and light multi-colored leaves. "It's called that because the flowering part of the plant looks like a rattlesnake rattle."

A Devil of a Leaf

Feature Plant: Devil's Walking Stick (*Aralia spinosa*)

LARRY: The devil has a few hangout spots on the CT: Devil's Step, Devil's Breakfast Table and Devil's Racetrack. So it is fortunate for the devil that his walking sticks can be found at many places along the trail. No one but the devil would want to use this small tree for a walking stick, as it is covered with sharp prickles.

Devil's walking stick deserves our attention for its leaves as well as it prickles. It has the largest leaves of any plant in temperate North America. To understand its leaves we need to know that the everyday concept of a leaf is not the same as the botanist's. For a botanist a leaf includes both leafy areas (blades) and their stems.

Stems are the support structures (petioles, rachises, petiolules). See the diagram on our website's page for this chapter. Everything, blades and support, that drops off trees is leaf. In the autumn the branches and twigs remain and the leaves fall.

The leaves and flowers are the non-woody part of the tree. In general, a leaf with no forking (thus only one blade) is called "simple." Examples of simple leaves include oaks and maples. A leaf with forking to support leaflets is called "compound." Examples of compound leaves include hickories, ashes and devil's walking stick.

The devil's walking stick leaf in the botanical sense is complex with dozens of blades (leaflets) and a repeatedly-forking support system. The forking may be irregular with up to three levels of forking. The leaf (the whole shebang) is up to a yard long and almost as wide!

The walking stick grows in many scattered places along the CT. Look for it in forest edges or somewhat-disturbed forests. Often it occurs in areas recovering from strip mining. It spreads from the roots and so creates colonies. These colonies are common in some areas but oddly absent from others.

Some say the name is based on the similarity of its leaf pattern to the rattler's skin pattern.

Because of the resemblance to rattles, healers once used these plants as a form of rattlesnake anti-venom. They thought that God would make the appearance of a plant suggest its purpose, a rule that they called the Law of Signatures. They believed that if God made flowers look like rattlesnake rattles or skin, He must have meant that they were for curing rattlesnake bites. They were wrong. Rattlesnake plantain does nothing for snakebites.

The Law of Signatures can be a nifty memory trick. Carrots, when sliced, look like eyes and help people to see at night. So people can remember to eat carrots for eyesight help. However, it doesn't always work. A daffodil bulb looks like a prostate gland, but eating one would kill you rather than heal prostate cancer. Kidney beans, named for their kidney shape, are no replacement for dialysis. We learn by testing. None of us can text God and ask.

The waters of Little Soddy Creek trickled. A bent strip of rusted metal leaned in a U-shape against a tree. Possibly it was an old rail. A chunk of coal sat nearby. The Soddy Mining Company once had mines and operations here. The mines were deep mines that tunneled into the ground rather than the more modern strip (or surface) mines that we had passed earlier.

A dedicated noticer named Jim Schroder had put up signs explaining the different ruins. If those signs had not been here, I would not have known what the ruins had been during the mining company's heyday. Water had flooded one of the mines. Decades of falling dirt had covered others, leaving only dents in the ground. Trees towered above everything now. Nothing remained of the miners' shower except a rusty pipe in a dry stream. The mule barn's building lumber had rotted like logs on the forest floor. Lichens and moss grew on the stone and cinder walls of the old company buildings. I wondered how long it would take for the road that brought us here or even the Sequoyah nuclear plant to become unrecognizable ruins like these.

Hot Water in Your Face!

BEN: We ended this chapter's hike at Hotwater Road. According to a legend, retold in Russ Manning's the Historic Cumberland Plateau, a woman fought with her drunken husband near there. She threw scalding water in his face. If we believe the legend, then someone felt like memorializing that domestic violence incident by naming the road after it.

A pile of tires lay by the side of the path. People called this stretch of the CT the "Trail of Tires," a name that did not do justice to all the other garbage around us. A rusty toy car parked next to a broken TV set with bright tangled wires. A drying machine lay at an angle on the forest floor.

People leave monuments that they intend for future generations to notice, like cemeteries, churches or pyramids. Then, there are relics like these, thrown in order to be out of everyone's way, but telling a more honest story for the noticers who spot them. Even if the tires would not last forever, they would last almost forever.

Dad said a Latin plant name into his voice recording device, then paused to look at the ground around the plant and added, "All kinds of junk." "Plants can be interesting in a garbage dump," Dad added.

When we got to Hotwater Road, thunder roared. Rain fell as we rode back to Dayton with my unused raincoat. The trash we saw on the Trail of Tires had been thrown down from this road.

The litterers who tossed the trash down had never seen the area below Hotwater Road as anything but a dump. A chain-link anti-littering fence, as tall as one and a half of me, ran along the road to stop people from chucking anything more. We wished we could take the litterers down to notice the beauty down below.

Discovery in a Dump?

LARRY: In the Trail of Tires area, nature's spiderwort (*Tradescandens sp.*) flowers contrasted with human trash. Normally our spiderworts are a deep blue color. Here the flowers were many shades of light blue and pink. Some were nearly white. They also were smaller in size and had long-haired leaf sheaves than other spiderworts I had seen. These plants may be a variety or species of spiderwort which has not been previously reported. It will take time to figure out how best to fit these plants into the spiderwort family tree.

Sources and Suggested Reading

Green Salamander:
Behler, John L., and F. Wayne King. *The Audubon Society Field Guide to North American Reptiles and Amphibians.* New York: Chanticleer Press Inc., 1995.

Niemiller, Matthew et al. *The Amphibians of Tennessee.* Knoxville: University of Tennessee Press, 2011.

General Sources:
Cumberland Trail Conference. *CTC's Guide to Hiking the Justin P. Wilson Cumberland Trail with Maps/Guides.* www.cumberlandtrail.org (accessed July 19, 2012).

Sequoyah:
The Sequoyah Birthplace Museum. "*A Brief Biography of Sequoyah*". 2009. http://www.sequoyahmuseum.org/index.cfm/m/5 (accessed May 18, 2013).

Eastern Box Turtle:
Bonin, Frank et al. *Turtles of the World.* Baltimore: Johns Hopkins University Press 2006

Burger, Kimberly and Melissa Jones. "Eastern Box Turtle: North Carolina Wildlife Profiles." Accessed June 4, 2013. http://www.ncwildlife.org/Portals/0/Learning/documents/Profiles/Eastern_Box_Turtle.pdf.

Behler, John L., and F. Wayne King. *The Audubon Society Field Guide to North American Reptiles and Amphibians.* New York: Chanticleer Press Inc., 1979.

Climbing Fern:
Cobb, Boughton. *A Field Guide to the Ferns and Their Related Families.* Boston: Houghton Mifflin Company, 1963.

Rule of Signatures:
Haskell, David George. *The Forest Unseen: A Year's Watch in Nature.* New York: Viking, 2012.

Hotwater Road:
Manning, Russ. *The Historic Cumberland Plateau: An Explorer's Guide, Second Edition.* Knoxville: University of Tennessee Press, 1999.

Mining:
Smith, Steve L. *The Good Old Days: A Short History of Soddy, Daisy and Montlake.* Soddy-Daisy: S. Smith, 1991.

Smith, Steve L. *The Good Old Days: A Short History of Soddy, Daisy, and Montlake, Part 2*. Soddy-Daisy: S. Smith, 1994.

Smith, Steve L. *The Good Old Days: A Short History of Soddy, Daisy, and Montlake, Part III*. Cleveland, TN: Derek Press & Penman Publishers, 2003.

Schroeder, Jim. "Little Soddy Mining Brochure." Cumberland Trail.org. Accessed September 24, 2014. http://cumberlandtrail.org/website/wp-content/uploads/2014/05/LITTLE-SODDY-MINING-BROCHURE-2.pdf.

Schroeder, Jim. "A Walk in History." Cumberlandtrail.org. May 10, 2014. Accessed September 24, 2014. http://cumberlandtrail.org/website/maps-and-guides/trail-segments/three-gorges/soddy-creek-gorge-section-1/a-walk-inhistory/.

Schroeder, Jim. "Mining History Synopsis of the Little Soddy Creek Valley on the Cumberland Trail." Cumberlandtrail.org. May 30, 2012. Accessed September 24, 2014. http://cumberlandtrail.org/website/wp-content/uploads/2014/05/Mining-History-Synopsis1.pdf.

BE A FROG

→ 8 ←

Big Soddy and Board Camp Creeks (Tuesday, May 15)
Hike 4: TN 111 to Hotwater Rd.
9.8 mi.

BEN: Dad watched my driving as I followed Dad's red truck with my white Camry. When few cars were around, I drove slowly by habit. When cars tried to pass me, I accelerated, thinking that I'd misjudged the proper speed. The other drivers didn't expect the speed-up. Some sped up even more to pass me. Others gave up.

"You're a bad driver," said Dad, more blunt than usual, as we rode in his truck to the other end of the trail, "and you'll probably get in a wreck soon." He was probably right. Still, after years of wanting to feel like I had improved, I winced when he said it.

LARRY: It hurts to be reminded of my harsh words. Driving is a focus of my fears.

BEN: A friendly man in blue with a white beard, a white ponytail, a water backpack, blue toe-shoes that followed the shape of his feet and a walking stick joined us.

"Hi, I'm Ed. I don't know if you remember me," he said to Dad. "We worked together on building this part of the trail."

"Nice to see you," said Dad, nodding his head and smiling a wrinkled smile.

Two dogs, both black labs, panted and trotted along with Ed on the trail. Sometimes they ran ahead of him. They were father and son but scampered together like best friends. Together as father, son, father-dog, son-dog and Ed, we climbed a stile, a steep wooden staircase over a fence.

"Have you seen anything unusual on the trail?" asked Ed.

"We saw a rattlesnake in March," said Dad, in a conversational not-frightened tone. "They're probably all out of their dens by now."

"I'm not worried about my dogs finding rattlesnakes," said Ed. "They've won almost every time."

The notion of anyone winning against a rattlesnake sounded about as

Two Days Digging on the CT

LARRY: Digging is a primal pleasure for me. You're messing with nature, but hopefully with little negative impact. Digging for garden or trail connects one to the earth. I have spent two days digging the CT, very little compared to most volunteers. If the ground is flat, trail building may not require digging. Flat ground is rare along the route of the CT; most of the trail must be dug.

The joy of building the CT has a number of components for me. Right at the surface is the physical struggle of moving rocks and roots. As you dig deeper the soil changes, becoming less mixed with plant material and more mineral. The rocks might go from sandstone to shale or vice versa.

Digging brings the pleasure of finding out what is hidden underneath. Often I found living creatures that would have normally been hidden below the screening of ground. Many of these animals also spend some time above ground, but it is a relatively short time for some like the 17 year locust.

Most of the critters are invertebrates—"bugs"—but not always. A Central Florida University student trail volunteer on alternative spring break found a slimy salamander. Slimy is an apt description of this species. It was a handsome creature, black with silver flecks. The student was proud of being comfortable with touching it despite the slime. Many years ago, I had a sad moment when I turned over a rock and broke the back of a delicate ring-neck

likely as winning against a tsunami, but I remained quiet and tried to record the conversation with my recording device. Being told I was going to be in a wreck soon did not put me in the best mood for talking. Besides, Dad kept chatting, eager to share every botanical concept relevant to the growing things around us, including the ones I knew by heart from having been his son. He pulled the branch of a rhododendron bush toward himself and squinted at the leaf intently through his field glass. Ed, one hand on hip, the other on his walking stick, looked over my father's shoulder. His gaze was more general curiosity, as if he wanted to absorb the investigative energy from Dad's mind, not just learn the leaf's species.

"I remember moving these big rocks," said Dad. "I did this one right here," said Ed, pointing to another hunk of stone. To others, these boulders would have just been rocks but not to my Dad and Ed. They could point to the trail the way parents point out their children.

---

snake.

Building the CT with simple tools is much more like pyramid building than modern road building with its big machines. I wonder if slaves felt any joy at creating the pyramids. I certainly felt joy from being a part of building the trail.

In my two days, I built about 40 feet of trail. I probably was close to average in my trail building speed. With a little calculation, I could tell that building the CT would take more than a lifetime for one builder working alone. Fortunately, many people have and will put their effort into the trail. I enjoy that feeling of being part of a group effort.

As we finished our section of the CT, we were pleased to see a group of backpackers using our newly-built trail, even though it was not yet marked with blazes. They ignored the trail blazes that would have led them on the current trail.

As I hike the CT, I see the effort of all the volunteers. I see the extra work to make those rock steps. The trail allows the hiker to flow through nature and focus on the environment rather than his or her feet. Attention can be placed on the natural world.

A red eft scampered below my feet on the damp, muddy, brown leaves. The color seemed more orange than red, but it stood out like a stoplight against the ground. Soon we saw the little crawling fellows everywhere.

"It's the terrestrial stage of the Eastern newt," said Dad to Ed.

"Amphibian" comes from the Greek *amphibios* meaning "double life." Yet newts, which are amphibians, live a triple life. They start as water creatures, move to the land and then back to the water. Each stage has a different skin and a different mode of living.

In their first life, they hatch in the water as larvae, with feathery gills and muted green skin. They search the water for worms to eat.

After a few months in the water, they start their second life. They become red efts with lungs ready to breathe the air. Red efts roam the land for up to seven years, feeding on a wide range of invertebrates like spiders and springtails. The land is a relatively safe place for them. Their flashy red skin sends the warning that they are poisonous to eat.

Back in the water, they live their third life as full-grown newts, diffusing oxygen from the water through their skin. Adult newts are ten times less poisonous than the efts. Now, they have flatter tails for swimming. They can eat many things including frog eggs and small fish. They are dull green but still keep red spots from their young, land-wandering days. Water is the place where they mate and place their eggs. Mama newts seal their eggs inside of a folded leaf.

The newt's life—Childhood, followed by a flashier youth away from home, followed by settling down and starting a family—seems like a human life. Yet unlike us, newts never know the love of parents during any stage of life after they leave their sealed eggs.

Not every newt goes through all of these stages. Sometimes a newt will skip the eft stage if the land is too dry.

I had intended to go out and explore like an eft but never thought that being with my Dad was the right way to do it. Sometimes I still felt like I didn't want my Dad there with me, especially when he pointed out things like my driving skills. Maybe I should have been a red eft, independent of parents. Yet being poisonous would mean nothing in a car crash. Maybe that's why red efts don't drive cars. Or it could be that they can't reach the steering wheel.

After seeing a box turtle by the side of the path, I explained my work with turtles and the process of sexing them to Ed.

"Where's the turtle penis?" he said.

I laughed to hide the fact that I didn't know.

A rusty truck rested by Boardcamp Creek. Its light blue coat had almost faded to white. Rusty dents the size of quarters decorated the door. Possibly people had shot at it. Twigs from trees above covered the folded truck bed.

"That's a hoopy," said Ed, "A truck they used for running moonshine."

Ed and his dogs headed back, but Dad and I kept going. We had enjoyed talking with Ed and sharing what we knew.

Water spilled off the cliff above us, right onto our path. The water had many voices: gurgling, striking and rushing. All of them sounded at the same time like a crowd of children on a school bus who were eager to go home. Another box turtle cooled itself near the water. A rainbow, or rather falls-bow,

Where's the Turtle Penis?

BEN: A male turtle uses a sperm-depositing organ that is similar to a penis. He tucks this organ in his shell near the tail most of the time, with good reason. It is a long, disturbing thing which I'm not showing in a family-friendly book.

Biologists have amusing debates about whether "penis" or "phallus" is the right word for this organ. It consists of a different type of tissue than the mammal penis's tissue. It's an example of convergent evolution, which is when unrelated species evolve to similar adaptations.

A male box turtle can travel a long way to find females during mating season. He greets a potential mate by bobbing his head up and down. He then bites her, climbs up against her shell and grabs onto her with his claws. If he falls backwards while still attached, the female drags him.

A sensitive eastern box turtle.

showed a faint view of every color the human eye can perceive. I stood under the drops. It felt right. I needed to do something pointless and wet. My stress from the morning washed off of me, at least for the moment.

Dad slipped on a damp stick. He accidentally pressed play on his voice recording device before almost hitting the ground. The recorder responded by saying a Latin plant name in a voice far too calm.

"Are your knees okay?" I asked as he got up.

"Trail's been pretty easy on my knees," said Dad. "I took two aspirin last night."

Dad came to a small tree with big flowers and called it *Stewartia ovata* to his voice recorder. I brought my head close to a flower on the tree and smelled it. The minute I was close enough, I could see ants crawling all over the flower. I jolted my head back and snuffed a few times to make sure that none of them had crawled into my nose. These wildflowers were riskier to sniff than the bouquets at Walmart. Out here, taking time to smell the flowers meant taking time to watch for ants.

We came to a bridge that looked like it was made with two telephone poles. What might have been the rail was tangled up on the side. A radiant green Carolina anole lizard sunbathed on the bridge. It turned brown after seeing me. I snapped a picture. It scurried away. Many people call them green anoles, but they can change color between shades of green and brown. I found another Carolina anole on the other side. Its skin was light green before heading into the leaves. Then it became a bluish shade of brown.

People used to assume that the color changes helped anoles to blend in with their surroundings. Anoles and their surroundings don't always match though. The sunbathing anole that I saw had been bright green on a chocolate-pudding-brown bridge until I spotted it. Instances like that have led scientists to come up with other explanations.

Scientists like Neil Greenburg of the University of Tennessee believe that stress hormones trigger the Carolina anoles' skin changes. The evolutionary reason for Carolina anoles to have mood-ring skin isn't clear though. Greenburg and others have suggested that Carolina anoles often change color as a way of signaling to one another. Often males turn brown in confrontations

Moonshining

BEN: Unlicensed moonshining thrived in the Cumberland Plateau decades after the national prohibition era ended. In 1956, an estimated 2,500 gallons of moonshine came from the mountains of East Tennessee each week. In April of 1955, federal agents found and destroyed 94 distilling operations in the region. Remnants of liquor-making, including distilling operations and hoopies, can still be found in various places along the CT.

over territory.

LARRY: Lizards changing color could be helpful for survival not as camouflage but by confusing pursuing predators.

BEN: "Shouldn't we go down those stairs?" I asked.

"No, I think that's just a side trail that leads down to the creek," said Dad.

We retraced our path back and forth without seeing a single blaze. Looking got so stressful that if I'd been a Carolina anole, my skin would have changed color. Instead, I just did the human thing. I gave up and made someone else do the work for me.

"You can handle looking for the trail," I told Dad. "I'm going down to the stream."

Big Soddy Creek was deep, wide and full of boulders of many different sizes. A pickerel frog squatted by the side of it. The frog had broad spots along its back. I tried to sneak in to catch a picture.

Jump.

The frog was on another rock. I stepped toward it.

Jump.

The frog dove into a pool.

Pickerel Frog (*Lithobates palustrus*)

BEN: Pickerel frogs often call from underwater. You can hear their low-pitched, grinding, snore-like sound and not see them. Odds are though, if you hear a pickerel frog, he's nearby, because the call is not loud. Pickerel frog males call in order to attract females. They mate in the water. The females are usually bigger than the males. Males' thumbs swell during mating season in order to hold females.

Adult frogs spent most of their time on land. However, they also jump into the water to cool themselves or avoid predators.

People often confuse them with leopard frogs. With a good enough look you should be able to tell the difference. Pickerel frogs have yellow thighs and spots that look like rectangles drawn by children, while leopard frogs have rounder spots and lack the yellow.

Pickerel frogs got their name because they were once used as bait for pickerel fish. Many other predators avoid them though, possibly due to toxins in their skin.

No more blazes! Will Ben Toon and Larry Toon escape the Land of Ribbons?

The Asian Connection

Feature Plant: Mountain Camellia (*Stewartia ovata*)

Disjunctions (splits) in plant distributions are intriguing mysteries to theorize about. It is hard to know for sure what happened long ago, but we can speculate on why there are gaps between areas occupied by plant relatives. The big question is "How did plant ancestors succeed in placing their descendants in widely separated areas?"

The gorgeous mountain camellia (*Stewartia ovata*) decorates the CT. Another *Stewartia*, silky camellia, grows further south in the US. Half a world separates these two southeastern US species from their nearest relatives in East Asia. All species in the genus *Stewartia* are found in these two widely disjunct areas.

The number of *Stewartia* species in China, Japan and Korea is 8 to 20 depending on your *Stewartia* authority while we have only the two other species in the US. The 8 versus 20 disparity shows how much botanists can disagree. One Asian species is the Japanese *Stewartia*. Perhaps you have a cultivar of it in your yard.

Evolutionary theory would say there had to be a common ancestor of the *Stewartia* species that somehow succeeded in having current descendants in both the eastern US and eastern Asia but not in between. It turns out that there are many groups of relatives that are split between eastern US and eastern Asia e.g. ginseng (*Panax*) and the trilliums (*Trillium*).

The popular theory is that a few million years ago, long before the

It swam back to the surface. I pulled my camera out again.
The frog plunged even deeper.
I gave up and walked back to Dad.

"I couldn't find a path. Maybe we should just follow the ribbons instead," said Dad gesturing to an orange one tied around a tree.

Builders had used ribbons instead of spray-painted blazes here because the trail was not quite done. It still needed a few bridges before the state and the Cumberland Trail Conference could call it finished.

The pickerel frog's stubbornness and quick jumping inspired me. Each bound took it somewhere new. It did not worry about ribbons, blazes or getting the right path. It did not fret about appearing too slow or a too fast. It did not spend hours stressing over the proper way to escape from me. It jumped.

....

most recent ice age, a widespread temperate forest stretched across the northern hemisphere. A land bridge west of Alaska (the Bering Straits area) connected Europe and Asia to North America. With time, the bridge disappeared and the climate changed, shrinking the area of temperate forest.

This left many groups of plant descendants separated into two areas of temperate forest half-way around the world from each other. Seeing the mountain camellia along the CT reminds me of that Asian connection.

Mountain camellia has a famous relative from Asia in a closely related genus: tea (*Camellia sinensis*) the popular beverage. Mountain camellia and tea are alike in their lovely flowers but unalike in the texture and caffeine content of their leaves. Tea has leathery evergreen leaves as opposed to Stewartia's softer, deciduous ones. I have found no reference to drug or drink uses for our native mountain camellia.

Mountain camellia is a small tree which, according to the books, flowers in June and July. In mid-May on our CT trek we saw some flowering. I suspect, depending on the particular year and the progress of climate change, we will see flowers even in early May.

If you find a shrub with large (about 3 inches across) showy white flowers along the CT, it's either mountain camellia or a magnolia. Our CT magnolias can be separated from mountain camellia by measuring the leaves. The magnolias have leaves longer than 5 inches while the mountain camellias have shorter leaves.

....

I slogged in my shoes and jeans through the cool knee-deep creek, which had no bridge. I strode ahead of Dad on the land. Nothing other than forward movement mattered to me now. I would be a frog.

The ribbon zone ended. We passed a CT sign on a tree and began to see white blazes once again.

"We're blazed," said Dad, "blessed with blazes."

"It should be pronounced blaz·éd," I said, "like the King James version."

Thunder rumbled in the distance. I didn't care about rain though. I was a frog.

A sign on a tree greeted us:

"WARNING:
ROCK HARVESTING AHEAD
Dangerous Equipment and Unstable Terrain in the area."

Do Plants Tell Time?

BEN: Plants grow, bloom and shed leaves with a schedule that doesn't have to be checked on a smartphone. Photoperiodism is the ability of some plants to tell time on the calendar by length of day or more often length of night. Scientists discovered it in a mutant ten-foot-high tobacco plant called Maryland mammoth. Studying mutant ten-foot-tall tobacco might seem like a sure way to find things that only apply to mutant ten-foot-tall tobacco. However, later scientists found that many other plants had the same pattern. Global warming may be too fast for some plants to adjust their calendars. These plants risk extinction. Mountain camellia, however, seems to be adjusting to the changing climate.

LARRY: As you might have guessed, some exotic plants here in the U.S. are adjusting their calendars more rapidly than the natives. This allows them to make better use of the extended growing season that comes with global warming. Thus they have a competitive advantage over plants with poorly adjusted calendars.

Heatstroke: Nature in an Age of Global Warming by Anthony Barnosky gives us a broad perspective on the effects on species to expect from warming. He uses the fossil record to illustrate past impacts to species, but he also notes that the current warming is unprecedented in its rapidity.

We saw no dangerous or even harmless equipment. The warning was from an earlier time when bulldozers ripped up the land.

Rock harvesting is exactly what the name implies: ripping stones off the ground and selling them. Native sandstone gives a more natural and rustic look to a wall, chimney, garden or mailbox support. People love the look of nature so much that they're willing to have other people tear up the land with bulldozers to get it for them.

The Lahiere-Hill LLC partnership had owned the mineral rights since 1951. So, in 2007, they blocked the CT with piles of discarded dirt from their rock harvesting operations.

Volunteers had fixed the trail. Sandstone rocks now guarded it from erosion. A fallen tree blocked the clay road that the rock harvesters had used.

Back at the motel, I researched pickerel frogs. Dad took notes on the plants he'd seen.

"So what was that plant you were supposed to remind me about?" he said.

"Spiderwort," I answered.

"No," said Dad, "New Jersey tea."

At left: Do plants tell time?

"Well," I said, "at least you remembered anyway."

Reading *Frogs and Toads of the Southeast* in the dim motel room light tired my eyes. I hopped into Dad's truck bed and read outside.

A middle-aged man with red hair and a two-inch beard walked toward me.

"Hi," he said. "What are you up to?"

I told him.

"It's a great thing your Dad's doing this for you, helping you out like that," he said, smiling.

"Well, I'm helping him too. We both want this book done."

"You should feel lucky. I know my dad thought I needed to fend for myself. Taught me farming was all that he did, but my mama helped me get through high-school, which was all she could do."

"I wanted to give my daughter all I could," he said, leaning against the truck. "I'm working to pay for her getting through college."

Climbing at Deep Creek

BEN: Near this hike's end, we followed a sign that said "trail." Soon though, we saw a sign that said "Southeastern Climbing Coalition," and knew it wasn't the main CT.

Climbers have known Deep Creek Crag at least since 2007. Back then, the climbers climbed secretly. When the Cumberland Trail State Park found out about it, they banned the climbers from bolting new routes. So, climbers walked with park officials down the trail and along the bluff, talking about the effects that climbing had on the land. The climbers and Cumberland Trail State Park made an agreement in 2009, letting climbers bolt new routes. The Southeastern Climbing Coalition works on helping climbers get better access to climbing sites. In 2011, just a year before our hike, they worked with the Cumberland Trail Conference and bought land for a parking lot and an access trail to the Deep Creek Bluff.

I don't know much about the climbing routes themselves. I'll let *Climbing* magazine's Cody Averbeck describe them for you:

"Deep Creek truly lives up to its name as the cliff rises straight from the stream bed, with psychotically overhanging cave routes where, at times, whitewater and evergreens blur in your periphery as you hang way out above a riparian rock garden."

"Where do you work?"

"I travel around and fix railroads." The railroad tracks ran just a block away, and the trains wailed as they went by every night. "I gotta earn a living. We all do. Just don't go crazy with it, for money can be the root of all evil."

Somehow I didn't see much risk of that happening in my life yet. I didn't have anywhere near enough money.

A car zoomed by us.

"Man," he said, "that mother-f__ drives fast!"

"Yeah, I know." I said. "Speed limit here is 45, I think. Everybody goes faster." For once, I got to complain about other people's driving. No one was around to call me a hypocrite.

New Jersey Tea (*Ceanosthus americanus*)

BEN: In spite of my forgetting it, distracted as I was by the pickerel frog, New Jersey tea is a beautiful shrub with small white clustered flowers. It is not, however, as closely related to Chinese tea as *Stewartia ovata* (see above) is. Instead its common name comes from its use as a hot beverage.

Sources and Suggested Reading

Asia-North American Botanical Affinity:
Wen, Jun. "Evolution of Eastern Asian and Eastern North American Disjunct Distributions in Flowering Plants *Annual Review of Ecology and Systematics* 30 (1999): 421-455. http://www.jstor.org/stable/221691.

General:
Cumberland Trail Conference. *CTC's Guide to Hiking the Justin P. Wilson Cumberland Trail with Maps/Guides.* http://www.cumberlandtrail.org (accessed July 19, 2012).

Box Turtle:
Naish, Darren. "Terrifying Sex Organs of Male Turtles." *Scientific American.* Last Modified June 8, 2012. http://blogs.scientificamerican.com/tetrapod-zoology/2012/06/08/terrifying-sex-organs-of-male-turtles/. (accessed July 18, 2012).

This lighthearted but accurate article offers a much more extensive discussion of male turtle sex organs and convergent evolution. It includes some not-safe-for-work photographs.

Bonin, Frank et al. *Turtles of the World.* Baltimore: Johns Hopkins University Press 2006.

Newts and Red Efts:
Mitchel, Joe and Gibbons, Whit. *Salamanders of the Southeast.* Athens: University of Georgia Press, 2010.

Niemiller, Matthew et al. *The Amphibians of Tennessee.* Knoxville: University of Tennessee Press, 2011.

Photoperiodism
Barnosky, Anthony D. *Heatstroke: Nature in an Age of Global Warming.* Washington: Island Press, 2009.

Nijhuis, Michelle. "Invasion! Climate is a game changer in the plant wars." *Smithsonian*, December 2013, Vol. 44, Number 8.

Thomas, Brian and Vince-Prue, Daphne. *Photoperiodism in Plants: Second Edition.* San Diego: Academic Press, 1997. Accessed 24, September 2013.

Wilkins, Malcolm. *Plantwatching, How Plants Remember, Tell Time, Form Relationships and More.* New York: Facts on File Publications, 1988.

Moonshining:
Durand, Loyal Jr. ""Mountain Moonshining" in East Tennessee." *Geographical Review* 46, no. 2 (April 1956): 168-181. http://www.jstor.org.
    This paper was my source for my statistics. "In 1956, an estimated 2,500 gallons of moonshine came from the mountains of East Tennessee each week. In April of 1955, federal agents found and destroyed 94 stills in East Tennessee."

Livingood, James W. *Sequatchie: A Story of the Southern Cumberlands.* Knoxville: University of Tennessee Press, 1974.

Yedell, Cynthia. "Ground Zero for Whiskey: Law Allows Production of Distilled Spirits in State." *Knoxville News Sentinel.* July 5, 2009. Accessed May 24, 2013. http://www.knoxnews.com/news/2009/jul/05/ground-zero-whiskeylaw-allows-production-distille/?print=1.

Carolina Anole:
Greenburg, Neil. "Deep Ethology: the Integrative Biology of Behavior" Last Modified March 2013. Accessed May 24, 2013. https://notes.utk.edu/bio/greenberg.nsf/989e1f6d00861f2a85257015006e192e/

fec0670b676b58b785256d2005771d6?OpenDocument.

Greenburg, Neil "Ethological Aspects of Stress in a Model Lizard, *Anolis carolinensis.*" *Integrative & Comparative Biology.* (2002) 42 (3): 526-540, accessed May 24, 2013. doi: 10.1093/icb/42.3.526

Here, Neil Greenburg goes into a great deal more detail about the chemical reactions involved in the changing of anoles' skin color. He explains the connection to stress hormones.

Jenssen, Thomas A., Greenburg, Neil and Hovde, Katherine A. "Behavioral Profile of Free-Ranging Male Lizards, *Anolis Carolinensis,* Across Breeding and Post Breeding Seasons. *Herpetological Monographs* 9 (1995) 41-68.

This pivotal study took the focus away from camouflage as an explanation of Carolina anoles' color changes. The researchers observed anoles changing color during confrontations with each other.

Losos, Jonathan. "New Study on Color Change in Green Anoles." *Anole Annals.* Last Modified February 24, 2012. http://www.anoleannals.org/2012/02/24/new-study-on-color-change-in-green-anoles/.

This blog entry gives a nice overview regarding the studies conducted regarding Carolina anoles and the resulting hypotheses.

Yabuta, Shinji and Suzuki-Watanabe, Akiko. "Function of Body Coloration in Green Anoles (*Anolis carolinensis*) at the Beginning of the Breeding Season: Advertisement Signaling and Thermoregulation."
Current Herpetology 30, no. 2 (2011): 155-158. Accessed May 24, 2013 doi: http://dx.doi.org/10.5358/hsj.30.155.

Rock Mining:
Cumberland Trail Conference/Tennessee Trails Association. "TTA/CTC Rock Mining News" Last Modified December 11, 2009. Accessed May 22, 2013. http://rockmining.blogspot.com/2009/12/state-company-reachtentative-deal-on.html.

This blog gave me the links to most of my other rock harvesting sources. It's a good place to visit for establishing a timeline of events.

Howell, Joe. "Appeals Court Reverses Ruling on Rock Mining Along Cumberland Trail Park." *Knoxville News Sentinel.* August 2, 2008. Accessed May 22, 2013. http://www.knoxnews.com/news/2008/ aug/02/appeals-court-reverses-ruling-rock-mining-along-cu/.

The reversed ruling described here was not the final word on the subject of rock mining, but this article gave me much of my background information. It told me about the damage in 2007 and the deed for mineral rights in 1951.

Paine, Anne. "Rock Harvesting on Cumberland Trail State Park." *The Tennessean*. Accessed May 22, 2013. http:// www.tennessean.com/ VideoNetwork/48994429001/Rock-Harvesting-on-Cumberland-Trail-State-Park? nclick_check=1.

Sher, Andy. "State, Company Reach Tentative Deal on Cumberland Trail Mining Dispute." *Chattanooga Times Free Press*. November 27, 2009. Accessed May 22, 2013. http://www.timesfreepress.com/news/ 2009/nov/27/state-company-reach-tentative-deal-on-cumberland/.

Rock Climbing:
Averbeck, Cody. "Deep Wisdom: A New Way of Thinking in the Old South." *Climbing*. 2005 May. http:// www.climbing.com/exclusive/features/ deep_wisdom/index.html (accessed August 29, 2012).

Tucker, Rachel. *The SCC Announces Funding for Deep Creek Climbing Access.* December 31, 2010. http://blog.rockcreek.com/archives/ the_scc_announces_fundraising_for_deep_creek_climbing_access.html. (accessed August 29, 2012).

Pickerel Frog:
Bailey, Kim. "Pickerel Frogs Found in Davidson County." *The Tennessee Conservationist*. March/April 2013. 24

Dorcas, Mike and Gibbons, Whit. *Frogs & Toads of the Southeast*. Athens: University of Georgia Press, 2008. Niemiller, Matthew et al. *The Amphibians of Tennessee*. Knoxville: University of Tennessee Press, 2011.

TO GET WET OR NOT TO GET WET?

→ 9 ←

Possum Creek (Wednesday, May 16)
Hike 5: Heiss Mountain Rd. to Retro-Hughs Rd.
9.5 miles

"Your driving is still not great," said Dad when I asked.

After crossing an overgrown logging road, I found a hemlock tree with a few tiny white spots the size of snowflakes underneath the needles.

"Hey Dad," I said, "I found our first hemlock woolly adelgid." He came over to the tree, looking at the spots with concern.

I knew from many other hikes with Dad that they would multiply. These white spots were the sign of one of the most freakish and fiendish tree-destroying creatures imaginable. They were hemlock woolly adelgids, tiny insects from Asia, no bigger than 1/32 of an inch. Woolly adelgids are an all-girls' club. They don't need men to churn out egg sacks containing up to three hundred eggs. Reddish-brown adelgid children creep out to find twigs near the hemlock's needles. After an adelgid finds the right place, she transforms. She becomes black and oval-shaped with a white waxy ridge down her back and on either side. She grows more of the woolly wax around her until it covers her completely, protecting her from danger.

When adelgids grow older, about half of them fly off to try and find a kind of spruce tree that grows only in Asia. Since they don't find it here in the U.S., they die. The ones who stay on the tree get to experience the joy of sexless reproduction, leaving a new generation of adelgid eggs in white-covered clusters of 250. Second generation adelgids find not-yet-sucked twigs on the same tree and cover themselves in white balls of wax. Then, they give birth to their own clusters of eggs which get blown by the wind to other trees. Hurricane level winds can sweep the eggs long distances.

It can take anywhere from four to ten years for a hemlock tree to die after adelgids start their sap-sucking. On sicker trees, needles would begin to turn yellow and drop. Branches would dry. None of that had happened to this tree yet. It was the first adelgid-hit hemlock tree we saw as we headed north, but it would not be the last.

The outlook for our hemlock trees is not good. A small portion of our hemlocks are being treated chemically to save them. In addition, conservationists have released adelgid-eating insects. Such releases of exotic species to control another exotic species are controversial.

A hemlock woolly adelgid's absurd life.

We passed lush clusters of plants growing out of a cliff on ledges. Plants clung to wherever soil could be found.

"I've been here before," said Dad. "In March these ledges bloom like flowerbeds." We were too late for most of the spring wildflowers here.

Water was everywhere, reminding me of my own thirst. It ran down algae on the rock walls, forming dripping clusters like slimy green icicles. I grabbed one with my hand, just to feel the squishiness.

Little Possum Creek, known for its rapids with dramatic names like Beat-n-Bang and Elvis's Truck Stop, ran below us.

When trail-building volunteers explored the Possum Creek area, they found a spectacular waterfall and knew the CT had to pass it. The volunteers found a group of kayakers nearby and asked them what they called the place. "Imodium Falls," said the kayakers. When asked to explain it, they said that it was named by another group of kayakers who wished they had taken Imodium, an anti-diarrhea medication before going over the falls. The name stuck. I wish I was making up that story.

Imodium Falls surges down from a curving ledge before striking a slanted rock in white sudsy glory (see the picture on our website or the cartoon at this chapter's beginning). After crashing off the rock, the water sprays into a pool. When I saw it, the water didn't look high enough to be safe for kayaks. Even when it is high enough, kayakers have to position their boats precisely the right way to make it over the falls safely. Still, the green pool below it was the kind of pool that shouted "Jump in me!" regardless of the waterfall's name.

"At times like this," I told Dad, "I wish I had brought my swimsuit."

"I guess you could swim in your underwear," said Dad in a just kidding voice from the other side of the pool. "Anyway we need to get moving."

I splashed water on my arms and face as we left. Then, I hiked in front of Dad, thinking maybe if I speed-walked far enough ahead, I'd have enough

The Garden Ledges

LARRY: I didn't expect the profusion of spring wildflowers I came upon on sandstone ledges in the Possum Creek Gorge. A joy! Most prominent were the trout lilies (*Erythronium americanum*) yellow flowers named for their leaves' resemblance to a trout's skin. Generally, I expect to find trout lilies on rich soils, especially over limestone, not sandstone. However, these ledges did have some things going for them. They got extra sun by facing south, and they were very moist, profusely dripping. Other species also occurring here in showy patches were shooting star, Carey's saxifrage, rue anemone and fine leaf toothwort. Of these, only the saxifrage is normally found in this rocky habitat.

time to take off my shoes and socks, put my hot, sweaty feet in the stream, let the current cool them, then throw my feet back into my socks and tie up my boots. Once Dad was far behind me, I left the trail and walked to the bank of Possum Creek.

It wasn't the first time that I had ever walked out ahead of Dad during a hike. Back when I was a child, my sister Jessie, my father, my mother and I would hike together with Dad's old friend Stan and Stan's daughter Robin. On those occasions Jessie, Robin and I would often run ahead of the adults. Jessie would make up elaborate pretend scenarios, based on books or movies she knew. Sometimes she would even cast the adults including my father as the villains and tell us to run away from them. It was different from the pretend games we played at home in which Dad participated.

Gently Down the Stream!
Whitewater on the Cumberland Plateau

BEN: Most of the streams that I've mentioned already, such as Possum Creek and Soddy Creek get used by paddlers according to a website run by Walden's Ridge Whitewater (www.waldensridgewhitewater.com) a company that sells whitewater paddling equipment. The legendary owner of Walden's Ridge Whitewater, Mark Cummock, discovered several of the paddling routes in the Chattanooga area.

Don't think that anyone can paddle down these creeks and rivers without practice and instruction. Walden's Ridge Whitewater's website has a warning that their information is incomplete and that whitewater is dangerous: "One of the contributors to this web site has personally helped bury 3 kayaking friends. This isn't a joke." Also, in 1996, a fellow died after getting pinned under his boat on Little Possum Creek. If you still want to kayak in whitewater after reading that, take lessons from an expert.

A recent video on the internet shows a kayaker descending Ozone Falls, which is over a hundred feet high. He lived! Ozone falls is on an unbuilt (as of this book) portion of the CT. See the plunge at http://www.grindtv.com/outdoor/post/kayaker-survives-100-foot-drop-in-first-descent-of-ozone-falls/.

Once we played a game based on *The Lion King*. During the game, Dad declared "botanical breaks." He relished those chances to share what he knew. Once we got away from him though, we were in Africa.

"That's not a rhododendron," said Jessie, after I referred to one as such. "It's a banana tree." She was tired of Dad's plant lectures. Pretend games became her way of escaping them.

The game I played now was not a pretend game so much as a strategy game of prove-Dad-wrong. I wanted to win, even if it was childish to be obsessing over wading.

From my spot on the bank, I looked upstream and noticed a low concrete bridge. If I dipped my feet there, I would still be on the trail and wouldn't miss Dad when he passed. I splashed my sweaty face again and headed to the bridge.

Dad stood there. I groaned. Maybe the gurgling of the creek was too loud for me to hear him passing at my earlier spot on the bank.

Near the bridge, the stream ran on bedrock. It was shallow enough in most places that it did not get anything but the soles of my shoes wet. Dad and I reacted to the stream by doing predictable things.

Dad: searching the habitat for unusual plants.

Me: Dipping my booted, socked feet into deeper cracks in the bedrock, hoping to give them some of that cool soggy goodness. It worked.

Days ago, walking wet from rain had made me miserable. Even at a pond earlier that day, I did not want to wade too deep for fear of slogging around in soggy pants. Now though, I did not mind squishing along in stream-soaked shoes.

We walked uphill through a pine plantation. People had planted pine trees here for pulp to be used in paper. It resembled a forest as much as a wheat field resembled a prairie. Annie Dillard wrote in *Pilgrim at Tinker Creek* that a wheat field was "unnatural and freakish." The same statement applied to the trees around us.

"I was at a conference once," said Dad to me, "and I called pulp plantations 'biodiversity deserts.' A forester got offended at that label. He probably thought I meant a biological desert, which is a different thing entirely." Being his son and having grown up with Dad's botanical breaks, I understood what he was saying.

The pine trees caught light energy in their needles and pulled carbon from the air. In that way, the plantation was no different from the wilder forest around it. The plantation lacked variety of life forms though, which was what made it a biodiversity dessert. Biodiversity refers to the diversity of life, not the presence or absence of it. The wild forests we had seen on the trail had leaves of many shapes and shades of green. They had logs, ready to be cannibalized by new generations, rotting on the ground. The plantation had nothing but pine trees, all the same age. They stood in rows like supermarket milk cartons.

Human control wasn't absolute here. There were breaks in the plantation. Small trees grew in clearings and in the understory below the tall pines. In one clearing, Dad pointed out some beaked hazelnut plants.

Nuts with Beaks

Beaked Hazel-nut (*Corylus cornuta*)

LARRY: As I write this, we have store-bought hazel-nuts in a mix of nuts for cracking on our living room coffee table and hazel-nut tea in a kitchen cabinet. There are at least 10 species of hazel-nuts or filberts in the world, and some of these species have been cultivated for commercial nut production. We have two wild species in eastern North America, beaked hazel-nut and American hazel-nut. I have eaten only one American hazel-nut because I have never found enough of them to get a real harvest. I remember that one as good to eat but not something to get excited about.

However, I did get excited about finding our other species, the beaked hazel-nut, along the CT. Beaked hazel-nut is scarce in Tennessee, unlike the common American nut. In fact, this was the first time I had seen the beaked species in Tennessee. Initially, I was unsure which hazel-nut species I was seeing. What I saw were shrubs averaging about four feet in height dominating the forest understory. Hazel-nuts spread from their roots. This spreading produces many stems to form colonies. Thus, these shrubs can spread without making nuts to seed the ground. Later, in a sunnier spot, I saw some nuts with the telltale beak extending past the nut. The beak is a pair of specialized leaves called bracts. The American hazel-nut also has this pair of bracts, but they don't extend past the nut to form a long beak.

The leaves of our two hazel-nuts are alternate simple with double toothed edges, i.e., edges with teeth and then teeth on the teeth. When nuts are present, the beaked hazel-nut is easily separated from the American hazel-nut by the beak. Without nuts, a hand lens will show that the American hazel-nut has twigs and leaf stalks covered with knobby hairs that are mostly lacking on the beaked hazel-nut.

After we returned to the motel, I changed into shorts. My pants were muddy and wet from the stream. I was willing to wreck another pair of jeans the same way if the next day proved hot enough.

Sources and Suggested Reading:

General:
Cumberland Trail Conference. *CTC's Guide To Hiking the Justin P. Wilson Cumberland Trail with Maps/Guides.* www.cumberlandtrail.org (accessed July 19, 2012).

Here, as elsewhere, we depended on the CTC site for major features along the trail, including the origin of Imodium Falls' name. Specific information, much of it relevant to plants, can be found at http://cumberlandtrail.org/website/maps-and-guides/trail-segments/three-gorges/possum-section/.

Hemlock Woolly Adelgid:
Hale, Frank A. "The Hemlock Woolly Adelgid: A Threat to Hemlock in Tennessee." https://utextension.tennessee.edu/publications/Documents/SP503-G.pdf. Accessed May 28, 2013.

Beaked Hazelnut:
Gleason, Henry A. and Arthur Cronquist. *Manual of Vascular Plants of Northeastern United States and Adjacent Canada, Second Edition.* New York: The New York Botanical Garden, 1991.

Whitewater Rafting:
American Whitewater. "Possum Creek, Little, Tennessee, US: Waldens Ridge to Bakewell." Last Updated September 27, 2010. http://www.americanwhitewater.org/content/River/detail/id/3587

Walden's Ridge Whitewater. "Little Possum Creek: Walden's Ridge Tennessee." http://www.waldensridgewhitewater.com/waldensridge/LittlePossum.htm. Accessed May 28, 2013.

Stredge, David. "Kayaker Survives 100 Foot Drop in First Descent of Ozone Falls." Last Updated January 18, 2013. http://www.grindtv.com/outdoor/post/kayaker-survives-100-foot-drop-in-first-descent-of-ozone-falls/

BEN'S BRIDGE (WELL, BEN HELPED).

⇀ 10 ↽

Rock Creek (Thursday, May 17)
Hike 6: Retro-Hughs Rd. to Leggett Rd.
9.6 miles

"This is a sensitive plant," said Dad as he touched the weedy plant. The leaflets on the part he touched closed up one-by-one, as if embarrassed.

Further down on the trail, I left Dad far behind me. What I wanted to see was further down in the Rock Creek Gorge. I strode ahead to find it.

A light rain fell as I climbed a wet trail ladder. A small rhododendron grew in a nook on a cliff. I knew its shiny leaves well from my many childhood hikes with Dad in the Smokies. Other rhododendrons grew on the forest floor to be tall bushes with many woody stems. This one though was different. The seed had fallen into soil too thin to support a full bush, but the plant grew here anyway. Although the rhododendron seemed out-of-place in the nook, it grew.

During my college's fall break of 2009 I, like the rhododendron, was thrown into a new situation, surrounded by strangers and working on projects I barely understood. Yet I did not feel out-of-place on the Cumberland Trail working at Rock Creek. Perhaps I could have. I had little idea of what I was doing. Yet I understood that we were working to build something that future hikers would enjoy. Our project was a bridge across Rock Creek, and that bridge was what I wanted to see. I thought back to my time that fall.

"What's the forecast?" I asked our leader, Tony Hook, while stumbling half-asleep out of my bunk-bed one morning.

"Forecast?" said Tony with a chuckle, already dressed and ready to go. "We get up at 7:00 AM, work and then head back."

At left: Former Cumberland Trail Conference director Tony Hook was dedicated to making the trail a reality, one day at a time. The conversation portrayed here really took place.

We stayed in a lodge used by Lutherans for a summer camp. Now it hosted a group of volunteers, young and old, all of us getting ready to work on the trail. Few of us knew each other, but everyone seemed friendly.

I had come with two other guys from my college for the week of fall break. I had decided to do it at the last minute after missing my chance to sign up for going to New Orleans or Georgia for volunteer projects. Then, as right after graduating, coming home to my parents didn't appeal to me. Even if I was still in Tennessee, the service trip would be a chance to see a new place.

The AmeriCorps NCCC Water Team 4 joined us. They were around my age and had worked on the Possum Creek Bridge at an earlier time, although since then they'd traveled to work on different projects, including one in New Orleans. They often talked self-deprecatingly about the isolated nature of "AmeriCulture," but they fit in well with the rest of us, a mixed group of young and old. We all worked together. We shared the same rooms and meals at the lodge. Sometimes the older volunteers would even laugh at the "South Park" DVDs that the younger volunteers played. Different generations brought different perspectives and different levels of experience.

Even though at college I was used to going to sleep at 2:00 AM and waking up at 8:00, here I went to sleep at 10:00 or 11:00 with everyone else. Trail building wore all of us out, and once I got used to the routine of rising at 7:00, it felt natural.

Every cool morning of that week in 2009, we carried lumber, tools, buckets of cement and pieces of metal scaffolding down to Rock Creek. As trail builders working away from roads, we couldn't use cranes to move our supplies. Some equipment was heavy. One volunteer compared the task of bringing it down to "carrying Godzilla." To help us with the weight, we put the scaffolding pieces on a zip-line system, letting them slide from tree to tree. Finally, we got our supplies down to Rock Creek. True to its name, the creek had tall, slanting boulders on its sides. It was shallow at this time of the year, with plenty of dry rocks for walking across and a few pools. We had to watch our step though. None of us wanted to slip into the chilly water and come out, clothes wet and teeth chattering, into the autumn air.

When Tony said to shove rocks into basket-like fencing, I shoved rocks into basket-like fencing. When Tony said to screw logs together with a power drill, I screwed logs together with a power drill. I did not need to know what we were doing so long as other people around me knew. Like the seed thrown into the nook on the cliff face, I adapted to my surroundings.

I worked wherever I could find work. Sometimes, I helped with the scaffold for the bridge. Other times, I moved rocks to build stairs for the trail

Sensitive Plant Reacts

Feature Plant: sensitive plant (Mimosa microphylla)

LARRY: How do plants avoid being eaten to death? Animals can use their ability to move in order to run away, hide from their predators and/or fight back with tooth, claw or hoof. Plants, on the other hand, can't run away. They generally try to poison their predators while feeding their pollinators and seed dispersers. I say "try" since the plant predators, herbivores, are always evolving to tolerate the poisons.

Some plants actually do move quickly enough to watch. The famous Venus fly trap closes its trap. The sensitive plant and some of its relatives fold their leaves. As you might guess from the scientific name, a sensitive plant's leaves resemble those of a mimosa tree, but the mimosa is twice compound rather than once. The sensitive plant is beautifully pink-flowered like the mimosa tree, but unlike the mimosa, it is armed with prickles.

on the bank. Still other times, I sat on a boulder, watching brown, orange, yellow and red leaves fall, while waiting for Tony or one of the AmeriCorps team to give me something to do. The experience reminded me of childhood summers when my mother, father, sister and I would put together jigsaw puzzles. We would take different areas, sometimes switching, until the picture was complete.

Not until years afterwards when I looked through photos of the process could I figure out the meaning of what we had done on the bridge. First, we cut down a tree near the site and made a wooden scaffold. Rocks wrapped in wire fencing held the wooden posts in place. Then, on top of the posts, we placed a metal scaffold, which supported work on the bridge.

I found a stream and put my memories of bridge-building aside for a moment. Earlier today, I'd searched in a stream for salamanders and failed. This was my chance to prove I could find one. The bridge could wait. So, I got my boots soggy and turned over rocks in the creek. Dad caught up with me.

"Finding salamanders was a hobby of mine when I was young," said Dad.

"I've done it once or twice," I said, "but I'm not finding many now."

Dad climbed down the sandy bank to me.

"These rocks are a little bit big, and you have to be careful, because under a big rock you might have a venomous snake. You want to stay behind it

---

Thigmonasty is the term for plants moving after being touched. Plants lack muscles but they can change water pressure levels (turgor). The leaflets on the sensitive plant close when water moves by osmosis away from the leaflet bases. This is much like wilting. Presumably the folding discourages some herbivores.

My first internet search (Bing, not Google) for thigmo**nasty** seemed to recognize the word but brought up only sites connected to **nasty**. There are many, many **nasty** sites! On my next try, Google's engine took me right to science rather than prurience.

The sensitive plant lives in disturbed open areas like the start of this hike. Watch for it about a quarter mile in from the Retro-Hughs Trail Head on the CT. You will spot it easily if it is in bloom. If you touch the leaves, they will fold gradually.

---

when you pick it up. Keep your fingers from going under it."

LARRY: I once moved a log and found a copperhead under it on the Kentucky Cumberland Plateau. Right before moving it, I said to my companions that it was a good log for a copperhead. See Chapter 12 for a discussion of coincidences. That was the only time I have uncovered a venomous snake by lifting wood or rock. I have also turned up scorpions under rocks on the Plateau.

BEN: He picked up a rock to demonstrate. "Nobody home. Put it down. Watch your fingers." He emphasized putting the rock down because I tended to stare under rocks for too long, thinking that the salamanders were just hiding somehow or that I'd just overlooked them.

"I just moved part of the trail," said Dad, amused that his rock had been intended to be a stepping stone. He placed it back where it had been.

"Oh there's one!" I shouted at Dad as a salamander wriggled away from me. I'd lost it.

"It's all right," said Dad, "You should be able to find more salamanders like that one. It's probably a dusky salamander, and there are lots of streams just full of those guys."

I wasn't as sure. In the time we had been hiking, most of the salamanders I had seen had been in plain view. Searching under rocks had turned up little until now.

Another one crawled away from me, this one bigger and purplish-brown. Dad thought it was another species of dusky. "Sometimes the only way they can tell them apart is by doing genetic tests or looking at proteins," said Dad.

Duskies are Confusing

BEN: If you turn over a stream rock near the CT and find a brown salamander with a flattish head, bulging eyes and a light line on either side of the head from eye to jaw, it's probably a dusky (genus *Desmonagthus*). The hard part is figuring out which species. It can be worse than fall warblers for birders. I narrowed these ones down to either seal salamanders or spotted dusky salamanders based on range, but the reported ranges are no guarantee. Also, telling the difference between the two species can involve looking at the colors of their toes, which is, needless to say, tricky even if you have one in your hand.

When we reached the bridge, it looked nothing like the place I'd volunteered three years before. Thanks to rain, the stream was deeper, had a stronger current and no easy way to get across other than the bridge.

More hands had worked on the bridge since I last saw it. Our scaffold of split logs, metal bars and wire-fenced stones was gone. In its place was a finished footbridge with stable boards and metal rails. The sandstone steps we shoved in place now stood in a longer staircase that stretched up the hillside.

Not a single board or rail on it was mine. Still, I could point to the bridge and say, "I helped build it." My part was tiny, like a grain of sand in a sandstone cliff. I had not been the trail's father, just one of the many people who raised it. Yet even that felt grand.

LARRY: The CT is an act of love. Love of nature and love of working together for a grand goal. The beauty of the well-built CT fits with the rock splendor of the Cumberland Plateau. The thousands of rock steps and many bridges showcase the pride and workmanship of the volunteers.

BEN: We climbed up the other side of the gorge. We followed the rim to the end. We were finished and ready to end another day of hiking.

Except we weren't.

Wait! The hike was not over. As we came to the parking area, Dad saw the sign marking the number of miles we had covered. It was far too high for what we had walked. Looking at the map, he saw that we'd been following a shorter trail blazed in yellow. We'd passed the official trail where it branched off, blazed in blue.

"Well," said Dad as we headed toward the truck, "I guess we'll just have to mention this in our book. Our Fresca awaits us." He pointed out that we had already skipped a roadside section of trail along TN Route 111 that he had already walked and did not find interesting.

"Maybe we should go back," I said, "just so that we can say we hiked it."

"Well," said Dad, "I suppose we could."

It started out easily, a shaded climb downhill along a falling stream. Then, we reached a steep uphill. By this point, I regretted taking the longer route. My gut felt about to explode, possibly with diarrhea. I should have stopped but felt too proud to wipe my butt with leaves and dig a hole, especially since we were almost back to our motel. I just wished we were closer. Meanwhile, Dad started talking about buying chocolate ice cream. Maybe he was ready to be back too.

Back at the motel, Dad told Mom on the phone that his knee had "never felt better."

Tomorrow, we'd rest and get ready in Dayton. The next day, we would go backpacking. Hopefully we'd feel up to it this time and not long for toilets or ice cream in the woods.

Sources and Suggested Readings:

On Dusky Salamanders:
Niemiller, Matthew et al. *The Amphibians of Tennessee.* Knoxville: University of Tennessee Press, 2011.

Mimosa microphylla:
United States Department of Agriculture. "Plants Profile for Mimosa microphylla (Little-Leaf Sensitive Briar)." USDA Plants Database. Accessed December 1, 2014. http://plants.usda.gov/core/profile?symbol=mimi22.

A New Exclusive Club?

Painted buckeye mixed with red buckeye (*Aesculus mutabilis*)

LARRY: In April you definitely do <u>not</u> want to use that shortcut mentioned above to the upper Leggett Rd. trailhead. You would miss a spectacular array of shrubby buckeyes in flower. Gregory Bald in the Smokies is famous for its azalea hybrid display while the CT has its dazzling display of buckeyes. These flowers are probably of hybrid origin rather than being actual hybrids.

Painted buckeye is yellow-flowered while the red buckeye is truly red. Joining their genes together, their offspring are every shade between yellow and red. These profusely-flowering shrubby buckeyes often flower less than two feet off the ground and can dominate large areas of the forest's understory. These shrubby buckeye stems spread out from the base then bend back to the vertical position.

In graffiti, an "x" between two people's names means that they are romantically involved. Perhaps this use of "x" is related to its use in biology to indicate a hybrid. We have the cross *Aesculus pavia x sylvatica* (painted buckeye x red buckeye). Hybrids are the offspring of two species, the parent species. The parent species here are painted buckeye and red buckeye.

The descendants of hybrids are said to be of hybrid origin and may be considered to be a new species that came into being by hybridization if

Thigmonasty:
Jaffe, Mordechai J., A. Carl Leopold and Richard C. Staples. "Thigmo Responses in Plants and Fungi." American Journal of Botany 89 no. 3. (March 2002): 375-382. doi: 10.3732/ajb.89.3.375.

---

they successfully reproduce.

Mules are the descendants of horses and burros. Famously, mules are sterile. So "mule" has become the term for any sterile hybrid. Our shrubby CT buckeyes do not appear to be mules since the flowers of all colors seem to be reproducing.

On hearing this, Ben took the reasonable position that painted and red buckeyes should be considered to be varieties rather than species. However, biologists are generally not so strict with the definition of species. This lack of strictness leads to species being a somewhat subjective concept. Since hybrids from these two buckeye species appear to reproduce well, their descendants have been considered to be a full species, *Aesculus mutabilis*, not a hybrid, which is written *Aesculus x mutabilis*.

The definition of species for sexual species is often based on the slippery concept of "strong" reproductive isolation, which rarely can be directly observed. A species, then, is an exclusive reproduction club with the possibility of some straying. Occasionally, the straying can lead to a new club. *Aesculus mutabilis* could be such a new club.

WON'T YOU TAKE ME TO MONKEY TOWN?

⇾ 11 ⇽

Dayton, Our First Stay-town.

BEN: "Let me get on your computer," said Dad. "I need to check my e-mail." He lowered his nearly hairless brows and exhaled as he looked at all of the messages on the screen. He would not have time to deal with all of them, given that we were hiking six days a week and writing and researching when we weren't.

Every night I would write in my blog about the trail. Then I'd put the link on Facebook and get distracted by other people's lives. Dad would turn off the light and plop into bed at ten. I usually got in bed a few hours after that. Often I was tired enough that it didn't feel too early.

The Scottish Inn sat in a newer, more sprawling side of town, near a Walmart where we bought frozen meals. The older part of Dayton was a section of brick buildings, many of them joined together. Even if one store sold video games and had Link and Mario painted on the window, I could tell the old downtown was built in a pre-video game era because of the lack of large parking lots. In the middle of it all, attached to no building, was the old Rhea County Courthouse. A green spire rose from its bell tower.

That courthouse had one moment of national fame: The Scopes Trial, or "Monkey Trial" of 1925. A teacher named John Scopes went on trial for the crime of teaching about evolution. Because of the trial, the town got dubbed "Monkey Town," by the media. The case made headlines across the country and symbolized a battle between old and new ways of seeing the world. Scopes later claimed he couldn't remember whether or not he had covered evolution in class.

Readers of this book can believe what they want, but we have our own reasons for believing in the evolution of species over time rather than in six-day creationism. For Dad, evolutionary ideas are important for understanding how plants fit into niches and how certain events, like the introduction of exotics or the recent warming of the earth, disturb those niches.

As his son, I grew up with stories about evolution. They take a place in my childhood mythology, right next to Dr. Seuss. Dad used to read to me from dinosaur books and walk with me between huge skeletons at natural history museums. Even now, thinking about it helps me to connect to my childhood days of asking Dad for the origin stories of everything around me.

Evolutionary theories allow people to ask and answer questions. For example: How did fireflies get glowing butts? To answer this question, a scientist might look closely at back-sections of beetles related to fireflies both current and fossil and delve into their DNA. At the same time, there's the related question of why. At the end of searching, I might find an answer: Fireflies glow to impress the opposite sex. With evolution, we can see the world's species, not as separate lines but as a family, with children going off in different directions and pursuing different lifestyles.

Tennessee's law in those days stated that it was a misdemeanor "to teach any theory that denies the story of Divine Creation as taught in the Bible and to

Ben Toon hikes with his extended family. The devices in the Toons' hands are voice recorders, not phasers.

teach instead that man has descended from a lower order of animals." The law's language is telling. The notion that some animals, such as human beings, are higher, or that others, such as ticks, are lower is a matter of opinion, not science. Terms like that were popular in the twenties though on both sides of the evolution debate.

William H. Hunter, author of Scopes' classroom textbook, used the terms in order to describe his own species, "man," as the highest creature, descended from old fashioned, lower, simpler ones. As if to show the ridiculousness of his reasoning, Hunter described, "the highest type of all, Caucasians," a statement that was never disputed in the Dayton trial. It would have been just as scientific to say, "The highest type of Caucasian is William H. Hunter."

Creationists wanted to go even further in thinking of humans as special. The notion that humans were in any of the same categories as the kind of creatures they caged, rode, ate or trained to ride unicycles in tutus disgusted them. This objection to evolution, encoded in Tennessee law, became a point in the trial, as seen here in this confrontation between Stewart, the state prosecutor, and Howard Morgan, a student in Scopes's class.

> *Stewart: I ask you further, Howard, how did he classify man with reference to other animals; what did he say about them?*
> *Morgan: Well, the book and he both classified man along with cats and dogs, cows, horses, monkeys, lions, horses and all that.*
> *Stewart: What did he say they were?*
> *Morgan: Mammals.*

Later, the famous defense lawyer Clarence Darrow tried to clarify matters:

> *Darrow: He didn't say a cat was the same as a man?*
> *Morgan: No, sir: he said man had a reasoning power; that these animals did not.*
> *Darrow: There is some doubt about that, but that is what he said, is it?*
> *(Laughter in the courtroom.)*
> *The Court: Order.*

Dayton has just as close of an historical connection to the Cumberland Trail's land as Soddy-Daisy does. Again, it's a history connected to the coal industry, but in Dayton, the coal history would influence an event far more famous than the Cumberland Trail itself.

An Englishman with the awesome name of Titus Salt Junior started the Dayton Coal and Iron Company. Salt had big dreams, buying over 27,000 acres near Dayton for coke ovens, coal mines, railroads, limestone quarries, company houses, company stores and even a Catholic school. He was ambitious like his father Sir Titus Salt who had invented a new silky fabric made from alpaca wool and gotten England's rich people to buy it.

Dayton continued to be a mining city long after Titus Salt Junior died. Three explosions shook the mines between 1895 and 1902, each one killing between 25 and 29 people. Compensation was expensive for the Company, especially when considered alongside other costs like equipment. At first the management responded to financial troubles by reshuffling the structure of the company, then buying new equipment. But the parent company, now in Scotland, caved in. Dayton Coal & Iron Co., Ltd as it was now called, was doomed. The Company's president committed suicide in 1913.

In 1922, George Washington Rappleyea, a name that could only be improved if it had "Sir" in front of it, took the lead of what was now called the Cumberland Coal and Iron Company. Rappleyea was from New York City. He had come to Tennessee to survey land for mining but got stuck in Dayton after a copperhead bit his foot. His nurse, Ova Corrin, married him and helped him get a job as company president.

He loved riding his horse through the East Tennessee countryside. Still, *The Chattanooga Times* called him "a stranger to the South and Southern ways." He supervised Sunday school at Five Points Methodist Church but didn't care for the more fundamentalist religion that some other people in the area practiced.

The men who worked under him did a little bit of coal mining, but mostly they cut up old furnaces and machines for scrap metal. It was not the best time for the company or the town.

Rappleyea came up with an idea that would save both of them: putting a local substitute biology teacher on trial for teaching evolution. The ACLU (American Civil Liberties Union) had offered to pay for the defense of anyone who challenged the law. According to many sources, Rappleyea hoped the trial could be a huge event that would draw publicity to Dayton and get investors interested. Probably to protect his own reputation, Rappleyea claimed in a July 1, 1925 AP story that he just wanted to test the law, a motive which was in keeping with his own belief in evolution. He probably had both of these motivations from the beginning.

It's tempting, especially for people in Dayton, to lay all of the blame for what would later become their public relations fiasco on Rappleyea, an outsider and non-fundamentalist Christian, but history is never that simple. In order to get the trial going, he needed support from others. He talked about his plan at F.E. Robinson's Drugstore, the town's unofficial center and a great place for ice cream sodas on a hot day. The famous northern journalist H.L. Mencken would later say of Dayton, "There is no gambling. There is no place to dance. The relatively wicked, when they would indulge themselves, go to Robinson's drug store and debate theology."

The folks at the drugstore, including the lawyer Sue Hicks who may have later inspired the "Boy Named Sue" song, agreed that the trial sounded like a good idea, even if they didn't agree with Rappleyea about evolution. After all, it would be great publicity for the struggling town and let people argue both sides. All they needed now was a defendant.

The Daytonians settled on the teacher and football coach John T. Scopes. He was twenty-four years old (my age) and just out of college. He'd been in Dayton for a year and intended to sell cars after the school year ended. However, he had a date, in his own words, with "a beautiful blonde" at a church social, and that persuaded him to stay in Dayton. It was the kind of motivation many animals share for their actions. Darwin would have understood.

A teenage boy found a sweating Scopes playing tennis and brought him to the drugstore. The people at the drugstore asked him if he'd taught evolution.

"I'm not sure," he said. "If it's in the textbook I did."

"Doc" Fredrick E. Robinson, the drugstore's owner, took Scopes's textbook off a store shelf and found the page on evolution. Perhaps he hadn't thought much before about whether he was selling illegal goods to children. To be fair, it was the official textbook for the state of Tennessee, making the law against teaching evolution confusing. The politicians who passed the Butler Act may not have intended for it to be enforced. It may have been all symbolic bluster, much like some of the more recent moral values laws proposed in Tennessee's Statehouse today.

Admittedly, this is not the only version of how the meeting took place. In fact, it's a pieced-together version dramatized by Kirtley F. Mather, who arrived in town later for the trial but wasn't there for this particular meeting. Other accounts, including the one by Scopes himself though describe it similarly as ending with the book being taken off the shelf and turned to the page on evolution.

Scopes agreed to go on trial. His father convinced him by telling him it would help the country. The only two things Scopes had to do for the court was show up and convince some students who had loved him as a teacher that they could still testify. He never had to testify himself. Supporters had already paid his bail, preventing him from having to spend time in jail. He did find the trial overwhelming though.

The trial was not really about him anyway, no matter how much some of the prosecution team would have preferred for it to be a simple case of "Is Scopes guilty?" It was about the Bible, Darwin's theory, big-name lawyers, shameless hype and, although many people didn't know it, the misfortunes of a failing coal company.

As much as Rappleyea supported science, he seemed to love attention more. He heard that Chattanooga was going to hold a trial of another teacher for teaching evolution and that they might get to hold the trial before Dayton. He then held a meeting of citizens to protest and discuss what to do if

Chattanooga succeeded. During the meeting, Rappleyea explained his views on evolution. A local barber yelled that his family weren't monkeys and bit Rappleyea. "Not a Monkey, but Bit," read the *Reading Eagle*, a newspaper in Pennsylvania. Rappleyea later said that he staged the biting in order to grab headlines like that one.

During the trial, Rappleyea helped the defense. He fixed up an old mansion to house the scientists who he wanted to testify about evolution. Only one of the scientists ever got to take the stand. Scopes lost and was fined 100 dollars. He won the appeal to the Tennessee Supreme Court because the judge had set the fine instead of the jury. Tennessee's anti-evolution law stood until the Tennessee Legislature repealed it in 1967.

Rappleyea succeeded though in his other goal of grabbing publicity for Dayton, especially after two celebrity lawyers, Clarence Darrow for the defense and William Jennings Bryan for the prosecution, came to town. It was the wrong kind of publicity though. When reporters came to the Rhea County Courthouse, they found a big "Read Your Bible" banner. It seemed like a blatant official bias. Similar signs hung throughout the city, and many fundamentalists came in to watch the trial, some from far away. During those days, the city took on a Christian revival atmosphere, one that looked ignorant of science in an age when Einstein was changing notions about time and space. The editorialist H.L. Mencken described the town as friendly, charming and hopelessly backwards.

"Two months ago the town was obscure and happy," he wrote, "Today it is a universal joke."

So, in 1927, just two years after the trial, the mines and coke ovens closed for the last time. A paper-making company called Bowater would later buy some of the old mining land. Even later, it would become part of Cumberland Trail State Park.

The trial brought new business to Dayton in a different way than Rappleyea had intended. Bryan, a famous attorney for the prosecution team, suggested the possibility of a school that would teach students based on Christian principles. After Bryan's death, people raised money and built Bryan College.

What people remember about the trial was its clash between new and old ideas. The fictionalized versions of the trial in the movie and play *Inherit the Wind* amped up the aspects of the trial that fit that image and changed the names of the participants for that reason. Many history books have a similar slant.

The typical way of talking about the Scopes Trial treats it as a human event, shaped by great men like William Jennings Bryan and Clarence Darrow. A statue of Williams Jennings Bryan stands outside the courthouse. Bryan had come to Dayton because he believed in humanity's special place in God's creation. Yet as someone interested in the relationship between Dayton and the natural world around it, I'd rather see a statue of the copperhead that bit

Rappleyea. Without that copperhead, or for that matter the prehistoric plants that formed the coal near Dayton, the trial might never have happened.

Perhaps creationists wouldn't mind me giving the copperhead credit. After all, the Bible also claims a snake was responsible for an historic event.

Like a fossil or a coal seam beneath a hill, the stories of the Dayton Coal and Iron Company, those tragic explosions and Rappleyea's role in the trial of the century lie buried in the museum under Dayton's courthouse. A small display explains it. While most of the museum's exhibits cover the trial, there are a few displays about other aspects of Dayton's past.

The museum is even-handed, accurately explaining both evolution and creationism. They also have both Darrow's straw hat and Bryan's pith helmet. Apparently lawyers dressed like safari guides back then.

After drinking our chocolate ice cream, which had melted because the freezer compartment didn't work well, we packed up all our things and headed off for a backpacking trip.

The trail took us through the woods past the brick arches of the Richland coke ovens, run by Dayton Coal and Iron. Now they looked like ancient tombs, looted of all of their treasures. Trees grew out of old foundations near mossy stone walls.

In these ovens, workers covered the coal in dirt. They lit the coal, sealed the entrances and let the impurities burn off of the coal for days under low oxygen conditions. Coke ovens' scorching heat could reach up to 3,600 degrees Fahrenheit. The end product, called coke, fueled the smelting of iron from hematite ore (see chapter 2).

I imagined the ovens at their peak burning tons of coal and glowing red. The land around them would have been barer with much fewer trees. During the Scopes trial, the national media had portrayed Dayton area as an isolated and backwards country town. The 1890s Dayton I saw in my mind now was nothing like that image. It was a Dayton of explosions. It was a Dayton of fire and slag feeding off a nation's demands for more coal, more coke, more railroads, rivets and steamboats. It was a womb from which an industrial country emerged, coughing and smeared with coal dust.

Sources and Suggested Reading

Scopes Trial:
Associated Press. "Scopes Case Not Started for publicity purposes; will test law." The Spartanburg Herald, July 1, 1925: 1.

Linder, Douglas. University of Missouri Kansas City. "Famous Trials in American History: Tennessee vs. John Scopes." Last modified March 5, 2008. http://law2.umkc.edu/faculty/projects/ftrials/scopes/scopes.htm.
    This website is a great place to learn more about the Scopes Trial. It was my main source for the life of George Rappleyea. It also helped me to put together information about Scopes himself and the textbook which he used. It was put together by Law Professor Douglas A. Linder of the University of Missouri Kansas City. The site was made with the general public in mind. It's not the best place for links to primary sources, however.

Larson, Edward J. *Summer for the Gods: The Scopes Trial and America's Continuing Debate over Science and Religion.* New York: Basic Books 2008.

Lesiak, Christine. *American Experience: Monkey Trial.* Directed by Christine Lesiak. Produced by Nebraska ETV Network. Performed by Linda Hunt. 2002.

Mather, Kirtley F. "The Scopes Trial and its Aftermath." *Journal of the Tennessee Academy of Science* 57, no. 1 (January 1982): 1-9. http://friendsofthecumberlandtrail.org/wpcontent/uploads/2009/11/im3511_20091103_1103161.pdf. (Accessed June 13, 2013).

University of Minnesota Law Library. "The Clarence Darrow Digital Library: The Scopes Trial (1925)." Accessed June 11, 2013. http://darrow.law.umn.edu/trials.php?tid=7.
    This website has photos and primary sources accessible as pdfs, including Scopes's textbook the trial transcript. The excerpt that I use here comes from http://darrow.law.umn.edu/documents/Scopes%203rd%20&%204th%20day.pdf page 125. Bryan's speech "The Bible and its Enemies" (quoted elsewhere) can also be found here at http://darrow.law.umn.edu/documents/Bible_and_its_Enemies_OCR.pdf.

Reading Eagle. "Origin of the Tennessee Monkey Law Test Suit." *Reading Eagle*, July 5, 1925: 6. Accessed June 12, 2013. http://news.google.com/newspapersid=xYkhAAAAIBAJ&sjid=yZcFAAAAIBAJ&dq=thurlow%20reed%20dayton&pg=4614%2C697281.
    My source for "Not a Monkey but Bit."

Dayton Coal and Iron's History:
    I owe a great deal to a small time line display at the Rhea County Courthouse, including Titus Salt Junior's initial developments, the explosions, the suicide of the company president and the connection of the operation to the

Scopes Trial. However it did not cover everything included here.

Reynolds, Pamela A. *Saltaire Village, World Heritage Site.* 2005. http://www.saltairevillage.info/saltaire_history_0001.html (accessed August 28, 2012).
    This web page gives a basic biography of Sir Titus Salt.

Shaw, David. "2 Saltaire Historians on the Dayton Venture." *Saltaire World Heritage Site.* Edited by Pamela A. Reynolds. May 5, 2012. http://www.saltairevillage.info/news-00245_2_Saltaire_historians_on_the_Dayton_Venture_2012.html. Accessed August 28, 2012.
    A British historian blogs about his time visiting Dayton and Dayton's history.

Simmons, Morgan. "Much to Celebrate: Guided Hikes Offered at Laurel-Snow Scenic Tract near Dayton." Knoxville News Sentinel. May 1, 2012. Accessed August 26, 2014. http://www.knoxnews.com/news/state/much-to-celebrate-guided-hikes-offered-at-laurel.

Coke Ovens:
Benton, Ben. "Mining History." *Chattanooga Times Free Press.* March 4, 2011. http://www.timesfreepress.com/news/news/story/2011/mar/04/mining-history/43958/. Accessed February 13, 2015.

Reneau, Michael. "Mining for History." *The Herald News.* February 22, 2011. http://www.rheaheraldnews.com/news/local/article_57c3704e-3b6c-56fc-a3b6-297aa53e86d7.html. Accessed February 13, 2015.

Terpstra, Sarah. "Coke Ovens." *The Friends of the Cumberland Trail.* Accessed June 11, 2013. http://friendsofthecumberlandtrail.org/history-and-culture/coke-ovens/.

"What is a Coke Oven?" *Wise Geek.* http://www.wisegeek.org/what-is-a-coke-oven.htm. Accessed February 13, 2015.

THOSE CRAZY AMERICANS

⇥ 12 ⇤

Laurel-Snow State Natural Area (Saturday and Sunday, May 19, 20)
Hike 7: Dayton Trailhead to Dayton Trailhead
11 miles

LARRY: Only a small part of the trails from these two days of hiking and exploring will be part of the main CT. At present, this CT portion is not connected to any other pieces.

⇥Forceful Hand Washing⇤
Saturday May 19

BEN: Wide Richland Creek ran parallel to the trail. It grabbed attention away from the ruins on the trail's other side (see Chapter 11). Boys in trunks and girls in bright bikinis strutted past us, eager to splash in the water. A century from now, Rhea County Courthouse might be forgotten and covered in moss, but if the stream still runs clean, people will swim.

We walked to a place with boulders the size of garden sheds, much smaller than some of the ones along the main creek. "Psalms 40:13" read a white spray-painted message on a rock. Psalms 40:13 is "Be pleased, O Lord, to deliver me. Make haste, O Lord, to help me."

We were ready to throw down our backpacks behind a boulder and explore. For the first time since we started the trek, we did not have to drive back to Dayton at the end of the day. We had two days here at Laurel-Snow State Natural Area.

At Laurel Falls, water fell from a high cliff. The sun shone from the top of it, blinding anyone who tried to look. The falls looked like a supernatural beam of heavenly energy. Below it, the stream flowed around and below boulders, these lacking graffiti, religious or otherwise.

I crawled down among the rocks, curious about what I might find in the wet places, dry places, pools and current below Laurel Falls. With a loud rip, a slight, previously unnoticeable tear in my jeans' crotch widened. No one was around to see.

Two bluish crayfish arms lay on a rock by the side of a pool, possibly torn off by a raccoon. A one-armed crayfish, possibly the owner of one of the arms, swam in a pool.

To avoid slipping, I searched for a dry route back up to the falls. A shaded tunnel between two rocks appeared safe until it started looking hellish. The skull of a broad-toothed animal, possibly a deer, stared up from the darkness with empty eye sockets. Dried but still-sticky fur stuck to the tunnel. Perhaps a predator had carried the deer, or flooding water had swept it. Maybe it chose to die away from predators, in a dark underworld, cast off from the bright light above.

My hands smelled of dried blood. So, after leaving the underworld, I thrust them under Laurel Falls before eating. The waterfall's pounding force would have put a sink faucet or even a garden hose to shame.

I'd slacked off about hand washing for the last few days on the trail, unlike at the trail's beginning. Dad, after all, had a point that drinking water should be saved. It didn't feel right though to eat with dead deer on my hands.

We headed up. On the cliff above the falls, pine trees grew around sunny patches of shallow soil, mosses, grasses and bare rock. Hairy blueberries grew here with other plants like the pink-flowered Carolina rose. The open areas reminded me of an abandoned parking lot. In reality it was a view of what might have been in a world without parking lots.

"This is how the Plateau might have looked before people came in and planted tree farms," said Dad. Intrigued by what we might find, we slowed our pace and scanned the ground.

Red imported fire ants from South America scrambled across the ground like business travelers in an airport. Fire ants may have come from South America, but it was once they got to the U.S. that they became global. Now they scurry the ground as far away as China.

Above the waterfall, Laurel Creek flowed across smooth bedrock. I waded out into the stream, while Dad walked along the shore.

The water fell down a knee-tall waterfall. Then, it splashed and gurgled down through a narrow channel. By the side of that channel, water sat still in a pothole, a remnant of a whirlpool that had once drilled slowly into the rock.

After spilling out of the channel, the water leveled out into a calm but moving pool. Different sizes and colors of tadpoles flitted about with their tails in the shallow water. The pool was like a multi-species amphibian nursery with no supervisor.

The pool ended, without as much as a ripple, on a ledge between two shadowy banks. It was the top of Laurel Falls. Beyond the edge, treetops shined in the sun. We stopped well away from the cliff's edge.

"It looks alright," said Dad, smiling nervously, "but I'm gonna have to avoid it out of principle. Things can happen around waterfall ledges." He mentioned a boy in California who got sucked down a waterfall by the current. His mother fell to her death trying to save him.

"You're right," I said, knowing that Dad tended to be, but wishing he wasn't. "Though right here there's nothing to worry about unless we get attacked by leeches. Are there leeches in pools like this?" I asked, more curious than frightened.

"I've heard stories about leeches to the north and leeches to the south, but I've never heard of leeches around here."

Dad noticed a jiggling shape in the pool, perhaps a leech. It treaded water by itself rather than heading toward my bare feet. The pool's fish and tadpoles looked too small for it to attach on. Maybe it wasn't a leech, or perhaps it was one of the non-blood-sucking types of leeches.

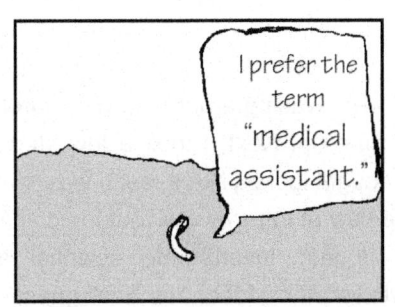

[Illustration: A leech in water with a speech bubble saying "I prefer the term 'medical assistant.'"]

Above: The only leeches used in surgery are European ones. New world leeches aren't great for that purpose. If they could talk they might claim otherwise.

We hiked back to Richland Creek and explored an old dam surrounded by slanting rocks. Then we set up camp.

I found a deep spot and swam. The water ran cold with a quick current. Once my legs started kicking, nothing mattered. Cold water was good because it felt real. It wasn't water from a faucet or a hot tub. It was cold water with a real current, pushed along by gravity.

Something squirmed in the water: a snake with bands across its back like a timber rattler, except they were colored orange. It coiled near a rock, deep in the clear stream. Then it wiggled under the rock to hide.

Leech Coincidence

LARRY: At age 40, I switched from math to ecology. The University of Tennessee allowed me to study up on and then test out of general chemistry and general biology. A few months after testing out, I lectured and led labs for general biology in UT evening school. I even lifted the chest flap on a cadaver to show students our organs.

My general biology lectures included several phyla of worms which we skimmed over. Worms are a weak area for me, but there are some stars in the worm phylum *Anellida*. Night crawlers are famous as bait and leeches as bloodsuckers (sangivores).

Not so long ago, doctors used leeches to let blood. Today, leeches are used to remove excess blood around surgery sites. Leeches occasionally attach to swimmers for some involuntary blood-letting. Because I had heard little about leeches in Tennessee, I have entered my state's waters with little fear of them.

Ben and I were wading around above Laurel Falls, and somehow the topic of leeches came up. Next, I took a few steps downstream to a pool. Something that I thought looked like a leech was swimming in it. You can see a video of what we saw at https://www.youtube.com/watch?v=90wWla_sAWI. Dr. John Smith, aquatic invertebrate scientist at Oak Ridge National Laboratory, has viewed the video. His best guess is a leech. An alternate theory is that it is a lamprey, an eel-like fish.

The video shows the mystery creature swimming by undulating side to side rather than up and down. Some of my fish scientist friends have the

It was a northern water snake (*Nerodia sipedon*). Northern water snakes gobble up minnows by night. People mistake them for venomous water moccasins and kill them, but northern water snakes lack venom. If bit, expect the bite to be bloody because the snake's saliva stops clotting. Still, a Band-Aid should take care of it.

True water moccasins, also known as cottonmouths, don't swim or crawl anywhere near the CT. This lack of cottonmouths may change with the climate, but don't worry about them yet.

For dinner, I poured boiling water and preserved salmon into bags of

....

opinion that side to side is lamprey mode and that up and down (magic carpet style) is the leech way to swim. Other have countered that the flattened body seen in the video is not lamprey shape. Let's assume the expert opinion from John is right. He has received support from others who have watched the video.

Ben and I very rarely speak of leeches, and we had never seen a leech before. So how do you explain this sequence of events: we talk about leeches and almost immediately see one?

Some choices for explanation: 1. God wanted to enhance our outdoor experience and so produced the leech. 2. The leech read our minds and wanted to show itself to interested persons. 3. It was just a coincidence.

I'm not ready to claim supernatural intervention or mind-reading exhibitionist leeches. It is not quite as strange a coincidence as it would seem. It certainly helps to be thinking of leeches to be able to spot one, but still, finding a leech after talking about them felt like an unlikely sequence of events.

There are so many possible strange coincidences that it would be strange if some of them didn't happen. A lot of low probabilities for events can add up to a high probability. In fact it is unlikely to <u>not</u> have strange coincidences in our lives. So unlikely that it would require supernatural intervention to prevent such coincidences. There were other *Twilight Zone* moments on our trek to be discussed later. I say look for and enjoy your coincidences, but you don't need to assume supernatural intervention.

....

dried rice and beans. It was tasty and filling if a bit spicy. It was the kind of fullness that slowed me down to the point of uselessness, hours away from bedtime. I'd forgotten my sleeping pad though.

"It's alright," I told Dad, trying to think positively.

"How is it alright?" he said, in a voice that sounded both amused and a little disturbed.

He had brought two pads for himself. Now, he gave one to me. I felt cold and tired enough to shove myself into my sleeping bag at 9:00 and give my flashlight to Dad. Out here, no computers, television or even books would keep me awake.

Dad wore his raincoat to keep warm. He struggled to sleep. It was not ticks this time. It wasn't leeches or snakes either. Maybe it was his lack of a second mattress that started his sleeplessness as he listened to the night's sounds.

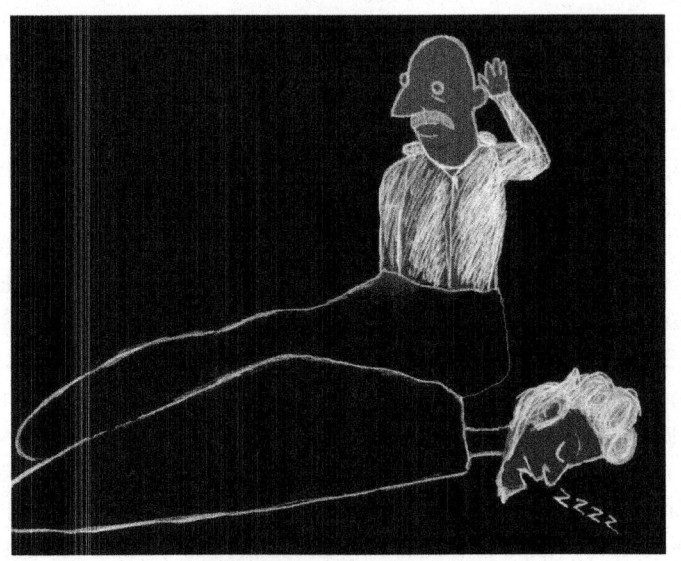

Listening to the night's sounds

↦Sandcastle in a Thunderstorm↤
Sunday May 20

BEN: I wriggled out of my sleeping bag, chewed oatmeal and slurped hot tea from my bottle. Once we got started, I hiked far ahead of Dad, clearing the cobwebs from his path. I did not care enough to change pants, so I kept the same pair of cool, damp jeans with a hole in the crotch from the day before. Soon Dad joined me in a grassy place of shallow soil above the cliff line.

LARRY: I would love to return to this area of spaced trees and grasses to spend more time studying the plant community.

BEN: A mother turkey and her children ran out of a depression in the ground. The spotted children, called poults, scattered into the grass. The mother circled us, fluttering up and down as if attempting to fly with a broken wing.

"Shouldn't she be hiding if she's injured?" I asked Dad.

"She's possibly faking it to distract us," said Dad looking up from the ground to watch. "The poults hide while their mother tempts predators to follow her." It seemed like an admirable sacrifice, although the mother turkey could still fly away if she was truly threatened.

I approached a small poult in the leaves and wondered if it felt glad to be away from its mother for a moment and experiencing independence. Probably it didn't. Probably it felt frightened of me.

Mom and Goyo, our international exchange high school student, were going to join us today. I checked my phone to see the time. It did not look right.

"Your watch adjusts to the time zone of the current cell tower," said Dad. "Did I say watch? I meant phone."

"What does your phone say?" I asked.

"My phone doesn't work."

"I meant watch."

Compared to Laurel Falls, Snow Falls was small. It fell from a rock overhang into a shaded grove. To get below it though, we had to climb down a steep slope.

When the slope got even steeper, I jumped down. Dad slid.

"Not that bad," I said. "You don't like jumping, do you?"

Dad laughed. "It's supposed to be a bad idea."

"Why? Is it worse than sliding?"

"More people get injured, I suppose, from landing badly after jumping."

"I jump anyway," I said. Sliding my behind on the ground meant fire ants and ticks could crawl onto me and bite me to shreds. Besides, jumping was more fun.

LARRY: I was taught to avoid jumping in caves. I witnessed one of the possible problems with jumping while caving. A rookie caver made a jump but delayed letting go of a rock he was using to steady himself. He dislocated his shoulder. He suffered intense pain as we struggled to get him out of the cave.

BEN: After some exploration below Snow Falls we headed back upstream. It was hot and sunny enough that I waded. Small fish swam. A blue damselfly with black wings stopped to perch on a branch.

This stream begged me to explore. Streams have that effect on me, as do trails, roads and railroad tracks. Since at least my middle school days, if something stretched further in either direction, I wanted to see where it went. Here, I couldn't walk far from where the trail crossed. Mom and Goyo would come any minute. Still, feeling the algae and the low cold water's current was better than looking at the stream and not exploring it.

"I didn't bring sunscreen," said Dad. "I'll just wait under this rock house."

Semantics for an Insomniac

Bitternut hickory (*Carya cordiformis*)

LARRY: The night sounds at Richland Creek Backpack Camp Site were like the day sounds but more striking to me with my sleeping-on-the-ground insomnia. The creek babbled constantly. Trains from Dayton whistled frequently. Also, immature hickory nuts pelted down, some hitting the tent.

Bitternut hickories drop mature nuts in the fall. The nuts I heard were dropping in mid-May. The botanical interpretation is that these trees have only enough resources to carry to maturity a limited number of nuts, so excess nuts must go. The term for this nut-dropping is the emotionally-charged word abortion. Perhaps a better word would be miscarriage since trees do not have minds to make choices. It is all semantics for an insomniac to ponder.

Evolution favors plants and animals that do the best at reproducing. Each plant uses its limited resources to make seeds. Each seed is supplied with food to get the baby plant started. Plants must share out the food resources between their seeds. Thus, more seeds mean less food for each. Each plant has a strategy for sharing available resources among seeds.

Seeds need food stores until they can produce or steal (as parasites) enough for self-sustainability. Orchids produce huge numbers of tiny seeds with minimal food storage while coconut palms produce a few very large seeds, coconuts, with ample stores. Interestingly, both species are good at long-range dispersal. Orchid seeds are carried on the wind while coconuts are carried on the oceans.

Generally, the parent plant must keep some resources for its own survival. One exception is the monument plant discussed in Chapter 14 which keeps no resources since it dies after producing seeds. Generally, the larger the plant, the more resources it has for reproduction. Thus, large

Dad sat in the shade, but soon his curiosity won. He ambled along the shore in search of plants. We stayed out of each other's way. Being alone with the stream, the damselflies and the fish was what I wanted. Dad would only be a distraction from the sense of freedom that wandering gave me.

Thunder rumbled. Clouds rolled toward us. Rings formed in the water from rain. I climbed out of the ankle-deep water, not wanting to be fried by lightning.

....

plants can do well both on quality and quantity. Hickory trees are an example of one such large plant producing many nuts with rich food stores.

The bitternuts that rained on our campsite would seem to be very wasteful since dropped nuts represent considerable investment of resources. Gardeners are familiar with flower abortion, but fruit/seed abortion is less common. An analogy of seeds to lottery thickets is useful. You buy a number of tickets in the hope that there are some winners that will cover the cost of all the tickets. Few tickets are winners. Similarly, few hickory nuts survive to produce more nuts.

This analogy is too simple for our hickory abortion since tickets are never "aborted." A better analogy is the enterprise incubator, a business that starts new businesses. During the incubation there may come a decision to pull the plug (stop investing in a new business). Note the mixed metaphor of an electrical egg. Anyway, the hickory tree that night was pulling the plug on many nuts. Presumably, the tree knows through evolution the right time to pull the plug. We can say that acting earlier would have saved resources, but this is Monday morning quarterbacking.

The hickories to look for along the CT are bitternut, pignut, shagbark, sand and mockernut. Another, less likely possibility is shellbark hickory, which occasionally grows in low areas of east Tennessee.

The most famous hickory, the pecan, is native to West Tennessee but occasionally escapes from cultivation in East Tennessee.

Jonathan Silvertown's *An Orchard Invisible, A Natural History of Seeds* is a fun, thoughtful and informative discussion of the evolution and ecology of seeds. He avoids the term aborted, though he does mention the concept.

....

LARRY: On the way in, Judy, my wife and Ben's mother, and Goyo had searched around the camping area for our hidden backpacks and found them. Hiding packs is a base camping skill, and we had failed at it.

BEN: Mom, Goyo and our mixed-breed dog Zeke arrived, all of them dripping. Goyo wore swim trunks in the hopes of swimming. We walked toward Snow Falls again, but soon the rain poured harder.

The five of us dashed through the storm. Zeke's brown eyes widened in terror at the lightning, Mom smiled nervously, Dad analyzed the landscape for shelter, and Goyo just ran.

We munched carrots and trail mix under a tiny rock house that had just enough room for the five of us. Not wanting to sit on damp sand, we all stood, except for Zeke, who dug and rolled around in it. To pass time, Dad told Mom and Goyo about the *Twilight Zone* leech.

"This is an adventure you can tell your friends in Mexico about," said Mom. "Those crazy Americans out hiking in the rain."

"The sky's gotten lighter all of a sudden," said Dad.

"You're an optimist," said Mom. Thunder roared as if it felt insulted by Dad's comment.

Standing still made the wet coldness worse. Tired of watching endless rain pound down like waves, I looked at the sand below my feet.

"We should make a sand castle!" I said, hoping to brighten Mom's and Goyo's mood. They said nothing, which I interpreted as yes. I pushed the sand into a tower. Zeke clawed the castle down and rolled around in the sand. Then, he shook every grain of sand from his black fur onto me. Goyo giggled.

"Those pants have a hole in a really inconvenient place," said Mom.

The rain lightened and stopped. Birds began to sing their sweet "no trespassing" songs again. Goyo led as we headed downhill. We crossed a fifty foot long, tall, old, wet, rusty bridge. After that, we walked up a slope on a tall bare boulder with only a cable for support. All of it was safe, even while wet, but dramatic.

Mom had brought watermelon, cold bottles of Sprite and swimsuits. By the time we got back, the rain had stopped, but she and Goyo were in no mood to cool down. Still, we ate our watermelon.

"Let's go out to eat," I said. We'd made Mom and Goyo suffer, and I desperately wanted to make it up to them. "We could try Chinese or Mexican. I'm sure you'd love some hot food after all that cold and wet rain."

"No, thank you," said Mom. "We'll just head home."

RC Crawling

LARRY: Ben has already described the Plateau sports of kayaking and rock climbing, but here we encountered a previously unknown sport, RC crawling. RC is for remote control and crawling refers to four-wheeling over rough terrain. We saw foot-long trucks, controlled by radio, climbing over pillow-sized rocks. We wondered about environmental damage but saw none in contrast to the effect of full-size ATVs when used in the wrong places.

Sources and Suggested Reading

Turkeys:
New York State Department of Environmental Conservation. "Wild Turkey." *New York State Department of Environmental Conservation.* Accessed June 12, 2013. http://www.dec.ny.gov/animals/7062.html.

Red Imported Fire Ants:
Collins, Laura and Scheffran, Rudolph H. University of Florida IFAS. "Red Imported Fire Ant—*Solenopsis invicta.*" *Featured Creatures.* Updated January 2013. http://entomology.ifas.ufl.edu/creatures/urban/ants/red_imported_fire_ant.htm.

Northern Water Snake:
Badger, David. *Snakes.* Stillwater: Voyageur 1999.
　　Badger's engaging book mentions the anticoagulant saliva of *Nerodia* and other facts about them.

Behler, John L., and F. Wayne King. *The Audubon Society Field Guide to North American Reptiles and Amphibians.* New York: Chanticleer Press Inc., 1979.
　　This may be a "disco era" book, as my girlfriend calls it, but it is still good at helping people identify species.

Beane, Jeffrey C. et al. *Amphibians & Reptiles of the Carolinas and Virginia.* Chapel Hill: University of North Carolina Press, 2010.

Brown, Gregory, and Weatherhead, Patrick. "Thermal Ecology and Sexual Size Dimorphism in Northern Water Snakes, *Nerodia Sipedon.*" *Ecological Monographs* 70 (2) (2000): 311-330. Accessed November 5, 2014, http://dx.doi.org/10.1890/0012-9615(2000)070[0311:TEASSD]2.0.CO;2.

Huheel, James and Stephen G Tilly. *Reptiles and Amphibians of the Smokies.* Gatlinburg: Great Smoky Mountains Natural History Association, 2001.

Fruit Abortion:
University of Basel and Swiss Agency for Development and Cooperation. "Why so Many Abortions of Flowers and Seeds." *Alpandino* accessed December 1, 2014. http://alpandino.org/en/course/18/18j.htm.
	Provides a good overview of some of the reasons behind fruit abortion.

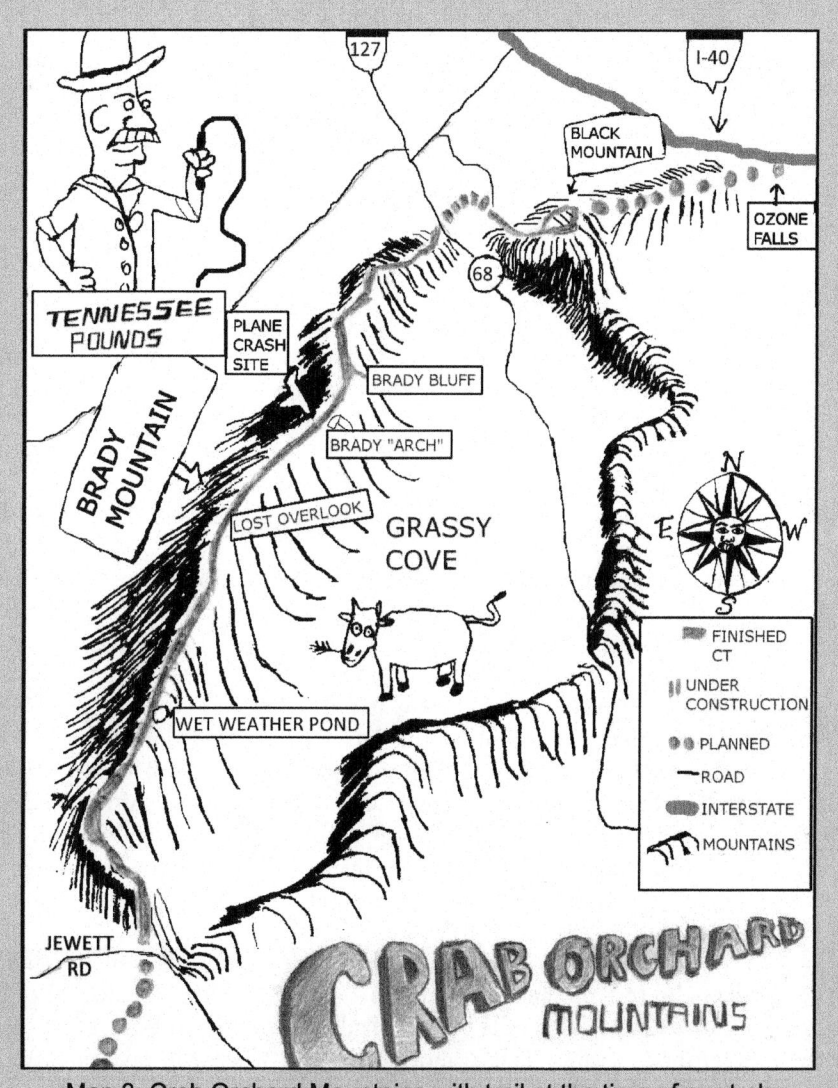

Map 3: Crab Orchard Mountains with trail at the time of our trek.

Interlude 2
Crab Orchard Mountains:
Not Just a Place to go "AWWW..." while Looking at Grassy Cove

BY LARRY

DESCRIPTION

The Cumberland Plateau has three groups of mountains sitting on top of it. The CT passes through all three.

The southernmost group is the Crab Orchard Mountains, reaching elevations around 3,000 ft. They run north from the junction (crotch) formed by the Walden Ridge leg and the main Cumberland Plateau leg. The two legs are separated by the Sequatchie Valley.

It is a line of mountains with deep gaps. These gaps carry roads. Starting on the south end the mountain/road lineup is Hinch Mountain, Jewett (Happy Top) Road, Brady Mountain, TN 68, Black Mountain, I-40, Crab Orchard Mountain. Much of the original Crab Orchard Mountains have long ago eroded away turning into the Sequatchie valley and Grassy Cove. This is strange! See the section at the end of this interlude for more details.

As you hike Brady Mountain you will have views of Grassy Cove to the east. Grassy Cove is a peculiar valley. Streams flow into it and then disappear into the ground. Thus, it is a gigantic sink hole, roughly 3 miles by 8 miles. It is one of the largest limestone sink holes in the US. The streams that disappear into the ground here come out several miles away in the Sequatchie Valley.

Presumably, Grassy Cove was the highest ground in the area and has out-eroded the rest of the mountains to become a valley. Most of that high ground (more than a cubic mile of rock) had to exit through the ground carried by underground streams. This is more believable when you take into account that most of the limestone was dissolved. So, it went to the Gulf of Mexico as hard water. The place where the water reappears from the ground in the Sequatchie Valley is called Devil's Step and is now part of Cumberland Trail State Park, though not currently connected to the main CT.

THE HUNT FOR RARE PLANTS ON THE CRAB ORCHARD MOUNTAINS CT

I found five species on the protected list. White-leaved leather-flower is a new species for me. See rare plant table at benandlarryincumberland.com.

HOW A MOUNTAIN ON THE PLATEAU BECOMES A VALLEY BELOW THE PLATEAU

How does an up-fold, the Crab Orchard Mountains, become a valley lower than the surrounding lands? First, the up-folding produces steep slopes which erode faster than the surrounding lands. Erosion should slow down as it makes the slopes less steep, but, by then, it has cut into softer rock (limestone). The limestone continues to erode and dissolve quickly since it is softer than sandstone. Thus, it turns into a valley faster than surrounding areas. So, the old mountain site is now lower than the lands that originally surrounded it. That softer limestone is exposed along the Cumberland Trail on the slopes of Brady and Black. Eventually all the Crab Orchard Mountains will be Sequatchie Valley.

WILDLY STROLLING ALONG

→ 13 ←

Brady Mountain (Monday, May 21)
Hike 8: Jewett (Happy Top) Rd. Trailhead to TN 68 Trailhead
7.8 miles

BEN: We had come to this part of the CT in April before the trek. Dad had stood at Jewett Road Trailhead ready to lead a group on a wildflower hike. No one was there. So, he decided to lead the hike with just me. Light rain fell.

On spring wildflower hikes like this one, I would often try to name all the flowers before Dad told me. I never succeeded though.

After about thirty minutes, we hiked back toward our truck. Before we reached it, we saw a group of about seven plant fans ready to go in spite of the rainy day. They had thought the hike started at 9:30 and not at 9:00.

Dad led the group up the hill, pointing out many wonderful red, yellow, white and purple flowers. Most of the group climbed up a hill with him in search of the prairie trillium. An elderly woman didn't feel she could climb further. She sat on a rock instead.

After missing it on the way up, Dad spotted the prairie trillium on the way back down. Its red petals were beginning to wilt. Still, finding a rare for East Tennessee species in bloom felt great.

We headed down with the woman who had waited on the rock. At first she held on to Dad's back for support.

"Maybe you should hold onto me," I said. "I'm the younger and more stable one." So, I helped her climb down. We explained about our planned book to her.

"Your book might sell more if it's controversial," she said.

"Well, it'll support evolution," I said. "Beyond that I don't know of anything close to controversial."

The One and Done Monument

Monument Plant (*Frasera caroliniense*)

LARRY: On the Brady Mountain piece of the CT near the Jewett Road trailhead, you will see clumps of large (mostly 7 to 24 inches long) leaves growing out of the soil. Each leaf has its own stem (petiole) coming out of the ground. This type of clump is called a basal rosette. If you look at them closely, you will find there are two types of large rosettes growing here. They are two different species. One is eastern shooting star (*Dodecatheon meadia*), a spring wildflower treat. It has some red coloration toward the bases of the leaves, and the flower stalks when present emerge from the rosettes. You may need to look closely to see the red.

The other is monument plant, also called American columbo. It lacks red coloring on the leaves. It emerges from the ground without a basal rosette <u>the year</u> that it flowers. "<u>The year</u>" is accurate since it blooms only once after waiting some years as a rosette. The monument plant flowers, produces seeds and dies. This one and done approach to reproduction is called monocarpic. Monument plant shares this trait with some species of bamboo, agave and salmon. Surely someone has written science fiction about a monocarpic race of humans.

Being monocarpic does not work well if you do it by yourself. The problem is that the main function of sexual reproduction is to mix genes. You can't do this by yourself. This means that monument plants in a local population should synchronize their flowering. Remember, this plant already has "decided" to flower before it emerges from the ground in the spring, since it comes out of the ground with a stalk. Just how this plant and others monocarps coordinate blooming is a bit mysterious.

In my experience, monument plants are not great at synchronous flowering. I often see populations with both flowering and non-flowering plants, though most often there is no flowering at all in a particular year.

I like the common name monument plant. It is monumental in its towering structure. It is our tallest spring wildflower (meaning here not a tree or a shrub) sometimes reaching 10 feet. Its flowers are a subdued greenish-white, but I find them attractive in mass or in close-up. It was in bloom in early May when we hiked by.

This time, with just the two of us, we could climb further up. The Cumberland Trail Conference map showed an airplane crash site within view of the trail near a rock arch. With the map's help, we were sure to find it just like we had found the prairie trillium.

A rough gravel road led us to the trailhead. Rocks stuck up from the road's surface, ready to pierce passing cars' oil pans. Dad drove my car on this section, making sure to position the tires on the rocks, so that the center of the car stayed safe.

We hiked up to an ATV road that ran through a large clearing. A pair of men unloaded an ATV from a pickup truck. One was older, with white hair. The other had dark hair and a thin mustache like mine. The two of them knew the area well. They'd not only seen the airplane before, they'd also seen signs of a more distant past.

"I'd say this is an old Indian campground here probably," said the older man. "Cause you can look around here and find plenty of flint where the Indians had worked. See, here's a piece of flint," he said, picking up a rock from

What exactly did they use arrowheads for anyway?

the road. "They were smart to make them, but they had to do that to survive."

We walked along on the top of Brady, past a shallow pond where dragonflies laid eggs and a dead turtle stank. Dad waded through the mud, eager to muddy his pants in the service of botany.

We walked through places where the blazes disappeared and shrubs covered the trail. Then, we saw the arch. Two boulders leaned against each other, leaving just enough room for someone to walk under them while ducking. After tall cliffs and dazzling waterfalls, Brady Mountain Arch felt overhyped. Still, it was a marker. We had an airplane to find.

So we hiked down the steep slope, holding on to tangled vines for balance and crunching through poison ivy, leaves, rocks, shrubs and fallen branches.

There was no sign of twisted metal. I began to scan the hillside for a

Brady's Wet-Weather Pond

LARRY: This is the kind of place that seems sure to provide botanical surprises because the habitat is so strange. I can't imagine that there are many natural-looking wet-weather ponds near or above 3,000 ft. on the Cumberland Plateau in Tennessee. To begin with, there is very little land at that elevation.

There was little standing water when we visited, but one could see that in wet weather the pond would have been about thirty feet across at a maximum. You could tell from the presence of wetland plants that the pond soil stayed wet for most of the year.

Here we found the quillwort. This is a fern relative that looks more like a rush than a fern. It produces its spores near the plant base. The base would often be under water.

This is a place I would love to visit again. We saw few wetlands of any type along the CT, but more may be lurking a bit off the trail. I hope to do more searching for them with their prospect of botanical surprises. Trails avoid wetlands for good reasons. Trail building in wetlands is hard and may damage the habitat.

single charred stump, thinking I might have missed something. Dad kept striding ahead and trusting his eyes.

"What if they cleared it out? What if there's nothing?" I said.

"We didn't come all the way down here to see nothing. We have to spot something out of the ordinary I guess. I think I see flagging. There must be some kind of a trail." He smiled.

"Why are you smiling?" I asked.

"I'm smiling about it being challenging," he said.

Having a purpose makes hiking more exciting. Some people look for wildflowers. Some people hunt for deer. Some people listen for birdcalls. We hunted for an airplane.

"Are you seeing some sign of a plane down there?" I asked

"No, just wildly strolling along."

We never found a single rusted metal scrap. Later, a commenter on our blog would tell us that the plane had been salvaged for its metal.

Tennessee Pounds and the Raiders of the Lost Airplane.

The common garter snake: a most frightening predator (if you're worm-sized).

Common Garter Snake (*Thamnophis sirtalis*)

BEN: We saw a skinny and agile garter snake on the top of Brady Mountain. Common garter snakes are beautiful, with stripes running down their backs. They slither away when scared. Unlike the slow rattlesnake with its very different defense, a garter snake can slide away from animals that might step on it. This particular one was in the process of shedding, with shedding skin all the way across the eye, limiting its vision. It might have been slow to run away for that reason.

If you grab a garter snake, it will probably spray musk on you, which is smelly but not harmful. It might bite like any wild animal with teeth might. Still, its venom won't usually hurt you, and there's no need to follow the directions we've laid out later on in this book for rattlesnake and copperhead bites.

Scientists used to think garter snakes had no venom. Actually, a garter snake has about enough neurotoxin to stun a small frog for a few moments. On large animals like humans, however, that kind of venom only has effects on people with allergies.

Australian molecular biologist Bryan G. Fry proposed that all snakes evolved from a common ancestor with the potential to be venomous, but only a few of that snake's descendants had use for venom and even fewer for powerful venom. The eastern garter snake supports that theory.

Still, the hike was worth it. For Dad it was particularly worth it because of the plants he found. For me, the view from an overlook of Grassy Cove below made it worthwhile.

I didn't just see trees, farmland and distant mountains getting bluer and hazier into the distance from Brady Mountain. I saw tiny cattle, circling birds and a truck moving down the road. Someone was driving that truck. It was real. If the truck was real, the valley around it was also real. I could feel the air and know that if I walked out too far, I would fall into it. The pictures I took from up there show none of that.

Reality's full expanse can be breathtaking. Stroll wildly.

Lily-of-the-Ridge and the Ultimate Incest Taboo

American lily-of-the valley (*Convallaria majuscula*)

LARRY: Lily-of-the-valley is a misnomer, at least for our native species *Convallaria majuscula*. Along the CT it occurs on the very tops of Brady Mountain and Cumberland Mountain, far from the valleys. *C. majuscula*, American lily-of-the-valley, differs from the garden variety lily-of-the-valley in being generally bigger but with flowers that do *not* stand up beyond the middle of the lowest leaf, as opposed to the garden species with flowers that *do* go beyond. Both species form large colonies, but colonies of the native species have plants spaced more widely at 6 or more inches, versus less than 4 inches for the garden ones. Different lengths of the rhizomes, the underground stems, cause the difference in the spacing. Still, if you know the garden plant, you will easily be able to identify the native as a lily-of-the-valley.

I have used the phrase *native* Lily-of-the-valley though some major authorities in the past have thought that our wild Appalachian plants are actually exotic, not native. The idea is that early European colonists brought over an odd form of this plant which then spread into the wild. This notion is quite unlikely, but it does illustrate the problems with determining or even defining nativity. That our Appalachian lilies of the valley are exotic is unlikely, because their distinct form is not reported from old garden stock of the region. Also, the Appalachian lilies are found in scattered remote locations.

Recent genetic studies have shown that the Appalachian plants are more closely related to an Asian variety rather than the European variety, the Asian connection again. Further studies are needed to see if the Appalachian form is better considered a separate species or just a variety of the Asian

Sources and Suggested Reading

General:
Cumberland Trail Conference. *CTC's Guide to Hiking the Justin P. Wilson Cumberland Trail with Maps/Guides.* Accessed July 19, 2012. www.cumberlandtrail.org.

---

plants.

Large colonies may be clones with most stalks continuing to be connected by rhizomes and genetically nearly identical. Each clone needs another genetically distinct clone close enough for pollinator to carry pollen between them to produce good seed sets. Self-pollination is the worst form of incest for plants. Little variation of genetic combinations is produced by it. Apparently genetic variation is very important for plants and animals. Outcrossing sexual reproduction for species is nearly universal, though often combined in plants with other forms of reproduction.

Lily-of-the-valley has a pleasing smell, presumably to attract pollinators. One chemical in that smell is bourgeonal, which is used for perfumes. Research has shown that mammal sperms have receptors on their surfaces for bourgeonal and will swim toward a source of this chemical at least in a test tube. This movement toward a chemical source is called chemotaxis. There would seem to be potential, then, for a fertility treatment using bourgeonal, but bourgeonal has not been found in human females. Still, similar compounds may be present that will work with the receptors. Currently, scientists are skeptical that this form of chemotaxis occurs inside organisms as opposed to the test tube.

When you see lily-of-the-valley in flower you can check one discovery about bourgeonal. Have people move their noses gradually closer to the flower until they can detect the smell. Males should be able to detect it from further away than females. Normally male smelling is less sensitive but not in this case. I haven't tried this exercise, but it could be fun.

Garter Snakes and the Evolution of Snake Venom:
Azelone, Marianne. "There's no Need to fear that Garter Snake." Nytimes.com. http://cityroom.blogs.nytimes.com/2012/06/05/theres-no-need-to-fear-that-garter-snake/ (Accessed May 7, 2014).

Graham, Donna. "Garter Snakes (*Thamnophis* spp.)" *Northern State University*. 1997. http://www.northern.edu/natsource/REPTILES/Garter1.htm.

Ohio Department of Natural Resources, Division of Wildlife. "Eastern Garter Snake." *Ohio.gov*. http://wildlife.ohiodnr.gov/species-and-habitats/species-guide-index/reptiles/eastern-gartersnake.

Zimmer, Carl. "Clues to the Origin of Snake Venom." *The New York Times*. November 22, 2005. http://www.nytimes.com/2005/11/22/science/clues-to-the-origin-of-snake-venom.html. (Accessed May 7, 2014).

Zimmer, Carl. "Open Wide: Decoding the Secrets of Venom." *The New York Times*. April 5, 2005. http://www.nytimes.com/2005/04/05/science/05veno.html. (Accessed May 7, 2014).

Zimmerman, Ryan. "*Thamnopsis sirtalis* Common Garter Snake." *University of Michigan Museum of Zoology Animal Diversity Web*. Last Modified 2013. Accessed November 12, 2014. http://animaldiversity.ummz.umich.edu/accounts/Thamnophis_sirtalis/.

On Lily of the Valley and Sperm:
Max-Planck-Gesellschaft. "Sperm cannot detect smells: End of 'Lily of the Valley phenomenon' in sperm research?" ScienceDaily. www.sciencedaily.com/releases/2012/02/120228102013.htm (accessed June 2, 2014).

Olsson, Peter & Laska Matthias. 2010. "Human Male Superiority in Olfactory Sensitivity to the Sperm Attractant
Odorant Bourgeonal." Chemical Senses. 427-432. Accessed June 2, 2014. http://swepub.kb.se/bib/swepub:oai:DiVA.org:liu-56471?tab2=abs&language=en.

A PLACE FOR EVERYTHING

⇾ 14 ⇽

Black Mountain (Tuesday, May 22)
Hike 8: Black Mountain Summit to Cox Valley Rd.
4 miles

BEN: On our way to Black Mountain, we passed a sand quarry. It was hard for me to grasp the idea of taking sandstone from cliffs to grind into sand, in a world with ready-made sand dunes. Sand like everything else has to be an industry these days.

LARRY: Special sands are needed for special uses.

BEN: We wandered from Black Mountain's misty summit, unsure of where the main Cumberland Trail started until we reached a point on our map: an old spring house used for keeping food cool. Its stone walls supported a metal roof. In the dark, below the roof, cool spring water trickled over the cement floor.

A mineralogist's summer house had stood near here. Nothing remained of it now though besides a chimney and the spring house. I doubt the owners intended for the springhouse to be a permanent monument. I would not care for the only lasting piece of my house to be a refrigerator.

From the springhouse, we climbed and then dropped down the cliff through a crack, another stone door.

On the other side stood a rock city, with blocky rocks for two story buildings and streets paved with leaves. This one had yet to get the flow of tourists and knickknacks that Rock City near Chattanooga had. This rock city's foggy emptiness gave it mystery. Fog blurred rocks and hid the world behind them. It made me eager to see what was beyond the fog.

A break in the sandstone layer exposed a deep pit in the underlying limestone. It looked like a ventilation shaft or a well, yet it was natural. Neither

Cave salamanders find cracks in the rock to be appealing homes.

of us could see the bottom. The pit stretched down into shadow.

A cave salamander, skinny and red, sat on the pit's wall in the half-dark. The Latin name is *Eurycea lucifuga*; *lucifuga* means "fleeing from light." Holding on to a rock wall like the cave salamander did would have been tricky for me. Living there would be even harder. Yet the salamander had adapted to life there. Possibly it felt as comfortable on its rock wall as I would on a couch. The salamander didn't move. It had no reason to fear us. If we'd gone clambering down after it, we would have probably fallen into the dark depths with no one around to rescue us.

We walked down from sandstone to limestone, which made Dad excited for the opportunity to see different plants. Limestone is also the kind of rock for caves, and our map told us we were coming close to one such cave, Windlass Cave.

LARRY: The cave is named Windless on one CTC map but Windlass on other maps. A windlass is a pulley devise which can be useful for saltpeter mining in caves.

BEN: A stream, which ran from the cave, held a gilled salamander larva. I shined my light in the cave, searching for more cave salamanders, and saw nothing. A sign warned me against going any farther due to "White Nose Syndrome Concern."

"White Nose Syndrome Concern" sounds scary but tells little about what the danger is. A casual hiker might run away from the cave in fear that he would wake up the next morning with an albino nose. In reality, white nose syndrome infects bats. It causes a powdery white growth on their noses. You might think bats with white noses look cute, like kids with milk mustaches. A more accurate comparison would be powder stuck on the nose of a cocaine addict.

What makes white-nose syndrome deadly is its ability to confuse a bat's mind and change habits. Bats normally fill up on insects during the warmer part of the year. They hibernate through the winter in dark places, hanging upside-down, surviving off of stored-up fat. Infected bats become restless and get their seasons confused. Flapping around in the cold weather, they search for food in vain. Then they die from starvation or freezing. Imagine such a life. All energy wasted with no reward. Over a million bats may have died between 2006 and 2009.

Bats save American farmers 3.7 billion dollars a year in pesticides by some estimates and those costs will pass down to food buyers without bats. Staying out of caves and abandoned mines is the least we can do to prevent the spread of the syndrome.

An ATV road led us across private land on the old CT. There is no current agreement with the land owners. I almost hoped for them to come out and scream at us to leave, but they never did. Back when we were hiking, the Cumberland Trail Conference was building a trail to connect more directly to the Brady Mountain section. At present that trail is complete.

Cave Salamander Mothers

BEN: From studying preserved mother cave salamanders in labs, researchers have found that the average number of eggs a female produces is much higher than the number usually found in one place in cave pools and streams. It appears that cave salamanders scatter their eggs in different places before abandoning them. For us, as a species with a different approach to raising children, this might seem neglectful, but from cave salamanders' evolutionary perspective, scattering makes sense. The mothers prefer not to put all their eggs in one basket.

A few drops of rain began to fall and we quickly moved ahead toward Cox Valley Road. A scarlet tanager fluttered around the trees, flashing bright red colors below the gray sky as we left the old CT.

A red salamander (*Psudotriton ruber*) lay dead by the side of the road. It was as wide as my thumb and the length of my hand. Grains of dirt covered it, ants crawled over it and a stump was all that remained of its tail. I grabbed it, wanting to pick it up and take a picture. Its dirt-covered body wriggled in my hand, not dead at all. Once I set it down below the road in the wet leaves, it scampered away, full of life and ready for its tail to grow back.

At the time I thought the salamander was too dry to breathe well and would die soon. Yet the air was moist and clouds covered the sky, so it survived.

LARRY: I think Ben rescued the salamander, but it is hard to figure why it didn't rescue itself by scooting off the roadside and into the moist leaves.

BEN: We drove back through Grassy Cove, a fertile valley in between the Plateau's higher places. Cattle munched on grass. Green and bluish mountains rose behind them. Out here, beyond Chattanooga's shadow, pastures replaced parking lots. Family-run general stores stayed in business, and Walmart dared not compete.

Bobby Fulcher, music enthusiast and Park Manager of the Cumberland Trail State Park would later introduce me to a folk song, dated to 1789 by a reference in the lyrics, about the people who made the Cumberland Plateau their own. The exact place referenced is hard to pin down, and there's even a version about the more famous (thanks to a computer game) pioneer destination of Oregon, which fails to fit the rhyme scheme. The song expresses well the mixed feelings that Grassy Cove's pioneers must have felt though.

When I first started away from you,
With sorrow, grief, and trouble too,
You gave to me the parting hand,
And wished me safe in the Cumberland Land.
When we were on the ice and snow,
It rained, it hailed--the wind did blow,
And some of us did mourn and cry,
To think with cold we all must die.
But bless the Lord, some relief is found,
We're landed here both safe and sound,
In a lonesome place but fruitful soil,
There's milk and wine, and corn and oil.

Russ Manning's book *The Historic Cumberland Plateau* tells of an 1801 group of settlers who tried to cross the mountains. Their wagon rolled out of control on a steep slope, leaving all but one of their mules dead. They abandoned their original destination and adapted to Grassy Cove's isolated valley.

I could relate to those stranded settlers. I had found myself back in East Tennessee against my will after trying to move away from it. Now, among boulders, mist and rolling mountains, I saw how magnificent experiencing Tennessee with my father could be. Maybe the red salamander felt the same way after being placed down against its will off the road. Perhaps it was not fear of me but excitement at being in a proper wet place that made the salamander dash back into the leaves.

The water that flows into Grassy Cove drains into deep caves, keeping the cove from becoming a large lake. Cove Creek flows through one such cave, Old Mill Cave, only to come out the other side of Brady Mountain as the Sequatchie River. Saltpeter Cave is even more famous. There, during the Civil War a local man named Andrew Kemmer mined for calcium nitrate, an ingredient in the Confederate Army's gunpowder.

These days, the Kemmers run two general stores. We passed them: J.T Kemmer & Son (since 1886 according to the sign) and J.P Kemmer & Son (since 1937), both small old buildings with gravel parking areas.

The inside of J.P. Kemmer & Son's General Merchandise smelled of old wood, like a true old-style general store. Paintings of cattle hung behind the cash register, along with a certificate marking the community's gratitude to the store. A small refrigerator with drinks stood nearby.

A glass bottle of Coke caught my eye. Glass appealed to me more than the typical plastic, possibly because glass was another form of sand, but also because it seemed distinctive and old fashioned. My wallet held a plastic debit card but no cash. Jim Kemmer had no card reader. So Dad paid for my Coke, along with a plastic bottle of juice for himself. At first, as usual, Dad did all the talking.

Business was not going well for Jim.

"Everything's going up," said Jim, "and we're making less." He was not the only one in the area who suffered from economic changes. He mentioned a plywood factory that "plum shut down."

Finally, because Dad seemed scared to, I asked him about the other Kemmer store down the street. Jim pointed out that his store sold different things, but he was vague on details that I, as a non-farmer, could understand.

On the way back I drove slowly, letting other cars pass me. It seemed too slow, but at least I stayed predictable.

"How was my driving?" I asked Dad as we walked back into the motel.

"Pretty good actually," said Dad.

We were in Dayton for one more night of blogging, Facebook updates, Walmart, microwave and mini-fridge. We'd be camping the next night in a place called Spider Den.

The two of us had adapted to the rhythm of hiking and returning to Dayton. It was too much of a rhythm. Maybe the desire to break up a routine only comes to humans and bats with nose fungi, but it's a pretty strong one. At Spider Den we would leave the city streetlights and enter a place where night is dark.

Grassy Ghost

BEN: After the Civil War, explorers found a Confederate soldier's hardened body lying on a stretcher in Saltpeter cave. No one knew who he was, why he died, or why he was so deep inside the cave, but the people of Grassy Cove gave the soldier a proper funeral and buried him in the Methodist graveyard.

Local children started to believe that his ghost haunted the place and they refused to go near it. As their school was nearby, it was a convenient superstition. Soon, for the sake of restoring calm, a group of men dug up the body and buried it somewhere secret. Now no one knows where it is.

Sources and Suggested Reading

General:
Fulcher, Bob. "Black Mountain: Rags and Riches." *Tennessee Conservationist.* July 2001. http://www.tn.gov/environment/tn_consv/archive/blackmountain.htm.
　　This article gives one of the best descriptions of Black Mountain that I have ever read. Among other things, it taught me that the springhouse was owned by a Cornell mineralogist.

White Nose Syndrome:
Puchmaille, Sébastien J., Pascal Verdeyroux, Hubert Fuller, Meriadeg Ar Gouilh, Michaël Bekaert, and Emma C. Teeling. "White-Nose Syndrome Fungus (*Geomyces destructans*) in Bat, France." *Emerging Infectious Diseases.* 16. No. 2 (February 2010). http://wwwnc.cdc.gov/eid/article/16/2/09-1391_article.htm

"A Mystery Bat Disease: Cute but Contagious." *The Economist.* May 21, 2009. http://www.economist.com/node/13702854. (Accessed May 7, 2014).

Bat Conservation International. BCI "Species Profile: Myotis Sodalis."

Batcon.org. http://www.batcon.org/resources/media-education/species-profiles/detail/2323 (Accessed May 7, 2014).

Grassy Cove:
Manning, Russ. *The Historic Cumberland Plateau: An Explorer's Guide, Second Edition.* Knoxville: University of Tennessee Press, 1999.

Cumberland Land Song:
Dixon, Jim, and Artful Codger. Lyr Req: Old Cumberland Land. October 9, 2009. http://mudcat.org/thread.cfm?threadid=124667. (Accessed September 12, 2014).
    This source is a discussion thread, not a scholarly source, but it does give some of the major variations in verses as well as links to various books. Attending a concert with Bobby Fulcher gave me much of the information I've used here.

Salamanders:
Behler, John L., and F. Wayne King. *The Audubon Society Field Guide to North American Reptiles and Amphibians.* New York: Chanticleer Press Inc., 1995.

Niemiller, Matthew et al. *The Amphibians of Tennessee.* Knoxville: University of Tennessee Press, 2011.

IN WHICH BEN IGNORES AN AERIAL YELLOWJACKET NEST AND MURDERS SNAILS

⇥ 15 ⇤

Piney River (Wednesday and Thursday, May 23, 24)
Hike 10: Walden Rd. to shut-in Gap Road
8 miles

⇥Sex, Snails and Cell Phones⇤
Wednesday, May 23

Much of the Cumberland Trail owes itself to a stiff-backed Englishman who was not around to see it or even hear plans. He was Sir Eric Vassettart Bowater who never did anything half-way and always stood up straight. Granted, World War I left him injured, so he had trouble bending over or slouching.

He took over his family's newsprint business but would not settle for just selling newsprint. His company had to be the biggest newsprint-making company on Earth, which in the days before iPads and Kindles meant more than it does now. By 1954 he succeeded, selling 1,000,000 tons of paper each year. American paper companies tried to stop him from building a mill and buying up land for pulp forests in Tennessee, but it was no use. By the 1970s the Bowater Company's land stretched for hundreds of miles across the Plateau.

Much of it is still in pulp plantations, but the Bowater Southern Paper Corporation designated some areas as Pocket Wilderness, with no development allowed except for hiking trails. These places later became State Natural Areas. We'd seen one such place at Laurel Snow.

Bowater Co. did not just build trails. They built dramatic trails. Before we started our month-long trek, we had hiked on a side trail at Piney River State Natural Area. I had climbed up a ladder to a craggy bluff at the trail's top. Chain-link fencing covers the ladder to stop hikers from falling, making it safe to climb. Still, it was too much for Dad. He bushwhacked his way up a slope, arrived at the same bluff and grinned at me from his side of the fence on top, not feeling like he had missed anything. He was here to look at plants, not to climb around on Bowater playgrounds.

In another handstand on the balance beam between adventurous fun and scaring people, Bowater named the campsite at which we would stay "Spider's Den Bluff," a name that sounded like something from *The Hobbit*. Neither I nor my father is scared of spiders, however.

Our neighbor Larry from Loudon kindly drove us to the start of the trail in a white van.

LARRY: Our thanks go to several friends who helped us with our car shuttles. They kept us from having to leave a vehicle overnight in places where we were worried about vandalism or theft.

BEN: The van sat low as he drove over bumps and rocks. Our neighbor Larry seemed like an alternate version of my father Larry. Both were bald and fascinated by plants, even if the Larry who drove us could not claim Dad's scientific knowledge. He stopped the van to take a picture of a butterfly weed.

"It's a darker shade of orange," he said. "It looks really special."

On the trail, I hiked ahead of Dad.

There are plenty of things to complain about with a backpack. You can whine about how a backpack is heavy. You can groan about how it makes you enjoy the forest less. You can curse the heavens for every log under which you have to duck your clunky and rigid-as-Sir-Eric-Bowater back. You can complain about how few animals you're seeing if your backpack makes noise. Or you can just head forward.

At White Pine Cascade, water fell over curving shale. We threw down our backpacks. Dad searched along the shore for plants. I waded deep into the water to look at fish in a green pool and on brown algae-covered rocks. Soggy pants seemed like part of the experience now. They had all day to dry anyway. We followed our typical routine, each of us following our own obsessions and not each other.

We joined up with each other on the shore and walked together. A thought hit me. For a trip that was supposed to be about the two of us spending time together and melding our skills, we had spent far too much of it hiking apart from each other or sitting in the motel room doing separate things.

During much of my time on the trail, the rhythms of walking had filled my head with its own thoughts, including pop-songs I only half liked. I walked in a state that was divorced from both Dad and the marvels of the world around me. Even when we did hike together, I would sometimes step on Dad's heels. I was so caught up in the rhythm of walking that nothing else mattered.

So I asked Dad a question. "You stopped to look at that one plant," I said, "was it anything special?"

"Large-leaved *Eurybia*, though I thought it was…"

Crunch.

"You just killed a snail!" said Dad.

Even with inches of rubber between my foot and the snail, I could sense its crushed gooeyness and shattered pieces of shell on my sole.

Dad called out every snail that crawled along the trail so that I would not kill them. Even though they were only snails, they mattered. They were peaceful enough that crushing them seemed like murder. They were big enough that killing them seemed like a sign of not paying attention. In the past I'd enjoyed letting my mind drift while hiking, but Dad always seemed to keep his mind on the trail. I'd try hiking his way.

In the stream, I picked up a rock, grabbed the crayfish under it and took pictures of her with my phone. She had a sack of dark eggs below her tail. Her pinchers groped my fingers as she writhed, finally managing to clamp me. She fought both for herself and for her unborn children. I could not admire her at that moment though. Pinching makes admiration hard.

The rock house of Spider-Den Bluff jutted above the fire circles of past campers. They'd built short tables and chairs out of rocks. Moss covered some of them, drinking water from the light rain that now pattered on us. True to the place's name, brown spiders lived under the rocks.

We didn't like getting our butts wet on the mossy rock seats, but they were all that separated us from the ground, which was even damper, as we ate lunch.

A wooden sign by the riverside said "Diver's End." A cliff loomed above it. The water looked too shallow for a diver to dive and avoid cracking his skull, especially if he jumped from the cliff. Maybe on rainier years the water got deeper, or possibly the sign was a playful joke by Bowater folks, stating that it would be the end for any diver who tried it.

As the rain stopped, we got up and explored sometimes apart, sometimes together, along the side of the stream, up the hill and sliding down, finding a dusky salamander with an orange tail, a piece of metal left over from old train rails and a small rock in the stream with a plant fossil, possibly another lycopod. Then we found ourselves in a dark hemlock forest. A red fungus grew like shelves from one hemlock. In future years when adelgids finish draining the hemlocks of their sap (see Chapter 9), these red fungi will lack much of their habitat.

A Not-So-Ephemeral Spring Wildflower

Feature Plant: Gaywings (*Polygala pauciflora*)

LARRY: This distinctive flower looks like a cartoonish airplane in pink to purple. They also come in white, but that's rare. The sepals are the wide wings. The petals form the fuselage with a fringed extension that resembles a propeller. Gaywings is a scarce beauty that gratifies the wildflower lover. It is a northern plant that has mostly eluded me in Tennessee, the southern end of its range. I have now seen the flowers in two Plateau gorges. Look for it along the CT on the Piney River/Dustin Creek section.

It is helpful to pick out this plant by the leaves without help from the flowers. Learning this method has allowed me to spot many populations I would have otherwise walked by. Many spring wildflowers give up on their leaves, dropping them as the tree canopy blocks out much of the light. The term for this is spring ephemeral. Gaywings keeps its leaves through the growing season. Thus it is not a spring ephemeral.

It has distinctive leaves. The developed leaves cluster at the ends of stems are only about 4 inches tall. They are oval-shaped, averaging about 1 inch long.

Another common name for this beauty is flowering wintergreen. **Watch out: flowering wintergreen and wintergreen are two species with similar leaves.** Wintergreen (*Gaultheria procumbens*) does have flowers, and they are attractive, though not as knock-you-out beautiful as gaywings/flowering wintergreen.

Wintergreen (not gaywings) is known for its aroma. Yes, it smells like toothpaste. It is evergreen, thus the name wintergreen. It is a sub-shrub, a very small shrub only 4 to 8 inches tall, while gaywings is non-woody and thus an herb to a botanist. Another name for wintergreen is teaberry for the wintergreen flavored red berries that make a nice tea. To separate gaywings leaves from wintergreen leaves, check the smell.

I reached into my pockets for my cell phone, hoping to take a picture. I found my Rite in the Rain pad, my pair of swim trunks and my recording device, but no phone.

"I'm sure I can find it," I said.

"Why?" said Dad, confused and almost laughing.

"Because it's not like there's anyone else out here to steal it," I said, wanting to be right. If I couldn't beat Dad at botany, geology, the history of forest fires or skill at striking up conversations, at least I could beat him at finding my cell phone. I'd lost it plenty of other times both at home and elsewhere. Still, I hoped my practice with snails and green salamanders had made me a better noticer by now.

"It's hard to find something small like that out here in the woods," Dad said. Still, he figured we had time. We walked back to the slope where we'd slid.

"Actually," I said "I remember where I last had it. I tried to take a picture of that fossil in the stream." So, we looked in the stream for either the phone or the pattern of the fossil plant.

Then, I heard a clunking sound like a plastic phone hitting something. Maybe a rock hit the phone. Maybe the phone slid backwards from behind my boot. I turned around and saw the phone, sitting like a black plastic pebble in the shallow stream and barely touched by the flowing water. Dad stared at the phone in awe, as though it had fallen from Heaven.

"This is another 'Twilight Zone' moment!" said Dad. "This time it's a phone and not a leech."

Back in the hemlock woods, we spotted something less awe-inspiring than a cell phone: white spots on a tree. The adelgids had claimed at least one victim here.

Back at the campsite, we ate macaroni. As the light dimmed, we talked about the asexuality of woolly adelgids and the evolutionary advantages of sexual reproduction. Dad described it as "cooperation between genes." Further, he said "It involves trying to mix up the genes and get new combinations."

"They used to say that aerodynamics proves that a bumblebee can't fly," he said. "Well, at first glance, evolutionary theory could be used to prove

Other Doomed Trees

BEN: Hemlocks are not the only trees that have ever been struck down in large numbers by pests. Long ago, many once-thriving American chestnuts died that way. Emerald ash borer has just started to hit Tennessee's ash trees. Disease hit dogwood trees too, but they survived and adapted.

that sexual reproduction would not be favored. That's the kind of thing you get into. Trying to use models and things that are too simple, you come up with results that obviously aren't right. Things have to be pretty complicated to make sense."

Don't Cry Wolf

Whorled Horsebalm (*Collinsonia verticillata*)

LARRY: As a person who cares about preserving our native plants, you might have expected me to advocate for giving legal protection for as many plant species as possible. I feel strongly that we should protect more of nature than we currently do. However, if we have species on our protection lists that aren't really facing extinction, the lists lose credibility. This may lead to the lists being ignored or circumvented. If we cry wolf and there is no wolf, we damage rather than enhance species conservation. In the "Walden Ridge Interlude," I suggested reconsidering the protected status for two plants of the CT.

Sometimes nature preservation should be based on issues other than the threat of species extinction. An example is preserving rare or old-growth communities of plants and animals. I would go as far as preserving all wild areas where there are very few exotic plants. Such areas are becoming rare.

I have long advocated for the state listing of whorled horse balm (*Collinsonia verticillata*), its genus apparently so named because of its use on horses' aching backs. Before my recent time spent on the CT, I had seen only scattered, small populations of this pretty plant with its pink flowers. Now I have seen thousands of individuals of this plant on protected state natural areas along the CT. I still delight in seeing it but no longer fear for its continued existence. Walden Ridge is the center of its range with out-lying populations as far as Florida and Ohio. I no longer call for listing it for protection.

In many cases, the more we look for a rare plant the more we find. Listing causes botanizers to look more, and many plants get de-listed this way. In other cases we look and find no new populations and discover that old populations have disappeared. Such plants are in trouble, but surely the plants at greatest risk are those that are so rare they will probably go extinct before they can be discovered and protected.

Then, we got off on subjects more difficult for Dad, like flying squirrels and whether we could see them in a hemlock grove like the one we were in now. Odds were they'd be in forests with more nuts.

"I've drawn some unpublished cartoons about a character called Lord Chipper who is a chipmunk. His favorite food is acorns, but that's not based on research," I said.

"That's probably pretty accurate for a chipmunk," said Dad.

"Although he's a giant chipmunk so he eats giant acorns, but you know this is fantasy," I said.

"Right, whatever," said Dad with a laid-back smile.

I sat in pants and socks that were wet from rain, moss and stream. With the sun behind clouds, the pants stayed damp. Dad had similar problems. He put his bare feet in his raincoat to dry them off.

"Maybe I should go swimming," I told Dad, "Even though it's cool out, my pants could use some time to hang up and dry."

"No," said Dad. "They'll dry more on you using body heat."

He was right, although I wanted him not to be right. Hanging around in wet pants felt miserable and even humiliating, reminding me of days back in preschool when I had wet my pants.

The sky was clear that night, which made me happy at first, but the air got colder. I walked to keep warm, holding my solar flashlight in the darkness. After coming back to the campsite, I distracted myself in true millennial style by playing cell phone games. Electronic music joined the sounds of frogs and insects. Before now, I'd been too much of a purist to play *The Simpsons Arcade* in the wilderness, but I could not stand being cold and wet without pretending to be somewhere else.

I shoved myself into my sleeping bag liner, threw my wet jeans off and tried to use them as a pillow. Being in underwear made me feel chillier. So, I pulled the wet jeans back on, put on a dry shirt, made a pillow out of my old shirt and two wet socks, and tried to sleep.

Maybe it was the coldness. Maybe it was the wetness. Maybe it was thinking about all the people who had possibly pooped in the woods by the campsite, even though we saw no sign of it. Whatever it was, a thought hit me. We were choosing to live like villagers in third-world countries. In the past, sleeping on the ground had been fun. Until now, I had not seen it as something uncomfortable, the way that Dad did.

⇥Watch out for Wasps!⇤
Thursday, May 24

BEN: I struggled to get out of my sleeping bag for fear of cold. After eating oatmeal, we started hiking. The heat rose to familiar sweltering Tennessee

Aerial yellowjackets on the bridge.

summer level. I crossed a suspension bridge as tall as four of me over a pool, marveling again at the Bowater Company's love of drama, but also at the pool. At last, I had a reason to use my swimsuit.

So, I hid behind a boulder as Dad wandered along the shore on the other side, looking for plants. Just when I had stripped down to my underwear, I heard someone walking toward the boulder, which did not block views from all sides. I grabbed my shirt, but did not have enough time to grab my pants before he arrived.

"There are wasps on that bridge," he said pointing to where I had just crossed. "I've done been stung already."

So, I swam across the pool. It was deep, clear and home to many fish. I stopped when I saw Dad on the bridge. "Watch out for the wasps!" I shouted.

He spotted the nest below the rail and crossed slowly, staying to the other side.

We hiked out to Dad's truck, my track record as a noticer more mixed than ever. Even if I'd seen my cell phone in the stream, I'd ignored a hornets' nest, until someone else had pointed it out.

LARRY: We think, based on an article in the *Tennessee Conservationist*, that though called hornets in ordinary speech, they are more properly aerial yellow jackets despite being white rather than yellow. The hornet is an uncommon exotic while the aerial yellow jacket is native. Aerial refers to having an above ground nest unlike other yellow jackets whose nests you can step on accidentally.

BEN: Back in Dayton, we shoved everything into my car. By now, Dayton felt like home to me. Still, I was happy to be leaving our corner of the town. It seemed decidedly un-quirky. Being near a Walmart Supercenter didn't feel like an adventure.

That night we would stay with friends. As we drove to their house, I was not sure if I could ever get used to meals that were neither frozen nor dried and rooms with decent lighting.

Sources and Suggested Reading

Aerial Yellow Jackets:
Taft, Joe. "Some Yellowjackets are Aerial Nesting." *Tennessee Conservationist*. July/August 2012.

Bowater's History:
Time. "Corporations: The Paper Prince." October 11, 1954. http://www.time.com/time/magazine/article/0,9171,936550,00.html#paid-wall.

Memorial University of Newfoundland. "Sir Eric Vansittart Bowater, LL. D." Accessed June 18, 2013. *Celebrate Memorial: History*. http://www.mun.ca/memorial_history/bios/EVBowater.html.

Van West, Carrol "Pocket Wilderness Areas." *Tennessee Encyclopedia of History and Culture Version 2.0*.

Whorled Horse Balm
Horn, Dennis and Tavia Cathcart, ed. *Wildflowers of Tennessee, the Ohio Valley and the Southern Appalachians*. Auburn: Lone Pine Publishing, 2005.

Map 4: Obed River section

Interlude 3
Obed River Section
Not Just a Place to Find Nemo

BY LARRY

→ ←

DESCRIPTION

The CT crosses three rivers, the Piney, the Emory (really the Obed) and the New. The Obed River is dissed (slighted) by what happens on maps at its junction with the Emory River. It is the bigger river of the two, so the water below the junction should be the Obed, not the Emory as the maps have it.

We include the CT along Daddy's Creek, the Obed River and the Emory River in our Obed CT section. The Obed CT section is the longest stretch of the CT that follows a stream's drainage, going continually along the right-descending banks of these connected streams.

The Obed and Daddy's Creek are fast-flowing streams where water levels can rise and fall rapidly. The scouring from the changing water levels maintains many open cobble bar habitat areas. Cobble bars are places along the banks of rivers in which cobble-size stones cover the ground. Some river bars are boulder bars with their larger rocks. Many rare plants grow on both cobble and boulder bars. Most of the CT stays well above the streams in this section. This design avoids flooded trail. You will need to leave the trail to explore the river and Daddy's Creek.

THE HUNT FOR RARE PLANTS ON THE OBED RIVER CT

Only one listed plant was seen along the Obed CT. Several others were seen on cobble bars not far from the CT. Go to www.benandlarryincumberland.com for the complete list.

FINDING NEMO BRIDGE

⇥ 16 ⇤

Hike 11: BreakAway Bluff to Nemo Bridge
About 4.2 miles and an undisclosed number through private land

BEN: "We had to design this house ourselves," said Elizabeth, as we stepped into the living room. "No one was willing to design a house that regulated its own energy."

The place seemed luxurious with separate rooms, separate showers, good lighting and, best of all, a meal of stir fried-shrimp and vegetables with peach cobbler for desert. Eating frozen and dried meals might not have been roughing it, but we tasted the contrast when we had a full home-cooked meal.

"Once two young men floated down the Obed on inner tubes," said Elizabeth. "They thought they'd come to a bridge or a road. But they floated for miles and miles without seeing one. They panicked, pulled their inner-tubes out of the water, wandered around in the forest and wound up here by pure chance."

LARRY: It is a long ways between road-access points on the Obed.

BEN: Our hosts told us of a private access point to the CT. This information allowed us to split what would have been a rather long hike. The next morning they lead us to this special access. I held my arms close to my body to stay warm in the cool morning air. The coolness would not last.

The hike would lead us down to Nemo Bridge, a former railroad bridge near the abandoned unincorporated community of Nemo, meaning "No one," in Latin. I don't speak Latin at all, but knew the name from *Illustrated Classics: 2000 Leagues under the Sea*, a book from my childhood. The Nemo of that book was a brilliant steampunk scientific mind and maestro organist who attacked ships and squid alike with his armored submersible. He was not the kind of man after whom people named inland towns.

Dad pointed out plants and animals like the yellow-black flat back centipede, a creature whose safety-colored back had graced our walk many times.

"Some people say they don't come out here because there's hardly anything to see," said Elizabeth. "It's amazing all the things you're finding out here." It was amazing indeed. Even the things I'd taken the most for granted could be fascinating and beautiful, including Dad's own knowledge and curiosity.

Though they did not feel like going the whole distance, Elizabeth and Carl came with us as far as Break Away Bluff.

The bluff was named in 1998 by volunteers who worked on this part of the Cumberland Trail during the Spring Break Away Program. Spring Break Away is an alternative spring break program for college students who want to do volunteer work during spring break. However, the name seemed fitting in other ways. Although we couldn't see it from where we were, from below, it looks like it was ready to break away, or like a piece of it already had. The rock jutted-out from beyond the cover of short hemlocks into a view of the river winding through the gorge.

"That's enough," said Dad. "You don't need to go any farther." His voice sounded nervous, but he never raised it. It wasn't the kind of "Can't let my son die!" panic that he had with the rattlesnake or the overwhelmed, hopeless tone he had when talking about my driving. He said it without strong emotion as if he was trying to mentor me in moderation.

As we started to leave the bluff, Carl grabbed his camera. "Come on back," he said. "We'd love to have some pictures."

My expression in the pictures was the eyebrow-raised but uninterested fake almost-smile of someone who would rather be looking out at the valley below than posing for a picture. The only picture of me that looked happy was one of me alone, surrounded by the misty trees behind me. Dad's expressions varied, but most of them seemed to either say, "Can I get back to looking for plants again?" or, "Will this bluff break away?"

We stopped at a sandy cove on the Obed River. Dad climbed through the knee-high cinnamon ferns, named for their cinnamon-brown spore-bearing parts, along the bank to look for other plants. I sat on a root, took notes and sketched the various plants and birds nearby.

The Obed did not sit low under boulders or look transparent like Piney River. It was deeper with a stronger current.

While neither at the bottom of the sea nor in the farthest reaches of space, the riverside was full of wonders. It was like naturalist adventurer John Muir said when he found the Emory/Obed, in his book *A Thousand Mile Walk to the Gulf*:

Ben Toon gets too close to the edge of Break Away Bluff.

"There is nothing more eloquent in nature than a mountain stream, and this is the first I ever saw. Its banks are luxuriantly peopled with rare and lovely flowers and overarching trees, making one of Nature's coolest and most hospitable places. Every tree, every flower, every ripple and eddy of this lovely stream seemed solemnly to feel the presence of its mighty creator."

Solemn seemed like the wrong word though. The now-bright sunlight made the cinnamon ferns' leaves a gaudy shade of green. They were about as solemn as neon-colored bikinis.

Dragonflies flew up and down over the stream, sometimes riding on each other to mate. A caterpillar crawled on my pant-leg. The stream roared down a string of rapids before flattening out into a steadier flow. It lapped about three inches at the cove's shoreline. Suds washed up into the cove, and I wondered if they were from a human or natural source. They did not ruin the place's beauty.

Two birds, belted kingfishers, made rattling noises as they swooped and rose back up. It was mating time for them just like the dragonflies. During mating season, a male belted kingfisher establishes a territory by chasing off other kingfishers. The male will often attract an arriving female by offering her fish. After sex, the two birds will often fly together, the female behind the male.

The Rhododendron from Hell or Heaven
Rosebay rhododendron (*Rhododendron maximum*)

LARRY: Southern Appalachian bushwhackers or off-trail hikers hate to find a dense growth of rosebay rhododendron between themselves and their destination. Getting through such shrub tangles takes energy and time. These tangles are traditionally called hells. When the rosebay is in flower, however, the hells are gorgeous enough to be called heavens.

Rosebay rhododendron is common along the CT. Hikers will most likely find it on moist lower slopes and stream bottoms on acid soils. Higher and drier on the slopes are other hells populated by the related mountain laurel (*Kalmia latifolia*), which is also heavenly in flower. Both are in the Heath family. These two heaths spread mostly from the roots but also use seeds.

Within a hell, few plants challenge the rosebay. This nearly complete dominance has sparked speculation that the rosebay has a subtle weapon, perhaps an herbicide against plants that would try to compete. This herbicide could be released from the roots or the fallen leaves. Plant chemical warfare is called allelopathy. There seems no reason to believe that evolution has not led to this sort of chemical competition, but it turns out to be hard to study scientifically. Studies of allelopathy in rosebay are not conclusive.

Getting at the truth is difficult in the field of ecology. Studies in the lab or garden setting can control for many of the numerous possible factors in nature, but they are unrealistic for that very reason. Complexities overwhelm studies in natural settings. Ecology is difficult to study, but we study it because it is so important. Long-term ecological research is especially important and difficult to fund. We need measurements of nature taken regularly with consistent methods over many years to spot trends and accurately record the impacts of rare events.

Long-term research shows that the areas dominated by rosebay are growing. We would expect this kind of domination from some exotic plants but not from a native like rosebay which has been around long enough to be in balance with other plant species. The observed rosebay dominated area extension does not appear to be related to climate change but might be caused by fire suppression. Does rosebay belong on our invasive pest plant lists?

Rosebay is in the genus *Rhododendron*. The genus *Rhododendron* is divided into evergreen shrubs (called rhododendrons) and deciduous leaved shrubs (azaleas). Note the awkward difference between *Rhododendron* in italics and rhododendron. The former is a genus and the later a sub-group of species in the genus. They all have delightful flowers.

Many people can recognize this genus when in flower because they are familiar with cultivated azaleas. We can use a simple key (an identification outline) to name the CT members of this genus. We will assume that you have seen azalea flowers and so will know when a flowering plant is a rhododendron. The simple key here will help you start to learn this genus. You begin with two choices called "1" and follow the indentation to get to a species.

Simplified CT *Rhododendron* Key

1. Evergreen leaves; leaves leathery texture ("rhododendrons").
    2. White flowers……………………………rosebay rhododendron
                                (*Rhododendron maximum*)
    2. Purple to pink flowers…………………..catawba rhododendron
                                  (*Rhododendron catawbiense*)

Note: Another purple species, Carolina rhododendron, has not yet been found in the Plateau.

1. Deciduous leaves; leaves not leathery (azaleas).
       3. Red, yellow or orange flowers……..Cumberland azalea
                                 (*Rhododendron cumberlandense*)
       3. Pink to White flowers
           4. Flowering with some leaves still folded at flowering time
               5. Leaves rather hairy underneath…southern pinxter
           (*Rhododendron canescens*) or roseshell azalea
                             (*Rhododendron prinophyllum*)
               5. Leaves sparely hairy underneath..pinxterbloom
                      (*Rhododendron periclymenoides*)
           4. Flowering with all leaves expanded….smooth azalea
                         (*Rhododendron arborescens*)

This key covers the species you are likely to see along the CT. Some long shots to run into on the CT are clammy azalea (*Rhododendron viscosum*) and Alabama azalea (*Rhododendron alabamense*). We saw neither. Clammy azalea would go to smooth azalea in the key but differs by having hairy stems. Alabama azalea would go to the two pinxterblooms but has a yellow blotch on the upper corolla lobe of the flower.

During our early May through early June CT trek we saw all the species in the above key flowering except the pinxterblooms which we were rather late to see. We saw southern pinxter on the Rock Creek CT during an April hike in 2013. Telling the southern pinxter from the pinxterbloom apart can be tricky. Only the pinxterbloom is colonial, spreading from the roots. At times it will actually form a ground cover. It does not flower in its low form but only as a bush. This difference in growth forms can help to differentiate them.

I was surprised to see catawba rhododendron in flower in a few places. I had thought of it as a Blue Ridge (the mountains of the eastern edge of TN) species rather than a Cumberland Plateau species. We were almost too early to catch the first rosebay flowers.

Update 2013: In May, while hiking on the Brady Mountain CT, Paul Durr and I found an azalea with light pink to deep pink flowers. Ben and I had not seen these flowers during the big trek the year before because that spring was very warm, and the petals would have dropped by the time of our visit. In 2013, at about the same time of year, they were quite showy. They appeared to be southern pinxter but had some odd characteristics: deep pink color, strong fragrance etc. We have concluded that the bushes are roseshell azalea. This is a new species for Tennessee. I was not able to come up with a simple way to separate southern pinxter from roseshell to use in the key.

The two birds I saw chased each other, swooping low over the water. One of them darted into the cove. The other stopped on a tree and turned its beak toward itself. I could not tell if they were mating or involved in a territorial squabble. As much as all the searching, swimming and prying around for things of interest had helped me to appreciate the other streams, it felt better now to sit still while letting my mind fly along the river with the kingfishers.

We moved on, hiking for miles. Just when we thought it would never come, the rusty camel-back hump of Nemo Bridge showed through the trees. The trail led us downhill through a campground where tents decorated an area of the woods. Girls in bikinis, boys in trunks and hikers with backpacks and fishing poles flocked around the site. Carl and Elizabeth had driven there to meet us.

Nemo Bridge was named for the community of Nemo, which was downstream from the bridge. The community of Nemo's namer gave it an "N" name to fit an alphabetical scheme, because it came after the stops of Lancing and Montgomery. The namer may have gotten the name from Jules Verne. It also reminded me of a newspaper comic called "Little Nemo in Slumberland" about a boy who traveled through the world of his dreams.

The bridge was finished in 1931. Back then, mills along the riverside used water power to grind grain.

"When we see a waterfall these days, our first thought is of horsepower," said William Jennings Bryan in his 1920s brochure *The Bible and its Enemies*. I had never thought of horsepower at any of the waterfalls or rivers we had seen. My thoughts had been more like John Muir's sense of innocent awe.

"People call it Wartburg Beach," Elizabeth told us. We looked down

Belted Kingfishers as Parents

BEN: The pair stays together throughout the season, chasing away other kingfishers that might come in. The male and female take turns kicking up soil with their feet to dig a burrow in the bank for their nest. The father digs for twice as much time as the mother. Both of them incubate the egg and both of them bring food to their newly hatched young. Kingfisher parents stay together until their children become experts at fishing for themselves. Then, they leave, each to possibly find a different mate the next year.

from up on the bridge as a family walked down from the sandstone cobble bar and floated by on inner-tubes. They floated on a deep and wide part of the river that gave blurry reflections of the sky and forest above it. We swam in sweat.

In the sweltering heat, I wanted to jump in the Emory River but had no swimsuit. There were too many people around for me to swim in my underwear or naked though. I could have kept my pants on in the water, but they were Dad's pants. He'd kindly let me use them because all of my other pants were muddy or ripped by now.

So I went back to the house and took a shower the way that boring civilized people do. As the water from the showerhead hit me, I thought about how peculiar showers are as an expected behavior. Westerners took centuries to consider bathing a good idea. Here in East Tennessee, early European settlers washed their hands and faces daily but probably only bathed once a year, standing in a tub of water and washing with a rag according to the Tennessee State Museum's website. The Cherokee before them had bathed in rivers though, sometimes as a religious ritual.

In Dayton, I questioned the value in staying at a motel close to a Walmart while trying to explore nature and the distinctness of the Cumberland Plateau. While camping, I questioned the point of staying in a tent. Now, I questioned the point of staying in a house with comforts that seemed weird in the long view of time and human evolution. I was grateful for the bed, the good light for reading frog books, the separate room and the shower. At the same time, I wondered if I needed them.

Regardless of any of that, I had to sleep rather than ponder. We would hike twelve miles the next day, including the part over private land.

Nemo's Flooded History

BEN: When Nemo Bridge was built, the Obed riverside area was recovering from floods that washed away mills and wrecked railroads in 1929. Even though some locals left, new mills and railroads rose, ready to take the place of the old. As if to laugh at them, the water rose again in 1940, sending people fleeing. This time, people learned their lesson and left. Nemo went the way of Atlantis, if Atlantis had become a popular swimming place. The name Nemo, meaning "no man," both fits and does not fit the place. Thanks to it being part of the Obed Wild and Scenic River, no man lives there, but crowds of men, women, boys and girls come to visit.

In the morning, we ate a big breakfast of eggs and fruit to get ourselves ready for twelve miles up and down hill.

"It's rocky and easy to slip," said Elizabeth. "Also, there are copper-heads. Even if I was in better shape, I wouldn't want to do this section."

"Copperheads should leave you alone if you leave them alone," I said.

"True," said Elizabeth, "but if you want to leave them alone, you have to first know where they are! They hide under rocks for shade. If one happens to slither out at exactly the wrong moment, and you step on him, be ready to get bit."

"We know snakes can be anywhere," said Dad, calmly. "We'll watch the ground."

More about the Obed Wild and Scenic River

BEN: The Obed Wild and Scenic River, managed by the National Park Service, includes a little over 24 miles of the Obed River, with parts of Clear Creek, Daddy's Creek and the Emory River. It almost got a dam instead of a protected status. The Tennessee Valley Authority assumed that a lake would bring more visitors and tourist dollars than a mere river. It took dedicated conservation groups like Tennessee Citizens for Wilderness Planning (TCWP) to talk them out of the notion and get the National Park Service interested in protecting this land.

The land that Scenic River area includes, though missing important areas of what TCWP initially wanted protected, is impressive. It is home to 13 species of crayfish and many fish, including the rare Cumberland Plateau musky. Roughly 800 species of plants, including the federally endangered Virginia spiraea and the federally threatened pink Cumberland Rosemary grow inside of park boundaries.

The park has outstanding rock climbing, paddling, swimming, fishing and hiking, with hunting allowed by permit. Much of the land just outside the National Wild and Scenic River's boundaries, including some of what we hiked here, is in the Catoosa Wildlife Management Area.

[Panel 1: "AT PINEY RIVER." — "MAN, SLEEPING ON THE GROUND IS WEIRD."]
[Panel 2: "LATER, IN WARTBURG." — "BEDS ARE WEIRD."]

Little Ben Toon in Slumberland

Sources and Suggested Reading

General:
Brill, David. *Cumberland Odyssey: A Journey in Pictures and Words along Tennessee's Cumberland Trail and Plateau.* Johnson City, Tennessee: Mountain Trail Press, 2010.

    This book includes great sections on a variety of topics relating to the trail. It was where I first found the quotation from John Muir that I used here.

Belted Kingfishers:
Bull, John and Ferrand, John Jr. *National Audubon Society Field Guide to North American Birds: Eastern Region.* New York, New York: Alfred A. Knopf Inc., 1977.

    While old, this source was my starting point for belted kingfishers.

The Cornell Lab of Ornithology. "Belted Kingfisher." *All about Birds.* Accessed June 18, 2013. http://www.allaboutbirds.org/guide/Belted_Kingfisher/lifehistory.

Kelley, Jeffery F., Eli S. Bridge and Michael J. Hamas. "Belted Kingfisher (*Megaceryle alcyon*)," *The Birds of North America Online.* Edited by A. Poole.

Ithaca: Cornell Lab of Ornithology, 2009. http://bna.birds.cornell.edu/bna/species/084.

John Muir:
Muir, John. *A Thousand-mile Walk to the Gulf*. Boston: Houghton Mifflin, 1916.
    This book is available for free online at http://vault.sierraclub.org/john_muir_exhibit/writings/a_thousand_mile_walk_to_the_gulf/.

Nemo:
National Park Service. "Stories." *Obed Wild & Scenic River*. Last modified June 4, 2013. http://www.nps.gov/obed/historyculture/stories.htm.
    This web page includes information about Nemo's name, the 1929 flood, and the establishment of the Obed Wild and Scenic River.

National Park Service. "Places." *Obed Wild & Scenic River*. Last modified June 5, 2013. http://www.nps.gov/obed/historyculture/places.htm.
    This page gives an account of the 1940s flood and its effects on the river's mills.

Baths, Beds (and Beyond):
Bryson, Bill. *At Home*. New York: Doubleday, 2010.

Mooney, James. "Cherokee Theory and Practice of Medicine." *The Journal of American Folklore*. 3, no. 8 (1890): 44-50 http://www.jstor.org/stable/533027?seq=6.
    This article gives Mooney's account of the "going to the water ceremony."

Tennessee State Museum. "Frontier: Everyday Life." *Tennessee 4 Me*. Accessed June 18, 2013. http://www.tn4me.org/minor_cat.cfm/era_id/3/major_id/25/minor_id/80.
    This site is a good place for answering questions about various periods in Tennessee history. I used it to learn about European settlers on the frontier and their hygiene habits.

Obed Wild and Scenic River/Catoosa Wildlife Management Area:
Lawrence, Ardi and Lawrence H. Lee *Natural Wonders of Tennessee Second Edition: Exploring Wild and Scenic Places*. Chicago: Country Roads Press 1999.
    This book explains the relationship between the Obed Wild and Scenic River and the Catoosa Wildlife Management Area.

Manning, Russ. *The Historic Cumberland Plateau: An Explorer's Guide, Second Edition.* Knoxville: University of Tennessee Press, 1999.
  Again, Russ Manning's book proved indispensable to us. It gives a much longer history of the attempts to save the Obed River from damming than we provide here. It also mentions the Cumberland Plateau musky, bald eagles and golden eagles.

National Park Service. "Plants." *Obed Wild & Scenic River.* Last modified June 17, 2013. http://www.nps.gov/obed/naturescience/plants.htm.
  This web page tells about Cumberland Rosemary and Virginia spirea. It gives the number of plants to be roughly 800.

National Park Service. "Crayfish." *Obed Wild & Scenic River.* Last modified June 17, 2013. http://www.nps.gov/obed/naturescience/crayfish.htm.

NOTICE OR ELSE!

→ 17 ←

Hike 11: BreakAway Bluff to Nemo Bridge
About 4.2 miles and an undisclosed number through private land

BEN: Today was not the day to look for rock formations, off-trail plants or crashed airplanes. Even though we'd read about a lovely formation called Devil's Breakfast Table, we figured we could skip looking for it. We had a long hike ahead.

According to legend, our starting point, Daddy's Creek had one thing in common with Hotwater Road: domestic violence. As retold in Russ Manning's *The Historic Cumberland Plateau*, a husband and wife were traveling through the area and bickering about something. Probably they had children, given that this legend would make no sense if they didn't. While they camped at Daddy's Creek, the husband hit the wife and won the debate, so the creek got named Daddy's Creek. Later, the wife got even by hitting her husband with a tree branch at a place that's now called Mammy's Creek. Like most legends, it probably stuck because it was amusing and not because it was true.

We walked quickly under the shade of trees and rock ledges. It was not Dad's style or mine to knock off miles like this, but we knew that today we had to. Noticing would have to wait.

Dad stepped across rocks while looking at the ground. Then, just as he was about to put his foot down, he did a double-take and kept his shaking foot raised, before slowly stepping back. He laughed nervously as the copperhead barely moved off the trail, just avoiding Dad's shoe. If the shoe had hit the snake, the snake could have bit back and left Dad screaming in pain.

"I thought I'd been watching the ground for dangers, said Dad, bewildered, "But I almost missed that one."

I stood back and captured a picture of the serpent, body camouflaged among the leaves with head against a gray stone. In typical copperhead manner,

Different reactions to danger

it never raised its head in aggression.

The brown hourglass-like pattern against lighter scales blended into the leaves of the forest floor. Once I saw the snake for what it was though, its shiny, scaly sleekness did not resemble the ground. With careful steps we headed forward, knowing that we had to be noticers now, or else get bitten.

"I found it hard to believe that it had not just been created on the spot or hatched from its mother, so unscathed and clean was its body, so unmarked from any passage," wrote Annie Dillard of a copperhead in her book *Pilgrim at Tinker Creek*. Her statement described the copperhead we had seen as well. By contrast, the fallen leaves, needles, rocks, sticks and shoots around the snake were in a flux of dead and alive, whole and decaying. I looked at Dad's face and saw that it was wrinkled. I put my hand on my nose and felt my produce scale scar. No matter how little I'd lived, no one could mistake me for a newly created body. I had experienced many things. My scars and flaking skin showed it.

The copperhead had experienced life's passage too, regardless of what Dillard thought. The skin looked unblemished and whole because it was shed all-at-a-time rather than in pieces like human skin and hair. The inside of a copperhead is like any other creature: a flux of chemicals growing older just like me.

When copperheads emerge from their mothers, they are not surrounded by eggshell. Instead, the young are born inside of transparent membranes which they rip open using a special tooth called an egg tooth. Other snakes use egg teeth to break out of their shells. Copperheads shed their egg teeth, a fact which gives me the odd image of a copperhead tooth fairy.

Copperhead egg tooth fairy.

We, unlike the copperhead, had many more miles to slog and couldn't rest under a rock when the day heated up.

The trail dipped down near a cobble bar by the river. "You can go swimming here," said Dad. "I know you really wanted to swim yesterday." He'd probably calculated the availability for naked swimming based on how far away we were from other hikers.

I splashed into the cool current. Nothing can replace the feeling of swimming naked and having moving water touch every part of one's body. My mind could not slither elsewhere. It stayed in the river, responding to the sensation. Dad felt like taking a picture. To make sure it'd be safe to put on our website, I posed behind a rock. As I climbed out, I felt happy for the water on all of my skin. I felt fresh, like I had replaced an old skin with a new one.

As I grabbed my water bottle to get it back in my vest, some of the water spilled. I knew I would regret it. The day would get hotter.

Heat makes a hiker notice a trail differently. A hot hiker chugs water from his bottle at first, but once he starts running low, he will learn how to make small sips go a longer way. Sun and shade become more than just scenery. They become sensations. When we walked under a cliff that had trees hanging over the top, I thanked the trail for leading us to a cooler place.

We followed an old road. Erosion had lowered the road beyond what any human would have wanted.

Because neither of us had time to stop for views or plants, we walked together and chatted about evolution, adaptations and how species related to each other in strange ways. Take cashews and poison ivy. They're not only in

Children who Bait with Tails

Copperhead (*Agkistrodon contortrix*)

BEN: A copperhead's venomous bite hurts, but it's rarely deadly to humans. Still, unless you want to feel acute pain for a long time, it's a good idea to avoid copperheads. You can tell them by their dark brown hourglass pattern on lighter brown scales, though you have to be careful. Their scales blend in with the forest floor, and unlike rattlesnakes, they use no sound to warn people. Possibly for these reasons, copperhead bites are the most common type of reported snake bites in the United States.

During the summer, copperheads live in shady places, such as the rocky area in which we found this one. They often hide beneath boards in the ruins of old buildings. After being bit, try to stay calm as being stressed will only make the venom spread.

Copperhead young have tails with yellow tips that resemble worms or maggots. Prey animals lunge for them, expecting to find a nice snack. Instead, they become snacks.

Vine Ben Toon relies on Tree Larry Toon for support.

the same family, but also both contain related chemicals that cause skin to itch. In the case of cashews, these chemicals can be found in the shell oil. By the time that cashews reach the store though, they've been roasted or treated so that they will no longer give people itchy skin. Cashews are the most popular nuts that are never sold in their shell.

Just because they are related does not mean they look like each other to the untrained eye. Cashews grow as trees in the tropics while poison ivy grows as either a shrub or a vine here in the U.S.

"I guess the advantage to being a vine," I said to Dad, with no clue what I was saying, but trying to be on his level, "is that you..."

"You rely on someone else to support you," said Dad, finishing my sentence, eager to support my learning.

"Though you'd be in the shade mostly," I added. There had to be a catch to living under someone else's shadow.

"Well, you can go over the top of plants," said Dad, lifting his hand. "You've seen kudzu do it."

I knew kudzu well. It is a rapid-growing Japanese vine that shows the darker side of using someone else for support. It covers trees, grabbing all of the light for itself.

By the time we made it up to Break Away Bluff, both of us plodded. Then I saw Carl waiting for us with a camera. Knowing that we were near the end gave me a surge of energy. I speed-walked toward him. Dad walked slowly to the end, holding his sweaty hat.

Sources and Suggested Reading

General:
Dillard, Annie. *Pilgrim at Tinker Creek.* New York: Harper Perennial 1998

Daddy's Creek Legend:
Manning, Russ. *The Historic Cumberland Plateau: An Explorer's Guide, Second Edition.* Knoxville: University of Tennessee Press, 1999.

Copperhead:
Badger, David. *Snakes.* Stillwater, Maine: Voyageur Press, 1999.
    Talks about egg tooth as well as young copperheads' tactic of baiting with their tails.

Beane, Jefferey et al. *Amphibians and Reptiles of the Carolinas and Virginia Second Edition.* Chapel Hill: University of North Carolina Press, 2010.
    Gives information regarding the appearance of both young and old copperheads as well as some behavior information and confirms the usually non-fatal nature of their bites.

Behler, John L., and F. Wayne King. *The Audubon Society Field Guide to North American Reptiles and Amphibians.* New York: Chanticleer Press Inc., 1995.
    This book gave me my information about copperheads' summer habitat, the non-lethal nature of their bites, and the yellow-tipped tails that they use in their youth. I've depended on other sources to confirm this information.

Gibbons, Whit. "How Dangerous Are Copperhead Snakes?" *North Carolina Cooperative Extension.* Accessed at http://www.ces.ncsu.edu/gaston/Pests/reptiles/copperhead.htm on September 17, 2012

National Institute of Occupational Safety and Health. *CDC-Venomous Snakes- NIOSH Workplace Safety and Health Topic.* February 24, 2012. http://www.cdc.gov/niosh/topics/snakes/ (accessed June 17, 2013).

Cashews and Poison Ivy:
Rosen, Ted and Fordice, Dawn B. "Cashew Nut Dermatitis," *Southern Medical Journal.* 87 No. 4 (1994): 543. http://journals.lww.com/smajournalonline/Citation/1994/04000/Cashew_Nut_Dermatitis.26.aspx.

WARTBURG: A TOWN IN SPITE OF EVERYTHING

⇥ 18 ⇤

Wartburg, Stay-town and Trail Town
Note: Just for the sake of doing so, we walked the part of the CT that runs past the courthouse. It was a short stretch in 2012.

BEN: The Cumberland Trail runs through Wartburg. Also, the town has a motel with Wi-Fi. So, we spent the next few nights there.

LARRY: I wonder if Wartburg will become a trail town like Damascus in Virginia or Hot Springs in North Carolina, both on the AT (Appalachian Trail). Through-hikers stop in these towns to re-supply and take a break from their hiking. If the Great Eastern Trail starts to compete with the AT, it could be a major economic driver for Wartburg.

BEN: The name Wartburg was a punch-line in Oak Ridge where I grew up. It sounded like a skin blemish and became shorthand for everything provincial or primitive to us Oak Ridgers.

    The further we drove into Wartburg, the more it looked like the old-fashioned idea of a town. Small houses formed tight blocks. Shop-fronts made of brick lined the streets. As if to make it feel even more nostalgic, the town had two video and DVD rental stores. I browsed through one of them, reminiscing about my childhood before Redbox and Netflix. Unlike some other Oak Ridgers, I love the style of Wartburg.

    Anyone walking on the Cumberland Trail in Wartburg will view the Morgan County Courthouse. Here, the city has put diamond-shaped

> **IN OAK RIDGE, WARTBURG HAD A REPUTATION.**
>
> "So, you're from Wartburg?"
>
> "Yeah."
>
> "If I brought a flashlight, would people in Wartburg think I was magic?"
>
> "SHUT UP."

I overheard the above conversation, typical of Oak Ridge's elitism towards Wartburg, back when I was in High School.

Cumberland Trail markers into the sidewalk to mark the trail's route. The courthouse's white clock tower stands higher than nearby buildings. "This is not just a collection of buildings" the layout says, "This is a town and a center of government."

German immigrants named Wartburg after the castle where Martin Luther translated the Bible into German. Elizabeth told me about plans to build a replica of the castle near Wartburg, Tennessee.

"Do you know the legend of Wartburg Castle in Germany?" asked Elizabeth before we left her house.

"No," I said.

"A man looked at a mountain and said "Wait, mountain! You shall bear a castle for me." In German, "Wait, mountain!" is "Warte, berg!""

"Warte" also means a watchtower, which is a more likely origin than a man shouting at a mountain to wait. Also, it's spelled "burg" meaning castle, rather than "berg" meaning mountain. However, the legend sums up the spirit of Wartburg, Tennessee: a town built only because one man wanted to build it.

According to Russ Manning's *The Historic Cumberland Plateau: An Explorer's Guide*, in 1842, a German immigrant named George F. Gerding bought the land on which Wartburg now stands and tried to make it a successful colony. Settlers poured in from Germany and Switzerland. They expected an already-thriving farming community but instead found a building called a "receiving house" with no indoor kitchen. The settlers cooked outside. Many of the Swiss and German seeds brought to Wartburg failed to sprout.

Gerding tried to direct the colony from a distance. When money didn't gush in, he moved to Wartburg and took over operations. The colonists planted grape vines and fruit trees with some success. They also set up furniture factories, including one that made pianos.

When the Civil War hit, Gerding moved to Louisville, Kentucky, figuring that it would be safer than Wartburg. While he was gone, soldiers from both sides sacked the Wartburg area for what food they could find. Guerrilla fighters, called bushwhackers, also did a great deal of damage. When Gerding returned, he found his colony abandoned and ruined. He sold it.

Some of the land became part of another colony called Rugby. Rugby today is now more of a museum meant to entertain and educate outsiders than an ordinary town. From what I saw of Wartburg, it did not seem to be going that route. While there were some offices in town that gave information about the Obed Wild and Scenic River and the Cumberland Trail State Park, there were also a few industrial plants such as Hereaus Precious Metals. The nearby Morgan County Correctional Complex employs many people as well.

While Dad bought food at a small grocery, I followed a sign to Wartburg's library. It was a one-story building with a small front porch. It looked like it had once been someone's house, and I felt guilty about not knocking.

"We don't have too many books about this county," said the woman at the desk. So instead, I read the local paper to get a flavor of Wartburg. One soft-news story struck my attention. It was about a petrified stump, presumably an ancient plant not closely related to today's trees. It is displayed near the elementary school. Miners had found it while strip-mining near Windrock Mountain.

Dad came back.

"Hi," he said, "Did you find anything?"

"Not really," I said.

"We should probably get moving," said Dad.

It was useless to argue with him. Dad bent to time's demands. I wanted time to bend to mine. This wasn't the first time our two approaches had clashed. It happened almost daily when I was a teenager. Because Dad often worked on his plant specimens from home, he usually cooked rather than Mom. He would always whip up some kind of meal by six. Often it would be beans with rice or spaghetti.

"Come and get it, or you'll regret it," he'd say in a whimsical sing-song voice.

"But I'm not done with homework yet!" I'd say.

I didn't love homework. I wasn't that strange. It was the opposite. I wanted to be done with it so that I could have the evening free. Having a later dinner time seemed to make 6:00 come later. Or perhaps I just wanted to argue with Dad about something.

"So how was the food shopping?" I asked.

"I couldn't find pita bread," he said, disappointed.

The Scenic River Inn, where we stayed, looked calculated to appeal to nature lovers with its walls of sandstone blocks. In the front yard, whirligigs spun and blocky wooden sculptures of black bears stood on their hind legs. The only thing it lacked was any view of a river. Probably someone named the motel after the Obed Wild and *Scenic River*. It must have sounded like a more comfortable name for a motel than "Frozen Head," another protected area nearby.

The microwave did not work. Two men came in to fix it while I sat in my underwear, writing about our hiking adventures.

Scenic River Inn felt less like a modern motel and more like a house. Our room had better lighting than the Scottish Inn. The sink and shower made rusty music whenever we ran them, but I learned to love the sound. The friendly clerk at the front desk sometimes worked in his pajamas.

Our room had a double bed rather than two single ones, because Dad wanted to lower the room rate.

"I pushed you in the tent," I said. "You're not worried about that here?"

"It was only twice," said Dad.

I tried to stay as far to my side of the bed as possible. People outside shouted, and a train rattled by. None of the sounds kept me awake. With enough time spent living by these hours, I was tired. Instead of staying up and posting to Facebook, I slept.

The next day's trail head required us to drive out into the boondocks. Mom and Goyo would once again be with us.

Sources and Suggested Reading

Wartburg:
Bell, Augusta Grove. *Circling Windrock Mountain: Two Hundred Years in Appalachia.* Knoxville: University of Tennessee Press, 1999.

Freytag, Ethyl and Glenda Kreis Ott. *A History of Morgan County Tennessee.* United States of America: Specialty Printing Company, 1971.
    I used this source to elaborate on most of the points outlined by Russ Manning. It's a more detailed history of the county, particularly its government.

Heat Moon, William Least. *Blue Highways: A Journey into America.* Boston: Little, Brown and Company, 1983.

Pollard, Jean. "Sharing the Past: The story behind CES's Petrified stump." Morgan County News. May 22, 2012.

Manning, Russ. *The Historic Cumberland Plateau: An Explorer's Guide, Second Edition.* Knoxville: University of Tennessee Press, 1999.

Sakowski, Carolyn. *Touring the East Tennessee Backroads: Second Edition.* Winston-Salem: John F. Blair, 2007.

WILDLY STROLLING ALONG

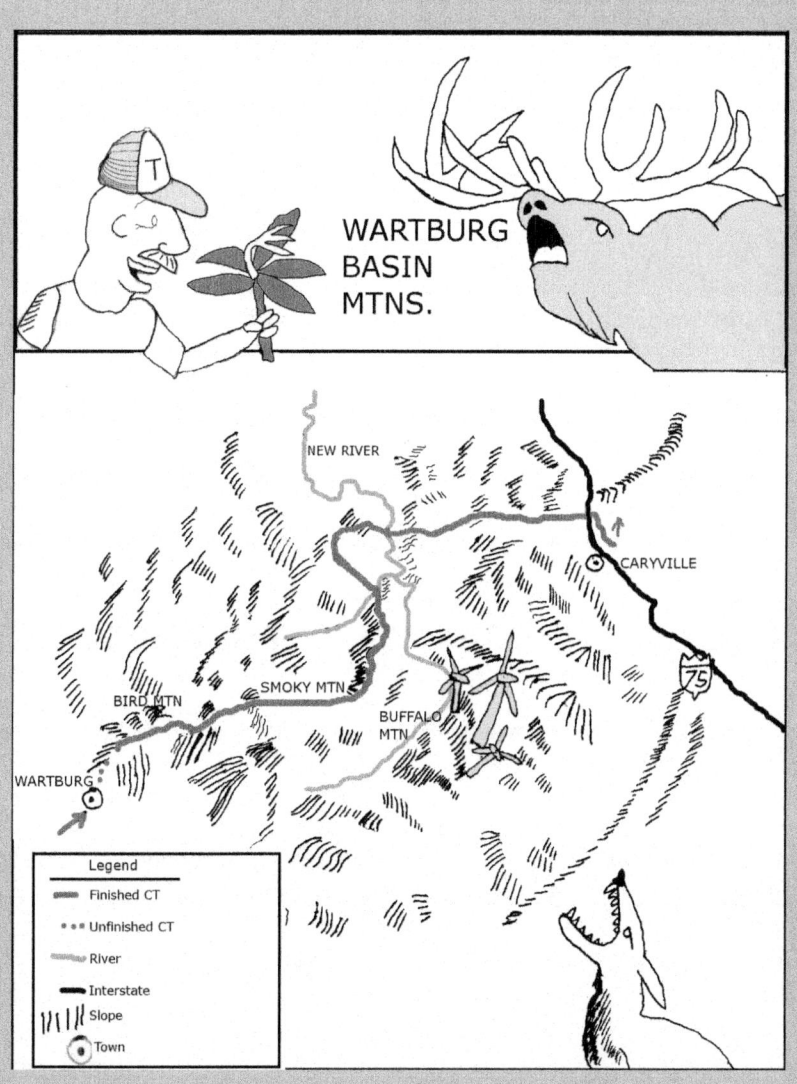

Map 5 Wartburg basin Mountains

Interlude 4
Wartburg Basin Mountains
From Basin to Mountains

BY LARRY

DESCRIPTION

This is our second group of mountains that sits on the Plateau. Collectively, the Wartburg Basin and Pine Mountain Fault Block Mountains are known as the Cumberland Mountains. The word "basin" in the name refers to the basin in which the sediments that formed into the rock were deposited. Later, a tectonic plate collision pushed the sediments up, and they eroded into mountains. The trail in this section goes from Wartburg to Caryville. The CT is complete in this section except for a few miles around Wartburg. There are views in this section where you see almost nothing but more Wartburg Basin Mountains in all directions. Much of the trail here is above 2,500 feet and occasionally above 3,000 feet. Elk live here. Many places along the trail show signs of past strip mining.

THE HUNT FOR RARE PLANTS ON THE WARTBURG BASIN MOUNTAINS CT

Tennessee Valley Authority (TVA) owns the mineral rights to areas along the CT for the Norma Road to Caryville portion of the Wartburg Basin Mountains. As part of a process to decide what to do with the mineral rights, I did a rare plant survey several years ago. The current trek survey did not add any rare species to that TVA survey for this section. Go to www.BenandLarryinCumberland.com for the list of rare plants in this section of the CT.

LOG AND COAL COUNTRY

⇝ 19 ⇜

Lawson Mtn. Part 1 (Sun. May 27)
Hike 13: Cave Branch Trailhead to Bowling Town Rd.
6.1 miles

BEN: Before we started the hike, we met up with Mom, Goyo, Zeke and the Callis family (Debbie, Charles and Chris). They would help us with shuttling. The Callises had been friends of our family since my childhood back in Oak Ridge. With other people to do the driving, I could take a break from driving on the winding roads and look at the scenery.

The area through which I rode, known as New River, is a series of communities along the New River and its branches. New River has none of Grassy Cove's big pastures. It's coal and logging country.

Coal and lumber ride out of the area on trucks, driven carefully on curvy roads. Earlier, going a different route through New River, I'd seen a mobile-home barber shop with a roof vent painted red, white and blue like a barber pole. New River intrigued me.

One man's intriguing is another's scary. An acquaintance from Clinton described the New River area like this on Facebook:

> *"LOL...the main thing about New River is that's it's a scary place...unless you live there or they know you...they sit on their porches watching the road to see if any unfamiliar cars drive by."*

She was not the only one in Anderson County who thought that way. Augusta Grove Bell reported in her 1960s oral history book *Circling Windrock Mountain* that, "New River has always been at the bottom of Anderson County's social heap." Everyone needed to feel better than someone else. People from Oak Ridge could look down on Clinton, Clinton could look down on Oliver Springs, which in turn could look down on New River by claiming, in words recorded by Bell "they be killing each other." She pointed out that people can get killed anywhere. What made the New River area unusual and potentially scary to outsiders was its remoteness. Many of its coal-mining communities shrank as strip-mining machines took over human jobs and the coal itself became scarcer.

The roads aren't busy, but it's hard to miss the coal and lumber trucks moving freight to the outside world. They move slowly.

We stopped by the side of the gravel road to start our hike. A giant dog near a trailer clanked on a chain and yowled at us. Zeke pulled on his leash, but Mom kept him back.

A man with dark hair and a stubby beard drove up on his ATV. It was his job to guard the logging equipment parked here. The trailhead was in a different direction from the equipment he was guarding.

"We've had people come in and steal gasoline from us," he said, smiling.

"Has anyone broken into your trailer?" I asked.

"Ain't a lot of people make it past my dog right there," he answered.

He was relaxed enough about the situation that he left to get ice cream.

"And watch out for snakes!" he warned us.

Volunteers had started to build a bridge across a stream here but had only gotten as far as one beam. With his arms out, Goyo walked across on the beam. I knew I would feel guilty for not crossing on it, even though it was just high enough off the ground that I could hurt myself.

"You don't have to cross that way," said Dad, who along with Mom and the Callis family had walked across the stream on stones.

I stepped onto the beam. I moved slowly, with arms out. I looked down at the stream below me, aware every minute of the possibility of falling. Dad looked on, worried as I made it across.

Chris and Goyo climbed up the long steep slope like quick mountain goats. Debbie and Charles lagged behind, sweating in the heat. Dad stayed near the back looking at plants. I hiked in the middle with Mom before catching up to Chris and Goyo.

Zeke, acting on the herding instincts that many dogs have, walked back and forth between the stragglers and the striders, changing his course every once in a while to chase after smells and animals. Climbing uphill was hard enough for me without trying to keep the herd together.

I finally caught up with Goyo and Chris, who were chatting about Mexico. We stopped to drink water and eat while the others made their way up toward us. By now, Zeke lay down on the leaves, panting.

"We'll get down to a creek here soon, Zekey," said Dad in his cute, talking-to-animals voice.

At the top stood the massive Pillow Rock, a boulder that resembled two giant stone pillows stacked on top of each other. Even though other hikers had spray-painted and carved their names onto the rock, it was still beautiful.

On the hike down, I picked up a branch and began to use it as a walking stick after seeing Chris do the same. I was young enough that a walking stick felt like a staff rather than a crutch. It was hard though to resist the temptation of shouting "You shall not pass!" Similarly, it was hard not to try to jump and swing on a broken grape vine. I fell almost immediately.

"Tarzan," said Goyo, laughing.

We hiked down to the bottom, and Zeke waded in the creek, just like Dad had promised. Now we were out of the shade on an old dirt road that led to a shuttle vehicle.

Inspired by both the heat and the man we met that morning, we stopped at the store to buy ice cream. I felt almost sick to the stomach from the hot uphill hike, but still wanted ice cream, mostly for the experience of buying ice cream from Hembree's Grocery.

Men sat on the Hembree's Grocery porch, chatting about the coal industry and the effects of politics on it. Once we got inside, we looked around and made our choices. Apples sat in crates near the door. The freezer was full of ice cream, some of it in unmarked wrappers. The man at the counter looked older than Mr. Kemmer and talked less. Like Mr. Kemmer though, he did not accept plastic.

"They call this kind of place a holler," said Mom to Goyo as we drove down the road. "The people who live here mine for coal. They are very poor."

Mom was simplifying things. Some of the houses looked nice. It made sense. Coal and lumber now require skilled machine operators, not to mention corporate bureaucracy. A trailer might be across the road from a two story house. I did not have time to ask the residents how they felt about it. All we could do was wave, and they waved back as they watched us pass. I failed to see how it was a scary place.

Sources and Suggested Reading

New River Area and Trail to Pillow Rock
Bell, Augusta Grove. *Circling Windrock Mountain: Two Hundred Years in Appalachia.* Knoxville: University of Tennessee Press, 1999.

Cumberland Trail Conference. *CTC's Guide to Hiking the Justin P. Wilson Cumberland Trail with Maps/Guides.* www.cumberlandtrail.org (accessed July 19, 2012).

Simmons, Morgan. "Reclaimed and Rugged: Cumberland Mountains' Coal Country Trail is Steep and Challenging." *Knoxville News Sentinel,* July 5, 2013: D1.

LAND OF GNATS AND RATTLESNAKES

⇻ 20 ⇺

Lawson Mountain Part 2 (Mon. May 28)
Hike 14: Bowling Town Road to Norma Road Trailhead
5.4 miles

BEN: The road to the trail wound back and forth. Normally, curves would keep me awake, but the repetition of curve after curve kept me on the edge of sleep.

We walked close to a pond's edge near some child-sized rocks.

"There's a newt right in front of you," said Dad, who stood behind me.

"Sorry, I can't see," I said, "I've got a bug in my eye."

I'd been rubbing my eye with my sweaty, sunscreen-covered hand. I opened my eye for a second and spotted the newt. It seemed to be glancing up at me from its spot in the pond.

Then, I heard a familiar rattling. Blinking quickly to get the gnat out of my eye, I saw a rattler. It slithered to coil under a boulder which acted as an echo chamber for the sound. Dad grabbed my shoulders to hold me away from the snake. No matter how much I'd strode ahead and left him behind, Dad was there to protect me. Even at 24 years, sometimes, I needed it. Unlike before, on our rehearsal hike in Prentice Cooper, I was grateful.

Rattlesnake bites can contain different amounts of venom. Sometimes their bites contain no venom at all. Also, timber rattlers in different regions have different kinds of venom. Some types of venom are nerve poisons, some cause bleeding, some cause both and others cause neither. So long as the venom keeps prey from escaping and deters predators, it does its job.

We wound back and forth up the mountain side, until we reached an old strip mine site. Before the strip mining, this place was a forest. In the days of the strip mine, it would have been a rocky desert. Because the law required it, the mining company revegetated, meaning that they planted new vegetation to replace what they removed. Now, the place was a field of thick grass with scattered trees that Dad identified as black locust trees. My now-clear eye was ready to look out at bluish mountains beyond us. The mountains didn't distract Dad from the ground though.

"It's mostly exotics here" said Dad, looking at daisies and other plants which did not impress him. Still, the place looked beautiful to me. Butterflies and ladybugs fluttered in the field and shined in the sunlight.

Even if Dad didn't think much of the disturbed ecosystem here, other creatures saw it as an opportunity. There were droppings that looked to be from coyotes, which we still hadn't seen, in spite of Dad's promise. A coyote had been here, perhaps scanning for prey among the grass and flowers. Human hunters had also left corn as bait to aid deer hunting, knowing that deer grazed in fields like this one.

We walked back down into the woods, a habitat with more native plants. It also had more careless insects that seemed to love landing in my eyes. In all the hikes before now, I'd learned to ignore spider webs while hiking, accepting them as part of the experience. Now, I felt guilty whenever I wiped a sticky web off my face. The spiders were doing us a favor by eating some of the gnats. I dodged some of the webs in gratitude.

The Red Queen Effect and Venom

"...it takes all the running you can do to keep in place!"
- The Red Queen to Alice in <u>Through the Looking Glass</u> by Lewis Carroll

LARRY: Why this variation in timber rattler venom described here?

If, by fortunate mutation, a rodent has cells that produce enough anti-venom to increase chances of surviving the rattler's fangs, then he or she should have more offspring, some of which should also have the anti-venom. You might think that this would lead to rodents that are safe from timber rattlers, but rattlers also evolve new venoms.

This type of co-evolution is called an arms race. In this case it's venom vs. anti-venom rather than armaments like teeth or claws. This form of evolution is a race that no one fully wins and never ends. Alice finds herself in this sort of a race held by the Red Queen. This gives us the evolutionary term "the Red Queen effect" coined by Van Valen.

The Red Queen effect suggests an answer to my question. Perhaps all the variation in venom helps the rattlers cope with rodents' evolving resistance.

On the dusty road of the drive back, Dad said that the curves almost put him to sleep too.

We passed graffiti on a bridge that shouted messages about land and energy politics. "Southern Coal Eats Ship," one side said. Someone, perhaps wanting to protect young eyes, had spray painted the last letter so that it looked like a cross between a T and a P. Another graffiti message on the other side read UMWA-SOCM. UMWA was in red and SOCM in green with a crude picture of a mountain.

UMWA stands for the United Mine Workers of America, a union that has represented workers in the coal industry for years. The UMWA had been powerful in the New River area during the deep-mining boom in the 1940s, but it's less powerful now. Once strip mining came in, many deep miners found themselves out of work and their unions weakened. Some of them tried to stop strip mining with force. To quote Augusta Grove Bell's *Circling Windrock Mountain* again, "sticks of dynamite had a way of getting thrown into strippers'

More about Venomous Snakes

LARRY: Yes, you may meet a copperhead or timber rattlesnake on the CT. They are not aggressive, but they will defend themselves. Once, while reading in a shelter I had built on the Cumberland Plateau in Kentucky, I brushed a copperhead off my leg without realizing what I had brushed. It took no offense.

Rattlers may or may not give you an audible warning. Staying on trails and watching where you put your hands and feet will help keep you from being bitten. Stepping on a venomous snake is definitely a bad step. As Ben stated above, the snake chooses how much venom to inject and sometimes uses none. This can give rise to belief in miracle cures for snake bite.

A few years ago, I was working for TVA in the Devil's Race Track area just off the CT with a fellow botanist who had been hoping to see her first rattlesnake. We stopped to have lunch on the rocks. Right below her rock perch were about six rattlesnakes. It is unusual to see more than one rattlesnake at a time. You may see multiple rattlers near the communal winter dens, during courting, or in this case when a mother is with her babies. Rattler eggs hatch inside the mom (which some people call "live birth"), and she stays with them for a week. Maternal care of this kind is rare for snakes or any reptile species.

trucks." By the late sixties the strippers dominated and continued to cut into the plateau. I follow Bell's usage of stripper to mean strip-miner, even though it tends to lead the mind in a different direction.

In the seventies, resistance to strip mining took a new form. SOCM, or "Save our Cumberland Mountains" started as a community group intended to address a wide range of issues. Under the leadership of a charismatic former deep miner named J.W. Bradley, SOCM narrowed in on lobbying for a full ban on all strip mining.

After failing to get strip mining banned, SOCM officially changed its position from wanting to ban strip mining to wanting to control it more strictly. Many strip mining operations chose to ignore laws and strip the land without a permit. Trying to stop these "wildcat" operations proved tricky for SOCM and dangerous. During this time period, J.W. Bradley got punched in the face during a permit hearing and several other SOCM members' houses burned down.

SOCM now addresses everything from pesticides to racism across the state of Tennessee. Since 2008, they've called themselves the Statewide Organizing for Community eMpowerment. Yet the Cumberland region

....

I moved to sit on another rock a few feet away. My co-worker stayed where she was, delighted to eat her lunch directly above the family of snakes.

I have some history with venomous snakes. At age 12, I nearly stepped on a rattler in my home state, Ohio. While living in Liberia as a Peace Corps volunteer, I went to see what was in a shed behind the house that I had rented. I found a cardboard box and carried it out with my thumbs inside it. To my astonishment, it was filled with a highly-coiled, nine-foot-long black cobra. The snake slithered out and went back into the shed. My neighbors later killed it with the proverbial nine foot pole.

Generally, the copperhead is more common than the timber rattler and can be found almost anywhere in east Tennessee. The timber rattler is confined to wilder areas that have rock den sites available. Some of the rattlesnakes in Frozen Head State Natural Area are yellow-orange, allowing them to be confused with copperheads. Copperheads, in turn, are easy to confuse with northern water snakes, which are common in east Tennessee but not venomous. Copperheads, rattlers and northern water snakes often share wetland habitats. Of the three though, only the water snake is routinely seen in the water. This non-venomous snake was discussed earlier by Ben.

....

remains a focus for them. They were involved in the struggle against rock harvesting mentioned in Chapter 6 and have continued to oppose strip mining for coal in various places.

So far, we'd wandered through land that had mild scars or dents from coal. The mountains we saw from the strip mine site looked solid and tree covered. Yet the next day's hike would be different. We would be heading through ripped and torn land, streams that ran orange and views of clear cuts where the trees had been shaved clear off in patches. Some hikers would dread that kind of hike. I looked forward to it. I wanted to see all that the Cumberlands contained, the ugly as well as the beautiful.

How to Care for a Snakebite Victim

BEN: People used to recommend cutting open the fang punctures and sucking out the venom, but these days, experts consider that to be a risky method. Instead, if you are with someone who gets bitten, take the following steps:

1. Call for medical help right away if you have a phone or radio. Make sure that the snakebite victim stays calm and stays still.

2. Note the time of the bite. If you have a pen or a marker, make a circle around the swollen area so that medics can check the rate of swelling. Don't worry about finding a pen or marker if you don't have one handy.

3. Take off any rings or anything else that might constrict the area.

4. Put the bitten area in a loose splint to slow movement. Do NOT tie a tight tourniquet.

5. If the bite area looks swollen, the snake was probably venomous.

6. Check temperature, pulse, rate of breathing and blood pressure.

7. If your hiking companion's skin is getting pale, raise the victim's feet and put a blanket over him or her.

Do not try to find the snake. As much as you might want more details on what bit your friend, you don't want to get bitten yourself.

Sources and Suggested Reading

Revegetation Laws:
Legal Information Institute. "30 CFR 817.111 - Revegetation: General Requirements." Cornell University Law School. Accessed December 2, 2014. http://www.law.cornell.edu/cfr/text/30/817.111.

General
Cumberland Trail Conference. *CTC's Guide to Hiking the Justin P. Wilson Cumberland Trail with Maps/Guides.* Accessed July 19, 2012. www.cumberlandtrail.org.

Simmons, Morgan. "Reclaimed and Rugged: Cumberland Mountains' Coal Country Trail is Steep and Challenging." *Knoxville News Sentinel*, July 5, 2013: D1.

Simmons, Morgan. "Controlled Burns Help Save Forests." *Knoxville News Sentinel*, April 28, 2013. http://www.knoxnews.com/news/2013/apr/28/controlled-burns-help-save-great-smoky-mountains/.

Tennessee Wildlife Resources Agency. "Elk Reintroduction Questions and Answers." Accessed July 17, 2013. http://www.tennessee.gov/twra/elkquestions.html.

UMW and SOCM:
Allen, Bill. "Save our Cumberland Mountains: Growth and Change within a Grassroots Organization." In *Fighting Back in Appalachia: Traditions of Resistance and Change,* edited by Steven L. Fischer. 85-99 Philadelphia: Temple University Press 1993.
    This is my main source for SOCM's history.

Bell, Augusta Grove. *Circling Windrock Mountain: Two Hundred Years in Appalachia.* Knoxville: University of Tennessee Press, 1999.
    Much of what I know about UMWA history comes from this book.

SOCM. "SOCM History." Accessed July 17, 2013. http://www.socm.org/index.cfm/m/60/pageID/22/fuseAction/contentpage.main/detailID/13.

Rattlesnakes in General:
Behler, John L., and F. Wayne King. *The Audubon Society Field Guide to North American Reptiles and Amphibians.* New York: Chanticleer Press Inc., 1979.

Falk, Ann. "Crotalus horridus." *Animal Diversity Web*. 2002. http://animaldiversity.ummz.umich.edu/accounts/Crotalus_horridus/ (accessed November 19, 2014).

New York State Department of Environmental Conservation. *Timber Rattlesnake Fact Sheet*. 2013. http://www.dec.ny.gov/animals/7147.html (accessed April 3, 2013).
   This article gives information about the life cycle of timber rattlesnakes as well as their habitat.

Saint Louis Zoo. *Timber Rattlesnake*. 2013. http://www.stlzoo.org/animals/abouttheanimals/reptiles/snakes/timberrattlesnake/ (accessed April 3, 2013).

Trott, John. *The Virginia Naturalist*. Kerney: Morris Publishing, 2006.
   While the articles republished here are old, John Trott writes in an engaging style.

Caring for Snake Bites:
Barish, Robert A. *Snake Bites*. February 2009. http://www.merckmanuals.com/home/injuries_and_poisoning/bites_and_stings/snake_bites.html (accessed April 19, 2013).

Minnesota Department of Natural Resources. "Snakes." *Minnesota Department of Natural Resources*. 2013. http://www.dnr.state.mn.us/livingwith_wildlife/snakes/index.html (accessed April 3, 2013).
   A PDF on this page is a good source of information on rattlesnake bites in particular.

Variation in Bites and Venom
Glenn, J.L., R.C. Straight, and T.B. Wolt. "Regional Variation in the Presence of Canebrake Toxin in Crotalus horridus Venom." *Comparative Biochemistry and Physiology Part C: Pharmacology, Toxicology and Endocrinology* 107, no. 3 (March 1994): 337-346. Accessed November 19, 2014.
   http://www.ncbi.nlm.nih.gov/pubmed/8061939.
   This article gives information about the different types of venom rattlesnakes can have depending on the region. It mentions four distinctive venom types with different effects.

Johnson, Steve A. "Venomous Snake FAQs." *University of Florida*. Published May 2, 2012. http://ufwildlife.ifas.ufl.edu/venomous_snake_faqs.shtml.

DESIRE

→ 21 ←

Arch Mountain (Tues. May 29)
Hike 15: Fork Mountain to Cave Branch
9 miles

BEN: Weeks before we started our trek, we went into a coal washing plant and got permission from the people there to use the Fork Mountain Road in order to reach this section. We probably didn't need to bother with permission.

While riding up that gravel road to the CT, we could see cliff-like high walls where people had strip mined. In some of these old strip mines, we could see gas wells and green tanks, controlled by electricity from mini-solar panels. Even though the coal had been depleted, the mine sites were still of use as sites to drill for natural gas. Natural gas will one day run out too.

We slapped on some sunscreen and started hiking. Once the mist cleared, the view of the surrounding mountains was a monument to tearing, bulldozing and chopping. Strippers had cut around the ridge tops, leaving improbable, round, hat-like peaks. Loggers had shaved off sections of trees and made dusty roads leading to the clear cuts.

Trees logged from forests like these had given me furniture and paper. Coal from strip mines like these had powered Oak Ridge's Bull Run Steam Plant, which in turn had powered the cassette player that I had listened to while falling asleep on many childhood nights, never once thinking about ripped-up mountains. Loggers and miners had wrecked places like this in order to satisfy people like me.

Yet people had also written laws, mandating that companies restore the land, as I mentioned in the last chapter. We want restoration for many reasons, but among them is an instinctual desire. One can tell a depleted land when one sees it: mud, dust, rock. Many people yearn for natural ecosystems instead.

The forest also wanted to restore itself, to the extent that an ecosystem can want anything. It's the nature of life to move back into bare areas and slowly re-establish itself, even if exotic plants often find moving back in easier than native ones do.

So the trail led us through human alteration, human attempts at restoration and nature's attempts at restoration. Grasses grew over old strip mined areas. Elsewhere saplings pressed up against each other with no canopy to shade them yet. They were the beginning of what would eventually become a forest with tall trees like we saw near other former strip-mined areas.

Ponds, where water had filled in strip-mined ditches, now teemed with duckweed. Mosses grew along their banks. Dad inspected these ponds with a little less enthusiasm than he had for the natural one at Brady Mountain. Still, they were habitats. They weren't just barren dents any more.

My desire to explore grew. I did not know what we would be seeing next amid the rugged, rocky re-vegetated land. Then, I heard thunder. My desire not to come back a wet mess again made me walk faster.

In a patch of forest, Dad, who hiked behind me, was delighted to spot two Luna moths mating. We have the photo on our website.

A power line stretched above the trail. It ran up and down hills until it reached distant Buffalo Mountain, where I could make out the small spinning shapes of wind turbines. They spun slower than whirligigs or pinwheels, suggesting their real size. Like coal and gas, they were another stage in humanity's quest for power.

Tennessee Valley Authority, a government corporation that provides East Tennessee's electricity, chose the depleted strip mine at Buffalo Mountain as a site for renewable energy production. They had discovered that some people want this renewable power and will even voluntarily pay more for it.

Some people complain that wind generators ruin views. Here, the view ruining had already happened long before the turbines.

Back when I was in high school, I liked spotting the same wind turbines from our hometown of Oak Ridge and never found them to be ugly. Then, as now, the sight of their giant spinning arms, visible so far away, made me feel small, in a good way, like the view from Brady Mountain or the sky from my front yard.

We walked on a bridge across a stream that had turned orange with bacteria fed by pollution. Looking at it made me feel divided. On the one hand, this stream, with its cloudy orange water and orange gunk collecting on rocks

Tilting at Wind Generators.

was ugly. On the other hand, the stream's out-of-the-ordinary orangeness stood out against the green summer leaves, making it fascinating and beautiful to me in a sick way.

Dad found something that excited him: a forest that looked older and more native than much of what we had seen. To me, at first, the site looked like just an ordinary forest, but to Dad, it was special, a place to enjoy and explore. After staring at the trees above me for a while, I did start to notice how tall and wide they were.

My own judgments of beautiful or ugly weren't the same as Dad's fascination about herbaceous layers. I could make ugly things like an orange stream beautiful with my mind. Yet I could not make an exotic-dominated field into a thriving habitat for native plants.

LARRY: Mature forest at higher elevation, 2,000 to over 3,000 ft. in the Cumberland Mountains are home to impressive herbaceous layers. See www.benandlarryincumberland.com for information on the plants of higher elevations.

BEN: I left Dad to his plants, only asking him about them from time to time. Salamanders were what I wanted. I yearned to find their secret homes. So, when we reached a clear stream, I searched. After lifting a few stones, I grabbed a yellow one with dark brown stripes. Likely, it was a two-lined salamander. Also likely, it did not understand my interest.

By now, my inexperience with salamanders bothered me. The yellow wiggling thing was not an "it" but a he or a she, even though I did not know which. I'd have to use the word "it" in writing, even though that word made the salamander sound lifeless, like a toaster.

The Two-Lined Salamander doesn't understand Ben Toon's Interest.

Two-lined salamander mothers will guard their eggs for more than two months until they hatch. Such behavior is a commitment to the future, with up to 100 unborn children to guard.

The native forest did not last. We passed through a forest floor that exotic Japanese stiltgrass (*Microstegium vimineum*) had conquered and carpeted, making the forest floor look like an overgrown lawn and replacing the native plants. Japanese stiltgrass probably moved into the United States because people used it as a packing material to protect Chinese porcelain. The first report of it in the U.S. was in Tennessee in 1918.

On a side trail, we found a small fenced area with a mysterious front gate that slid down guillotine style. It was baited with corn. A trail camera, mounted on a tree, watched us as we wandered around the corral. The camera seemed odd even here in such an altered landscape. The next day, we would we learn its purpose.

Further down in a logging area, we saw a logger who was taking a break from work. He was blond, well-tanned and rugged-looking. Dad told him that we'd come from Fork Mountain.

"I don't know that I'd feel like walking that far," he said.

"Actually," said Dad, "we're going to be doing a series of hikes going all the way to Virginia." The logger opened his mouth in amazement.

Maybe our walk seemed crazy to some people, even if we were splitting most of it into day hikes. We weren't the first to walk through the Cumberlands and study them though. When the naturalist John Muir had passed through the Cumberland region on his trek to the gulf, he met a baffled frontier farmer. Unlike our logger, who had been impressed, Muir's farmer scolded him.

"Picking blossoms doesn't seem to be a man's work in any kind of times," the farmer had said.

"Well you know Solomon was a strong-minded man, and he is generally believed to have been the very wisest man the world ever saw," said Muir. "And yet he considered it was worthwhile to study plants."

Muir added, "We are told that he wrote a book about plants, not only of the great cedars of Lebanon, but of the little bits of things growing in the cracks on the walls."

Our next hike would not have appealed to the logger or the farmer, although it might have appealed to John Muir. It was a long hike that Dad's plans failed to split into shorter pieces. Nature had already ruled out breaking it up as a backpacking trip. The seep near the camping site would be dry. So instead we decided to do the whole trip in a day. We had found ourselves feeling less tired these days than after our first hikes. Our next hike might break us.

Sources and Suggested Reading

Wind Power:
Lienhard, John H. *How Invention Begins.* New York: Oxford University Press 2006.

Buffalo Mountain:
Environmental Protection Agency. "A Breath of Fresh Air for America's Abandoned Mine Lands: Alternative Energy Provides a Second Wind." Accessed July 17, 2013.
http://www.epa.gov/superfund/programs/recycle/pdf/wind_energy.pdf.

Mens et Manus.net. *TVA's Buffalo Mountain Wind Power Plant.* Last updated November 17, 2007. http://www.mensetmanus.net/windpower/.
      This site provides a negative and non-scholarly view about the Buffalo Mountain wind farm. I include it here only to provide the opposite opinion of my previously listed source. Some people, like me, like wind power. Other

people don't.

Two-Line Salamander:
Behler, John L., and F. Wayne King. *The Audubon Society Field Guide to North American Reptiles and Amphibians.* New York: Chanticleer Press Inc., 1979.

Mitchel, Joe and Gibbons, Whit. *Salamanders of the Southeast.* Athens: University of Georgia Press, 2010.

Niemiller, Matthew et al. *The Amphibians of Tennessee.* Knoxville: University of Tennessee Press, 2011.

Japanese Stiltgrass:
The University of Georgia Center for Invasive Species and Ecosystem Health. "Invasive Plants of New England: Japanese Stiltgrass." Accessed July 18, 2013. http://www.eddmaps.org/ipane/ipanespecies/grass/microstegium_vimineum.htm.

Invasive Plant Atlas of the United States. "Japanese Stiltgrass: Microstegium vimineum." Last updated July 15, 2013. http://www.invasiveplantatlas.org/subject.html?sub=3051#maps.

USDA Forest Service. "Microstegium vimineum." Accessed July 18, 2013. http://www.fs.fed.us/database/feis/index.html.

John Muir:
Muir, John. *A Thousand-mile Walk to the Gulf.* Boston: Houghton Mifflin, 1916.
   This book is available for free online at http://vault.sierraclub.org/john_muir_exhibit/writings/a_thousand_mile_walk_to_the_gulf/.

PIGS AND BLOOD BLISTERS

↦ 22 ↤

Frozen Head (Wed. May 30)
Hike 16: Fork Mountain to Park Headquarters
Over 10 miles

We passed the now-closed high security Brushy Mountain Prison. Martin Luther King's murderer had done time there. At one point, prisoners from Brushy Mountain worked at a coal mine nearby. The prison abandoned that idea after prisoners sabotaged mining equipment and took their guards hostage.

Today's hike would take us through land that was once the prison's property in Frozen Head State Park. We started at Fork Mountain trailhead, the same starting place as our last hike, but this time we were going the other way.

Dad, now hiking in front, turned back to face me. "Quiet," whispered Dad, "Feral pig." The black shape of a hog walked in front of us as we crept toward it, both of us hoping for it to stand still so that we could look at it. It dashed off the trail, a black blur. It wasn't a lazy barnyard creature but a feral hog of the forest, ready to flee the footsteps of invading humans. According to Professor Billy Higginbotham of Texas A&M University, feral hogs can run up to 30 miles per hour.

If it felt cornered, it could have charged at us, mauled us, or bitten us. The last of those possibilities might be brutal, as, again, according to Higginbotham, hog jaws can crack nuts or the bones of the carcasses they scavenge. None of these possibilities were likely, though. Feral pigs, like many feral and wild animals, prefer to be left alone. The best thing is to stay out of their way.

According to John L. Meyer's 2013 study "Wild Pig Attacks on Humans," only four fatal wild pig attacks have ever been reported in the United States. Hikers should avoid chasing wild pigs, feeding them or getting in the path of a running pig. Also, avoid injured pigs, as they are understandably irritated.

Other hogs cooled off in the shade further down the hill from us. Though I could see them with my binoculars, none of my pictures could capture them. They couldn't be held in the hand like toads or salamanders. They'd adapted to being hunted by humans and knew to avoid us.

Even when we could not see the pigs well with the naked eye, we could hear a chorus of loud squeals from them. Once Dad told me what it was, I could not confuse the pigs' call for anything else. Appropriately, a group of feral sows and their offspring is called a sounder, though granted, yakking human children and parents can be just as noisy. The two of us tried not to be a sounder.

Frozen Head's pigs are mostly of feral origin, meaning that they were farm pigs that had adapted to living in the wild. The domestic pigs lived unfenced in herds in the old days to be rounded up for harvest. Farmers often branded them like the cattle of the old west. Their other ancestors were Russian wild boars that hunters introduced.

Pigs had used these woods for fewer years than humans. Now though, they had made themselves at home. They'd torn through the forest floor for roots and grubs to eat. They're destructive creatures.

Hog Parenting

BEN: On average, a feral sow's litter is between five and six piglets. Sows tend to have one litter per year, starting at age 13 months. As with mother bears, a feral sow will defend her litter. Keep that in mind when encountering them.

"Ke-eeeeer!"

"Sounds like a red-tailed hawk," I told Dad. The red-tailed hawk call is distinctive, evoking large distances and majesty. Hollywood often uses it for the call of the bald eagle or even the vulture. Neither bird in reality has a similar call.

It was a fact that I remembered from my time volunteering at the Clinch River Raptor Center back in High School. The Clinch River Raptor Center, run by Katie Cottrell in Clinton, took care of injured birds. Mildred, the Raptor Center's red-tailed hawk with an injured wing, couldn't fly, so releasing her back into the wild wasn't an option.

I had fed her by hand in order to train her for educational programs. She perched on a long glove that covered my arm. I kept my hand raised to prevent Mildred from walking further onto my arm and digging her talons into my skin. Her sharp beak yanked and ripped bloody meat from the dead mouse in my gloved fingers. As her adopted father, I enjoyed every minute of it. It was like raising a fierce, feathered flesh-ripper for a daughter.

Red Tailed Hawk (*Buteo jamaicensis*)

BEN: Red tailed hawks live above open areas in trees or power towers so that they can see their prey. Not all red tailed hawks have the rusty-colored tails which give the species its name. They do, however, always have distinctive white chests.

Humans have muscles that can change the shape of the eye's lens so that we can see things that are close and things that are far away. Red tailed hawks' eyes are even better. Not only can red-tailed hawks change the shape of the lens, they can also change the shape of their cornea, allowing them to see eight times as far as we can.

Mating begins at age three. Red tailed hawks are monogamous, with only one partner for life. Male and female red-tailed hawks usually fly around in circles together before mating.

Sometimes they fly over fields to search for prey. At other times they scan the ground from treetops. They swoop down and grab small rodents and birds from the ground.

Red-tail hawks build their nests high atop rock ledges or tall trees. They lay two to three eggs. Fiercely territorial, they often compete with great horned owls for nesting space. Both species eat the others' young.

I felt happy to know more than Dad about something other than turtles.

As if to continue the theme of my high school days, I found yet another box turtle. I've not mentioned all the turtles found along the trail in this book, because on paper, finding turtle after turtle gets repetitive. In practice

Some Plants that Reinforce My Humility

Feature Plants: Green Violet (*Hybanthus concolor*) and goldenseal (*Hydratis canadensis*)

LARRY: I thought I knew the habitat for green violet: forests with soil derived from limestone. Well, as far as I know there is no limestone high in the Cumberland Mountains, but we saw many green violets there as we hiked the CT. Perhaps there is some calcium in those rocks to make the soil resemble limestone soils. The more experience I have with plant species, the less I'm sure of where they will turn up.

The green violet is an inconspicuous plant. It is in the violet family but not in the genus with the violets we enjoy as spring wildflowers. The flowers are green. Most flowers have evolved colors that stand out in the world of green they live in. This makes it easier for their pollinators to find them. I wonder who pollinates the green violet. Perhaps their vision is different from the usual bees and butterflies that pollinate other flowers.

Years ago, I had seen goldenseal in the Cumberland Mountains where sandstone dominates and not with limestone as it is supposed to be. I had guessed it must be there as a remnant of an abandoned herb garden. We discovered to the contrary that goldenseal grows widely scattered along the CT in the same areas as the green violet, thus a double surprise.

Goldenseal is a famous medicinal herb. This was brought home to me in an odd way by some college students. I had been leading them on a nature hike. When we came to some goldenseal, they told me that it was useful to cover up drug use when urine is tested. Goldenseal, like ginseng, needs to be protected from overharvesting for sale to herb wholesalers.

I want to spend more time along the CT in the lush high elevation forests of the Cumberland Mountains. I'm sure there are more botanical surprises for me there.

though, it's anything but repetitive. No two are alike. The beautiful patterns on their shells range in color from yellow to every shade of orange.

I heard this one hiss when closing her plastron, the lower part of her shell. The sound comes from the air leaving the turtle's lungs, an action which makes closing the plastron easier. I'd forgotten that they hissed though, during all the time I'd been looking at them on the CT. Apparently, I'd forgotten to listen.

The box turtle in my hand was so flat on the bottom that I knew she was female without a doubt. Maybe some of the females that I had found earlier on our trek had actually been males, because the bottoms of their shells weren't nearly as flat. After putting the turtle down, I thought about those other turtles and how confident I had been when looking at them. Now I wasn't sure.

I felt kinship to Dad. Dad seemed to know more than I did, but ultimately it was what he didn't entirely understand that kept pushing him to search along the trail with his crazy son in tow. Green violets and goldenseal had fascinated him today and other days, as he kept seeing them in soils that didn't seem right for them.

Soon, we saw neither white blaze nor clear trail. There was a flattened path, but it was muddy and several trees had fallen over it. We walked back and forth a few times hoping to find a white blaze. I decided to follow the mud trail, splashing through mud puddles. Dad followed me until the trail waned. We found ourselves forcing our way over fallen logs and through bushes.

We decided to follow reddish-orange blazes that we'd skipped earlier because they were not white. The red-orange blazes led us around the edge of the Frozen Head Park.

"What if this isn't really our route?" I asked Dad, fearing the lengthening of an already long hike. "What if you're just taking us this way because you wanted to explore it?"

"Only subconsciously," said Dad with a joking smile.

We sat down and ate at a campsite with picnic table. The site had a seep. Right now, the seep held less water than the mud puddles I'd slopped through earlier. We would have had to lug our water with us this far had we gone camping here.

LARRY: There is a water source about half a mile from the CT in this area. Coffin Springs is on an orange-blazed side trail. The orange and white blazes run along together as you head north on the CT. When they split up, follow the orange to the spring area where the trail meets a road. The spring looks like a coffin with the lid pulled back about 5 inches. It may take a while to find.

BEN: Castle Rock, the formation we approached next, was tall, but many of the cliffs we had seen before had been much taller. This big rock was special because it was climbable without climbing gear. Dad stayed below.

Foot on bump, notch in rock, notch in rock, then up into a shallow, leaf-filled crack in the rock about the height of my knees. I pulled myself out of it with my arms. It was easy, even if I was already tired.

On top, away from the edges, Castle Rock resembled the forests below. Only when close to an edge did I realize how serious it would be to fall off.

Dad, hiking below, yelled at me to come down. We had a long way left to go.

Both of us felt tired. Neither one of us felt like outpacing the other. We were not expecting it, but this hike wore on us more than any of the others. Dad's left knee felt fine, but his feet gave him trouble. So did mine.

Being worn out makes everything more dramatic. An uphill becomes a dreaded uphill, especially after long stretches of downhill hiking. A downhill becomes a chance to let gravity take over.

As we walked along a pond, thorns from an exotic species of rose ripped cuts into my arms, like the tusk of a sow defending her litter. Perhaps this ripping was what Seal meant when he sang "Kissed by a Rose."

While walking up and down on the dirt path, I knew I needed to motivate myself. "We might make it down," I said out loud. "What am I talking about? We *will* make it down," I said, laughing.

We left the main CT at Ross Gap dropping off Byrd Mountain on a side trail. Later during the fall, Dad hiked the main trail beyond Ross Gap for

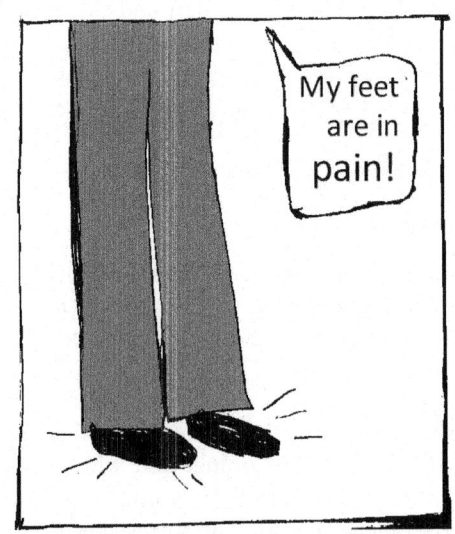

Larry Toon accepts the glory of victory and the agony of de feet.

probably less than a mile to a sign reading "Trail End." Perhaps soon the trail will go on to Wartburg.

Finally we reached the park headquarters and passed the tents pitched in the field. Neither of us could have been happier to grab Frescas at the car.

Back at the motel, Dad found a blood blister on his foot. Thankfully, the next day was free since we had just done two days' worth of hiking in one day.

Sources and Suggested Reading

Brushy Mountain
Bell, Augusta Grove. *Circling Windrock Mountain: Two Hundred Years in Appalachia.* Knoxville: University of Tennessee Press, 1999
       This book is also a great source of information about the history of feral hogs in the area as well.

Freytag, Ethyl and Glenda Kreis Ott. *A History of Morgan County Tennessee.* United States of America: Specialty Printing Company, 1971.

Sakowski, Carolyn. *Touring the East Tennessee Backroads.* Winston-Salem: John F. Blair, 2007.

Feral Hogs
Higginbotham, Billy. "Coping with Feral Hogs: Frequently Asked Questions- Wild Pigs." Last Modified August 2013. http://feralhogs.tamu.edu/frequently-asked-questions-wild-pigs/. Accessed December 30, 2014.

Henry, John. "Feral Hogs: A Growing Problem in East Tennessee." Last updated November 1, 2001. http://www.wbir.com/rss/article/240250/2/Feral-Hogs-A-growing-problem-in-East-Tennessee.

Humphrey, Tom. "Commission, Wild Hogs Both Facing Eradication in East Tennessee?" *Knoxville News Sentinel.* October 22, 2011. http://www.knoxnews.com/news/2011/oct/22/commission-wild-hogs-both-facing-eradication-in/.

Mayer, John J., "Wild Pig Attacks on Humans." *Wildlife Damage Management Conferences -- Proceedings. Paper* 151 (2013). http://digitalcommons.unl.edu/icwdm_wdmconfproc/151.

Nelson, John E., Peter M. Heis-Pavlov and Sigrid R. Heis-Pavlov, "Sus scrofa: Population Structure, Reproduction and Condition in Tropical North-Eastern

Australia," Acta Silvatica 5 (2009): 179-188. Accessed December 30, 2014. http://www.nyme.hu/fileadmin/dokumentumok/fmk/acta_silvatica/cikkek/Vol05-2009/16_heise_pavlov_et_al_p.pdf.

Taylor, Richard B., Eric C. Hellgreen, Timothy M. Gabor and Linda M. Isle. "Reproduction of Feral Pigs in Southern Texas." Journal of Mammology 79: (1998) Accessed December 30, 2014. http://www.jstor.org/stable/1383024.

Red-Tail Hawk
Dewey, Tanya and Delena Arnold. "ADW: *Buteo jamaicensis*." Accessed July 18, 2013. http://animaldiversity.ummz.umich.edu/site/accounts/information/Buteo_jamaicensis.html.

Enature. "Red-tailed Hawk Buteo jamaicensis" Accessed July 18, 2013. http://www.enature.com/fieldguides/detail.asp?allSpecies=&searchText=Red-Tailed+Hawk&GroupID=&cmdSubmit.x=9&cmdSubmit.y=6&curGroupID=1&lgfromWhere=&curPageNum=1.

Sinclair S. *Extraordinary Eyes: How Animals Seeced the World*. New York: Dial Books for Young Readers, 1992.

Wilson, B. W. et al. *Scientific American: Birds*. San Francisco: W. H. Freeman and Co, 1980.

RETURN TO DEVIL'S BREAKFAST TABLE

↠ **23** ↞

Daddy's Creek Area (Thur. May 31).
Slow, Rambling Exploration Day
No new miles covered, but see text box.

BEN: On our day off we decided to look for the Devil's Breakfast Table with Elizabeth and Carl. It had eluded us on our first trip to Daddy's Creek. We couldn't find it this time either.

Maybe it was the lack of medication. Maybe it was the foot-blistering, leg-aching, trail-losing, rose-thorn scratching hike we had done just one day before. Today, I searched around to find things that would distract me from my tiredness. We had time to be distracted. After all, we were not trying to cover ground.

Devil's Breakfast Table.

We leisurely strolled up Daddy's Creek. A log lay across our path. I crawled under it and kept crawling for no reason.

"I guess I'll just crawl this whole thing," I told Dad while feeling the dirt under my hands.

"Yeah, a new sensory experience," said Dad, while walking far ahead of me.

The trail took us away from soil and onto the pebbles of the riverbank. On two legs again, I sniffed a plant with a reddish flower. It smelled distinct but pleasant. I thought of how human languages have such specific words for colors, but few words for smells.

"What's this one called?" I asked Dad.

"Sweet shrub," Dad answered.

Sweet seemed as good a name as any for the shrub's smell.

[Comic panels:
- Panel 1: "THIS IS ME WITHOUT ADD PILLS." (TRUE).
- Panel 2: "I thought you were always crazy, like me!" (ALSO TRUE).
- Panel 3: "WE ATE ON AN OUTCROP OVERLOOKING DADDY'S CREEK." "WE GAVE UP ON FINDING DEVIL'S BREAKFAST TABLE, BUT WE ENJOYED WHERE WE WERE."]

The above conversation between Ben and Carl actually took place.

"This reminds me of the tundra," said Carl as we sat down on an exposed rock outcrop that stuck up from the earth like a boulder. Like the tundra, a treeless landscape with frozen soil found in the far north, this outcrop teemed with lichens. As Dad had taught me long ago, lichen is two living things, an algae and a fungus, growing together. Lichens can look brushy or like patches of green, yellow or white on the rock. For these algae and fungi, survival of the fittest meant surviving together.

The most striking one here was *Cladonia* or reindeer lichen in English. It bristles up in whitish clusters, sharing the rock with flatter, greener lichens. Someone associated it enough with the tundra to call it reindeer lichen, even though it can live far away from any reindeer on a hot Tennessee summer day. Elizabeth noticed another thing growing on the rock. It looked like uneven roof shingles. I knew it as rock tripe, another lichen. "Is it true that you can eat this," she asked.

"Yes, you can," said Dad, from on top of the outcrop. "I've seen it listed as a starvation food. You'd probably only want to eat it if you were starving."

I'd eaten rock tripe before. It had the taste, texture and nutritional value of a newspaper that had been left out in the rain, then dried. I liked it.

I munched on my sandwich slowly, taking time to savor the grains. A fish the size of my forearm moved slowly through the water at a slow pace, switching to faster at moments that seemed random to me. Up here on the rock, I no longer felt the need to bang on signs, crawl, or sniff. Up here, I could just be tired and watch the wonders of the world around me.

We stopped at Carl and Elizabeth's house. They gave us a delicious snack of pineapple upside down cake and milk as we chatted about many

Back to the Devil Again

BEN: We did not find Devil's Breakfast table the first or second time around, even though we were standing right in front of it. We came back in November and found it. The leaves no longer blocked the view, so we could see the Devil's Breakfast Table from the bridge across Daddy's Creek. It was a thick and wide sandstone slab supported by a far-too-narrow base of shale.

We got even closer by scrambling across rocks toward it. The rocks, fallen pieces from above, were scattered in no formal pattern, stepping stones with no intention of being stepped on. My foot slid through leaves that gave way in a crack between rocks. I panicked, thinking I'd find a rattlesnake in such an opening. Still, I kept going until we arrived at the table, without a single rattlesnake stopping us. After all, they'd mostly gone into hibernation by then.

Someone had set up a rope for climbing up to the top of it and had even left litter on top. Still, it looked too risky for either of us. Historians think the early settlers called it the Devil's Breakfast Table because it looked like it was about to topple. Only the devil could have thought such a table was a good place to eat. Yet, humans, being the devilishly clever creatures they were, had strung a rope up there and eaten without a single sign of even loosening the structure. The soil and fallen leaves on top supported a pine tree.

We climbed on top of the hill above the table and took a picture from above. From above, the table looked slanted even though it had looked like a level table from below. The slanting was just an illusion because of the hill itself being slanted. If I had only seen the table from above, I would never have known how flat or how difficult to reach from below it was.

LARRY: The Table with its shale pedestal looks to have formed by a chunk

different things.

"I wonder about the invention of fire," said Dad. "What would have happened if people back then decided it wasn't such a good idea to cook their food?"

"We wouldn't have frying," said Carl. "It would be so much better for health."

"I've heard sugar would not pass the FDA if it were invented now," said

......

of hard sandstone breaking off from the nearby cliff and landing on the softer shale which was then protected from erosion by the chunk. Eventually the Table will fall and slide down to Daddy's Creek as the shale erodes away leaving insufficient support. Perhaps some of the many large rocks by Daddy's creek were once "table tops". My imagination conjures a possible time when there were many devil's tables, a devil's restaurant, each on its own pedestal. What a fantastic landscape there might have been! The current table appears to defy physics by not toppling.

BEN: We saw a sign for a piece of the trail going upstream from the bridge. This piece of trail was not shown or mentioned on the CTC website at the time. We had not yet hiked it in May when we supposedly hiked the entire built trail. After heading down it for a while, we saw why it was not on our map. It started out strong, white-blazed with a finished-looking bridge. Soon though, we found ourselves climbing over logs, scraping through rhododendrons and being pricked by thorns. I'd learned not to mind hikes like this. The flagged but un-blazed, un-built trail was a far better metaphor for my life's journey than a perfectly maintained trail could ever be.

We came down to Daddy's Creek a bit upstream from the bridge and thought we might be able to make it back along the bank to our truck. A steep cliff jutted into the stream, making it a hard route.

Dad, not as afraid of cold water as of heights, climbed and bounded across the jutting rock. I'd learned some cautiousness since our first trip, so I figured I'd only follow Dad if he found a way to the truck from where he was.

"You'd have to swim if you wanted to keep going from here," said Dad. I took his word for it.

......

Elizabeth while putting her fork into the pineapple upside down cake.

We said goodbye and thanks to Carl and Elizabeth. After stopping in Wartburg to see the town one last time, we drove to Caryville, our next town.

The most direct path, TN 116, would have taken us along New River and out of the Plateau at Lake City. We had taken that route when we were scouting motels and trailheads, before we started our month long trek. It was an intriguing route. It kept us on the Plateau and then in the towns that once depended on the Plateau, like Rocky Top (formerly Coal Creek), site of a heated battle over convict labor, and Fraterville, with an associated mine that exploded, killing 216 people.

We didn't go that way. It wasn't just because we had gotten stuck behind a pair of slow moving coal trucks on the earlier trip. It was more that we were tired of country roads making us dizzy or putting us to sleep with their repeated curves.

So instead, we took route 61 away from the edge of the crinkled Plateau and into lower country. I already knew the towns around here. They were in the orbit of my hometown, Oak Ridge. We drove through Oliver Springs, past the roller rink where I'd fallen down at friends' birthday parties when I was young. We drove through Clinton where I had volunteered at the Raptor Center, feeding dead mice to wounded hawks and kestrels. All these places took on a new context now. All the gorges, rivers, fields, mountains and hollers of our travels were close to places I knew. Back when I left for college, they seemed like generic small towns with nothing distinctive about them. Now, I wondered about their histories as distinct places.

Maybe it was because my mind was now used to exploring small towns as unique and complex places. To an ant, an anthill can be as elaborate as Tokyo or New York City, and an antlion might be as terrifying as the clawed and fanged beasts that a human might fear.

We drove onto I-75, one of the least blue highways imaginable. When I was first learning to drive, I avoided the interstates. Dad told me that I needed to master driving first, and I agreed. These days though, driving the interstate felt easier than driving the back roads. It felt too easy, a long predictable line that never zigzagged and wobbled.

I'd ridden with Mom, Dad and my sister Jessie past Caryville on I-75 countless times on my way north to family reunions in Ohio. We never stopped there on those trips, but I still loved it. The drive past Caryville had everything a young boy could love: a tall green statue of a dragon, a billboard shaped like a Christmas tree and a rock formation that looked like a jagged roller-coaster.

Caryville was where we would stay. We'd have time to explore it. As it turned out, the town was far quirkier than even I had imagined.

Sources and Suggested Reading

Rock Tripe:
Encyclopædia Britannica Online, s. v. "rock tripe", accessed July 18, 2013, http://www.britannica.com/EBchecked/topic/506217/rock-tripe.

Devil's Breakfast Table:
Mattheny, Jim. Namesake: Devil's Breakfast Table in Cumberland County. Last updated February 11, 2011. http://www.wbir.com/rss/article/157604/2/Why-do-they-call-it-that-Devils-Breakfast-Table.

Cladonia:
Munger, Gregory T. "Cladonia spp." Last updated 2008. Accessed July 18, 2013. http://www.fs.fed.us/database/feis/lichens/claspp/all.html.

Fraterville Mine Disaster:
Williams, Kate. "Tennessee State Library and archives: Disasters in Tennessee: Fraterville Mine Explosion. Accessed July 18, 2013. http://www.tennessee.gov/tsla/exhibits/disasters/fraterville.htm.

Lake City:
Bell, Augusta Grove. *Circling Windrock Mountain: Two Hundred Years in Appalachia.* Knoxville: University of Tennessee Press, 1999.

HERE THERE BE DRAGONS AND GHOSTS

→ 24 ←

Caryville, stay town and former trail town

BEN: We ate at Shoney's. Dad and I had eaten there many times during my childhood, though not often recently. As a child I'd eaten so much there once the buttons had popped off my shirt.

"I think I'm going to have a desert course next and end with salad," said Dad. Even at the buffet, he bushwhacked off the expected trail.

We settled into the motel. We had gained an extra day by not backpacking at Frozen Head.

From the hilltop parking lot of the motel, we could see and hear the cars on I-75 roaring by like a stream. Molded vehicles of metal, plastic and rubber ran in a constant stampede, burning fuel that came from corpses of the ancient biota. The interstate made roadkill of every critter in its path. From our motel in Dayton, which was away from interstates, we had heard trains. Here we heard only cars.

In Caryville, a looming, bright-green dragon, about the size of seven Ben Poundses shows his teeth to the cars below. Named George by his creators, he stands upright with small arms like a T. Rex in one of my childhood dinosaur books. Thunder Mountain Fireworks Factory built him as an attention-grabbing mascot. Like many billboards and signs near busy highways, he's big and eye-catching in order to lure passing motorists out of their cars. He means more than that to me, though.

When I was younger and would have needed far more Bens to reach the top of him, my family would pass Caryville on the way to visit my Grandma, Dad's mother, in Ohio. After passing that dragon, I would see long jagged lanes of rock going down the Cumberland Plateau in a formation called Devil's Racetrack. I-75 drifted on from there into Kentucky. To my young mind, that dragon symbolized being far from home and out toward the wider world, like a sea serpent on a map. Here there be dragons.

To Thunder Mountain Fireworks Factory's owners, a fire-breathing mascot seemed like the perfect thing for a fireworks store, even if a real fire-breathing dragon would be the last thing they'd want nearby. Speaking of that, Thunder Mountain Fireworks met the fate that all fireworks store owners fear: It caught on fire. Colored sparks flew everywhere as it burnt.

The firefighters could not save the store, but they loved George too much to let him die. They kept a hose on him at all times. He's now a mascot without a purpose.

After resting at the motel, Dad and I stopped to visit George. He stood in front of empty, cracking pavement on one side and tall, tree-covered hills going off into the distance on the other side.

The lack of a store made the dragon more beautiful. With his bright green body, yellow alligator-style belly, claws and spikes, the dragon was a monument to imagination and effort, even if it was all geared toward selling fireworks. It made me want to lean my back forward, curve my fingers into claws and roar to the mountains beyond me. Dad probably thought I was still acting like a three-year-old. I didn't care.

Coming up with the idea of the Cumberland Trail was just as imaginative as coming up with the idea of using a dragon to advertise. The trail used to run through Caryville, down sidewalks and past houses. This old route for the trail still has signs marking it. We passed a few of them on Caryville's residential streets. Plans changed, and the main trail took a different direction than its parents once imagined. Now it narrowly avoids Caryville. It passes nearby to the north, crossing Old Tennessee 63, also known as Royal Blue Road. Red Ash was a community on that part of the road that the CT crosses.

"Supposedly the Red Ash stretch of road is haunted." I told Dad. One story went that a worker died near the coal tower and his ghost haunted the place. Since then, people reported other ghastly things nearby, including ghost women, ghost trains, cult rituals and a red man with horns and goat legs.

"That last one was probably just a man in a costume," I told Dad. I knew the real devil had better things to do, like eating breakfast and racing on his racetrack.

Dad had been to Red Ash before. "I was riding down to Florida from Cincinnati to visit my grandparents when I was little," said Dad, "I remember little hovels along that road."

"The road kept showing up in my dreams," he added. "They weren't scary dreams. Still, you say it's haunted. Well, it has haunted me."

Dad and I rode together in the truck down Red Ash Road. We passed a gravel lot full of non-spooky logging trucks and a railroad loading area. I felt disappointed.

We passed an old railroad bridge. "I've heard something about a ghost train here," I said. "You know, there are ghost trains and ghost ships, but how come you never hear about ghost cars or ghost airplanes. Or what about ghost space ships? Are the ghosts just too lazy to invent new technologies?"

LARRY: The CT does have a ghost car. Online I saw a story about a ghost car seen on Graysville Mountain Road which the CT will have to cross when it is built through that area.

BEN: Everything else near Tennessee 63 from then on was forest and railroad. Dad's hovels were nowhere to be seen. Then, we reached a coal washing plant.

"The last time I was here, when I was working for TVA, this coal washing plant was inactive," said Dad. The plant now had a yellow gate, a few trucks and piles of fresh coal.

"Well, maybe these are ghosts, driving around in ghost trucks, cleaning ghost coal," I said, laughing at how non-spooky that scenario would be. Apparently, the washing plant had just opened again because there was new coal to wash.

I would hate to spend my afterlife driving a coal truck. Some people count themselves lucky to get stuck in work routines, but continuing them after death would be taking it too far. If I had to be stuck in any kind of routine as a ghost, hiking would be my ideal one. I would float around, exploring mountains and rivers, never getting tired.

Dad scanned without success the edges of the road for the site of the old run-down houses from his dreams and memories. "The hovels were among the trees," he said, looking by the side of the road. The trees swayed in the wind. We found no sign of the houses.

Back in Caryville, we stopped in an old brick part of town at a store called "Lilly's Candyville." The store's inside looked like beautiful chaos with lots of candy in colorful wrappers and boxes, including giant gummy bears on sticks and gummy hearts in bags. The floor was made up of interlocking colorful pads like a children's playroom. To continue the chaos, the store had a picture of Jesus, a dream catcher and a statue of Budai, the fat, laughing future Buddha figure popular as a good luck charm in Chinese restaurants.

If I'd still been the boy I was when I passed that dragon in my childhood, I would have been eager for sweets. Instead, all I bought was a pack of gum to stop me from eating all the Triscuits in our room.

And so we ended our day of exploring a town from both of our pasts. I felt closer to Dad after knowing the places that lived on in his dreams, even if they could not stay the way he remembered them any more than the fireworks store could have been saved. The world had moved on, just as both of our lives had since our first memories of Caryville.

We'd spent enough time driving and sitting for Dad's blisters to get

Haunting the CT

better. Our next day would be mostly downhill. Our feet were ready to move again.

Goyo and Mom would be joining us again. Their first hike with us had been so wet that we had to hide under a rock house and Mom had commented on the hole in the crotch of my pants. Their second hike with us had been hot and steep. Maybe this time they'd love the Cumberland Trail.

Sources and Suggested Reading

General:
Bollan, Dallas. Caryville through the Ages." Accessed July 18, 2013. http://www.tngenweb.org/campbell/hist-bogan/caryville-yrs.html.

Campbell County Chamber of Commerce. "County History: Caryville." Accessed July 18, 2012. http://www.campbellcountychamber.com/county_history/caryville.aspx.

Dragon:
News Sentinel Staff. Caryville Fireworks Blaze Prompts Evacuations, Closing of I-75. Last updated May 31, 2011. http://www.knoxnews.com/news/2011/may/31/caryville-fireworks-store-fire-closes-part-i-75/?partner=RSS.

Red Ash Community:
Note: As many of these sources tend to deal with occult or paranormal happenings, they may not be the most reliable. However, they are fun.

Find the Data. "Red Ash Tipple, Campbell, Tennessee." Last updated July 12, 2013. http://mines.findthedata.org/l/58553/Red-Ash-Tipple.

Haunted Red Ash. "Haunted Red Ash Coal Towers in Carryville, TN." Accessed July 18, 2013. http://hauntedredash.wordpress.com/2010/05/02/haunted-red-ash-coal-towers-caryville-tn/.

P., Tama. "Red Ash Coal Towers Caryville, TN-An Eerie place, but is it Haunted?" Updated February 16, 2010. http://paranormalspectrum.ning.com/profiles/blogs/red-ash-coal-towers-caryville.

Strange USA. "Haunt in Red Ash Cemetery, Caryville, TN, 37714." Accessed July 18, 2013. http://www.strangeusa.com/Viewlocation.aspx?id=9164#sthash.fau1xpaO.dpbs.

CREATION

→ 25 ←

Big Bruce Ridge Eastward (Saturday, June 2)
Hike 17: Big Bruce Ridge to Cove Lake
4 miles

"And whatsoever Adam called every living creature, that was the name thereof."-Genesis 2:19 King James Version.

We started at a place called Big Bruce Ridge, or more grimly, Frenchman's Grave Gap. A cool breeze moved through the trees as we stumbled down the hill.

Goyo wore shorts. "Watch out for those plants" said Dad, pointing to the jagged-edged leaves of stinging nettles. They have hairs that inject an itch-inducing substance.

"Why?" Goyo asked.

"Because they sting," said Mom, also wearing shorts.

Goyo did not let the warning bother him. Whenever he passed through a nettle patch, he kicked his knees up and ran through them. Then, afterward, he would stop to scratch himself.

"Are you okay?" I asked him as he scratched himself.

"Yes, I am okay," said Goyo in his clear but accented English, sounding annoyed at being asked.

Goyo got ahead of me, and my parents lagged behind. I stayed in the middle. It was an almost-all downhill route. The trail took us along a stream which ran in a cascade by our side. It was not a single waterfall but rather a narrow string of skips and falls over rocks. The water moved with gravity in will-less mindless motion, not worried for a minute that it was on the wrong path.

A Special Find

Interrupted fern (*Osmunda claytoniana*)

LARRY: This fern is rare enough in Tennessee to make it a special find for me. Look for it above 2,500 feet in the Cumberland Mountains. I have seen this fern on Black Mountain and right beside the main CT as you drop off Bruce Ridge toward Caryville.

It has a couple of lovely relatives, royal fern and cinnamon fern. Both are more common than the interrupted in Tennessee. At lower elevations look for these other two species in wetlands. The higher the elevation, the more likely you are to see the cinnamon fern growing in moist forests in the same habitat that the interrupted fern uses while the royal ferns stick to wetlands. Wetlands are distinguished by soils that are filled with water (saturated) for months during the year.

Change of habitat with elevation occurs for many species. Note the example in the paragraph above. Many of our spring wildflowers which normally grow in sheltered moist forests within less than 50 feet of a stream can be found all over Cumberland Mountain tops. Cooler temperatures with higher elevation reduce evaporation. This effect, along with mountain-top fogs, makes moist habitats common in the mountain areas.

The leaves of ferns are called fronds. My friend, botanist Dr. Leo Collins, recites a fern-centric pun, "With fronds like these who needs anemones." The dissed anemones are wildflowers. Fronds come in two types, those that produce spores (fertile) and those that don't (sterile). Spores are functionally like seeds in that they disperse their species.

The sterile fronds of cinnamon and interrupted fern are very similar. This similarity means that it is easy to walk by an interrupted fern and think it is a cinnamon fern. When fertile fronds are present, hikers can easily separate the two species. The fertile fronds of cinnamon fern are totally different from the sterile fronds. The fertile fronds of the interrupted fern are like the sterile except that some of the middle leaflets are brown and shrunken, interrupting the frond. So when you are hiking in the Cumberland Mountains, take a second look at what are probably cinnamon ferns to see if there are fertile fronds. You might find an interruption.

[Cartoon: Three ferns labeled INTERRUPTED FERN, SENSITIVE FERN, and MARGINAL FERN. The sensitive fern says "What I meant was... DON'T INSULT MY FRONDS!" The marginal fern says "Sigh. CAN'T ANYONE NOTICE ME?"]

Fern Support Group

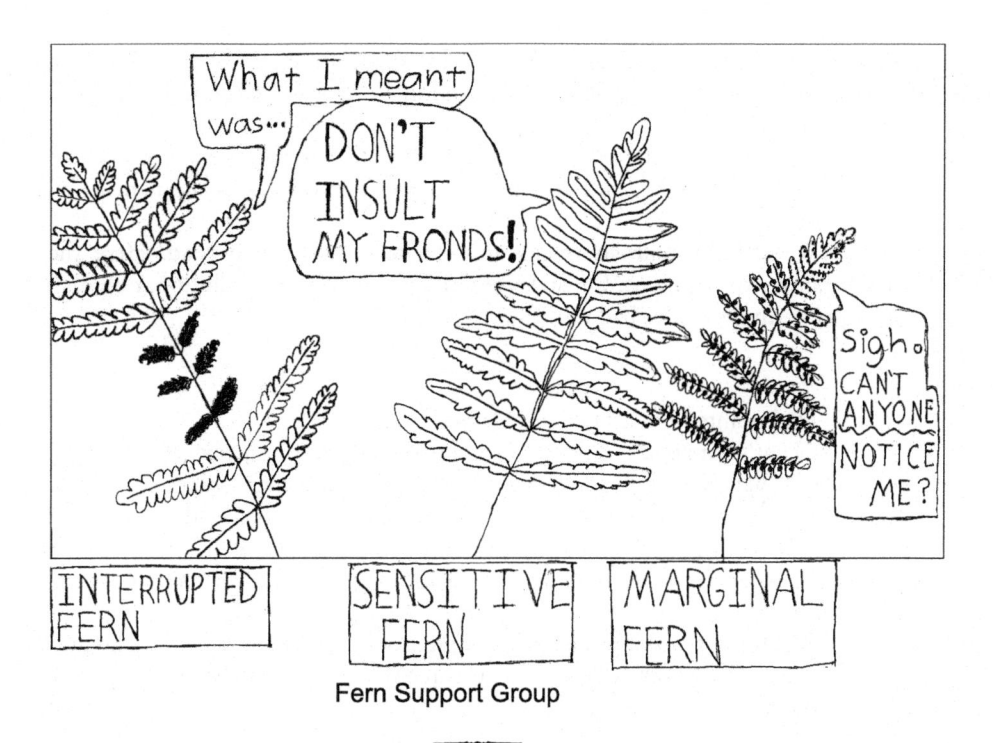

I picked up a red eft. It wiggled whenever I loosened my hold on it. The minute I opened my hand, it climbed out onto my arm, jumped down and scrambled away.

Rather than getting scared stiff or dithering, the salamander ran away. I could not say the same thing about myself. In high school, I'd once slowed down on a left-hand turn after worrying that I was heading into the wrong lane on the road ahead of me. A pickup truck plowed into my car, totaled it and its driver broke her leg. I rode with her in the ambulance as she cried "How could this happen to me?" in sobbing shrieks.

Dad supervised me the next few times after that, commanding me to look before turning, but to turn decisively after looking. It was like I had gone back to my early days when he let me drive my Mom's car around the Roane State parking lot. Many years later, he bought me my own car. It was technically still his, even when I used it to drive far away from him. He knew I couldn't afford the insurance cost. We create our own lives. Yet it helps to have support from the rest of creation. For me, that includes the people who created me. Keeping my distance from my family was not what I wanted to do.

We hiked together along the tracks of an old railroad that ran beside the haunted Red Ash Road. One track looked shinier, newer, and possibly still in use. The other was rustier, older and abandoned. People had seen ghost trains here.

I balanced on the rail. It worked well until I took out my recorder so that I could say, "Look! I'm balancing on a rail." At that exact moment, I fell off.

We left the railroad tracks and crossed the haunted road. Here the stream ran down below us. Once devoid of life due to mine pollution, now fish and aquatic invertebrates had returned.

Dad pointed out a Frazier's Magnolia.

"That's a magnolia?" asked Mom, used only to the species that grew in lawns. Mom had gaps in her own knowledge, even after many hikes with Dad. Later, we came to another magnolia, the cucumber magnolia. Dad pointed out its smaller leaves and lack of lobes at the base. It got its name because its fruit looked like a cucumber. According to Dad, all magnolias had fruits that looked like cucumbers.

We did not make the world, but we can describe and label it. The idea in Genesis's creation story of the first human choosing the names for everything appeals to me.

Naturalist in the Garden.

Now down in the valley, in limestone country, we walked under an interstate bridge. Cars above us sounded like airplanes zooming over us to their far-off destinations. Each car sounded like it needed to go somewhere quickly. We did not.

"Monster poison ivy" said Dad, pointing to big clusters growing along the banks beside us. Nearly every other plant that had taken over this space was exotic except the poison vine.

People do not hike in order to see the interstate. Yet seeing it and hearing it from below was a powerful experience. Before now I knew the interstate as the fast route, a limbo between places, but not as a place under which one could stand. In a way my perspective from under the interstate was anything but unique. To any deer, vulture, coyote, squirrel or opossum, the interstate was just another fixed object and not a route for traveling at all. To see the interstate as part of an ecosystem was to see it as a nuisance, not a convenience.

A turquoise damselfly with black wings landed on a branch. We had not been counting the different kinds of insects that we had passed because neither of us knew the first thing about them. The damselfly did not need us to know about it to be beautiful. Damselfly and dragonfly eyes have several thousand facets or ommatidia in their eyes. A damselfly can also see colors that we humans cannot. So we will never know how we looked to that damselfly.

Insect's view of the BLTs

We joined the Cumberland Trail Builders' Reunion picnic at Cove Lake State Park. Bob Fulcher, Park Manager of the Cumberland Trail State Park, grinned as he played his guitar with a bluegrass band. Then, he came up to the microphone and started calling on people to speak.

Group leaders, surveyors, builders, maintainers and Boy Scout leaders spoke. We heard stories about the struggles in creating the trail. We heard about a golf course with strict rules about trail-building across their land. It seemed reasonable until the golf course built a golf cart path that broke many of their own rules. Judge Harry, who had done maintenance work talked about the constant struggle to keep the path clear. "Nature has a force all of its own," he said. Nature's forces were a problem not just for sections that had already been

What Some Trail Builders Had to Say

Gary Grametbauer, surveyor and designer: I got involved in 1999 and spent many a day along those mountains keeping records of what was there, where the trail could go and where it shouldn't go. It was really rewarding. I got a lot of scars to show for those years. I got to see a lot of places that very few people ever get to see. At the same time it was for such a good cause because once I learned what the project was about, I said, "This is something really great."

Jim Schroder: On the way out that first night I got asked, "Jim, what are you doing here?" because obviously I was really out of shape at that time. But I stuck with it and ended up doing the Soddy Daisy signs, trail design and survey work, of seventeen or eighteen miles which are now open to the public, some of it pretty scenic. I probably have been involved with building trail and investigation work on about every section of the trail, from Cumberland Gap all the way down to the south end of Signal Mountain.

Judge Harry: I'm a member of the Cove Lake Hiking Chapter and came down here to East Tennessee in 2008. I really could not believe the beauty here. In New York City and the suburban area of New York, you really would have to get in a car, travel for a couple of hours, pay ten dollars in tolls and fight traffic to find some wilderness or relative wilderness, and here it's in your back yard. I remember as a kid, summers you'd go into the country and run wild. You'd find frogs, see butterflies, and every day I get up here in Nor-

built, but also for flagging. "Often in a year or two the flagging is gone," said Gary Grametbauer, who had surveyed and flagged many miles of trail. Another volunteer talked about his fear of snakes and how working on the trail had helped him to overcome it. Beyond building and maintaining the trail, there was also the task of raising money for it, which often came down to finding businesspeople that hiked.

I'd noted, as I walked the Rock Creek Bridge, how my work on it was just a small pebble in the conglomerate that was the Cumberland Trail. Now I started to see just how many such pebbles were needed to create a mountain. It was not a matter of a vulture flapping his wings and accidentally pushing the earth into a trail. It took time and sweat.

People told of how the effort involved in building the trail was worthwhile and how it would open up new land for people to enjoy and

....

-ris, I feel like I'm in camp. It's a great feeling.

With the Cove Lake Hiking Chapter, we have been trying to deal with the maintenance of the trails. Nature has a force of all its own, and you can have a trail built and within a month or so, briars have moved in, branches have come in and trees have fallen. So we have set aside one day a week every month to give back to the community of the trails. Just recently we worked on putting a ladder up on a section of the Cumberland Trail, and it was marvelous to see what a bunch of twenty to thirty people could do, lifting generators, climbing a mountain and providing comfort to hikers so they don't have to scale the stone wall. I feel blessed to be here.

Del Truitt, Vice-Chair, Friends of the Cumberland Trail: What we've got on the Cumberland Trail is in my mind much more than the Appalachian Trail. Because we've got so many local folks involved and so many volunteers that it's such a vital part of the core of communities up and down the line, as well as communities all around the Southeast. It's much more than a trail. It's a way of life.

Ann Hook, Tony Hook's wife: I just support Tony as much as I can, whether it's work on the trail or wash his clothes.

Jim Schroder: I've never met anybody on the trail who wasn't a good friend.

....

explore. It was an act of love for nature and for future generations. Yet it was also a bonding experience with people in the present.

Bobby, who had seen our blog, called us both up to the microphone. We stood together. Compared to all the people who had dedicated years to the trail, we didn't have much to say.

"I really haven't done much for the CT," said Dad. He mentioned his rare plant survey, but downplayed its importance. It made sense to be humble here, but I couldn't let his thoughts be the last word. I gestured to Dad for the microphone.

"Well, I've done some work on the trail," I said. I talked about the feeling of satisfaction and awe I felt at looking at my own finished bridge. The audience applauded.

Before leaving the trail builders' reunion, I stopped to talk to Park Manager Bobby Fulcher about our next day's hike. It would lead us past a jagged rock formation called the Devil's Racetrack then back down to Cove Lake State Park.

"If something is big, monstrous, awesome in scale, it might be called the Devil's Breakfast Table, the Devil's Haystack, the Devil's So-and-so," said Bobby. "The Devil's Racetrack name has been used from here to the British Isles for these narrow bands of rocks that people can just imagine what a treacherous thing it would be if you were actually racing on it."

"Watch out," joked Dad as he passed Bobby and I. "He'll hold you down with questions for the rest of your life!"

Sources and Suggested Reading

Dragonflies:
Borror, Donald J., and White, Richard E. *Peterson Field Guide Series: A Field Guide to Insects America North of Mexico.* New York: Houghton Mifflin 1998.

Grrlscientist. *30,000 Facets Give Dragonflies a Different Perspective: The Big Compound Eye in the Sky.* July 8, 2009. http://scienceblogs.com/grrlscientist/2009/07/08/30000-facets-give-dragonflies/(accessed November 30, 2012).

University of California Museum of Paleontology. "Introduction to the Odonata: Dragonflies and Damselflies." Accessed July 18, 2013. http://www.ucmp.berkeley.edu/arthropoda/uniramia/odonatoida.html.

Cumberland Mountain Region.

Interlude 5
Cumberland Mountain:
More like a Ridge

BY LARRY

➜ ⬅

DESCRIPTION

When a rug is pushed, parallel wrinkles form perpendicular to the push. The high places of the Appalachian region, including the Cumberland Plateau, are broad wrinkles formed by a push from the southeast. That push came from the plate on which Africa sits.

Sediment layers start out horizontal because they are deposited by gravity. As sediments are buried, the pressure from the weight on top turns them into rock layers. These layers can be bent (wrinkled) and even broken by the plate collisions. The breaks are called faults.

Large blocks of rock can be split out and pushed over the top of other rock layers. The CT runs up onto such a block, the Pine Mountain Fault Block. It is very roughly rectangular, 125 miles by 15 miles. Pine Mountain is the northern edge of the block while Cumberland Mountain is the southern edge. To me, Cumberland Mountain is too long to be called a mountain. It should be called a ridge.

Generally, the southeast-facing slope (the scarp slope) of Cumberland Mountain is steeper than the northwest-slope (the dip slope). Along the scarp slope several sandstone layers have been bent from the horizontal to nearly vertical. The Devil's Racetrack that you see from I-75 is the protruding of these layers from the southwest corner of the fault block. Two vertical layers continue to protrude but to a lesser degree as you hike the CT to the northeast.

THE CUMBERLAND MOUNTAIN TREK

We took three short hikes to do the entire CT on Cumberland Mountain as shown on the CTC website, but at the time we hiked there was a huge, 30 mile, missing trail piece between the Lafollette area and the Cumberland Gap area. The old CT did or does continue on along the crest of Cumberland Mountain to the Gap. Gene Smith, who I met while hiking, has hiked this gap in the CT walking mostly on ATV roads and seeing some of the old CT signs.

Much of the land has now been acquired so the trail building for this long stretch is underway. Ben and I had a chance to chat with the state park trail-building crew as they started in to build the 30 miles of trail. They and others to come will take about four years to build all the way to Cumberland Gap.

You can access some very lovely old CT by making a reservation for McCloud Mountain Restaurant. Your reservation allows you to enter this private area. The old CT runs east from this development past a CT access trail and on to an impressive natural arch.

CUMBERLAND MOUNTAIN RARE PLANTS

My first work as a field botanist was a rare plant survey (1988-89) of Cumberland Gap National Historical Park. I was the main author of a National Park Service document covering that study, <u>Rare Plant Assessment and Checklist for Cumberland Gap National Historical Park</u>. I'm still amazed the Park service hired me, as I had little on my resume at that point in my botany career to show I could do the work. I must have been the lowest bidder.

I found six Tennessee listed rare plants during my original work. We saw none of these as we hiked the CT in the national park. This illustrates that though there are many rare plants along the CT, there are many more in the public lands surrounding the trail. Go to <u>www.benandlarryincumberland.com</u> for a list of rare plants along the Cumberland Mountain CT.

HIKING WITH THE DEVIL

→ 26 ←

Cumberland Mountain east of I-75 (Sunday, June 3)
Hike 18: Eagle Bluff to Cove Lake
6 miles.

BEN: We'd hiked on this part of the trail in the summer before my freshman year of college. Mom and my sister Jessie had joined us then. Dad's left knee was not giving him trouble yet. He was already planning a book. All of us, even usually-long-pants Dad, walked in shorts through grass and brambles along I-75. Then we climbed uphill while carrying heavy backpacks. After we returned, Jessie swore that she would never backpack on the Cumberland Trail again. Dad got a kidney stone probably as result of dehydration on this backpack. However, the trip appealed to me enough that I felt like returning.

This time we split the hike into two downhill hikes from Eagle Bluff. We'd cover the same distance with less strain and more time for wild strolling.

We walked on an ATV road from Eagle Bluff. We followed the ridge-top along lanes of raised rock. Our path led us right between and sometimes on the jagged lanes of sandstone that are so prominent at Devil's Racetrack.

Wild blueberries thrived here. Another bush also looked like a blueberry bush to me. I munched on the berries. Dad, not content to just eat, looked at its leaves with his field glass.

"This is a huckleberry," he said. "See how it glistens?"

He gave his field glass to me.

"See these golden dots?" said Dad. "I usually get my eye much closer to the lens than you do." I put my eye straight on the lens and saw the golden specks. "Look at a blueberry leaf properly," said Dad, "It doesn't have those spots." The seeds were chewier than the blueberry's seeds but still delicious.

When we actually reached the top of Devil's Race Track, an American

Devil's Racetrack.

Ben & Berries

BEN: We found seven succulent kinds of wild fruit: highbush blueberries, lowbush blueberries, huckleberries, dew berries, blackberries and raspberries. Here is my quick guide to some of them, based on what Dad told me during the hike.

Blackberries

As the name implies these are black when ripe. They grow on bushes. When you pick them, a core comes off with the fruit.

Raspberries

Our wild raspberries in Tennessee are also black when ripe, but to the north or in the grocery store you will find red ones. Only the fruit comes off, not the stem or core

Dewberries

These fruits look like blackberries but grow on vines, not bushes. They have a tangy taste.

For more on blueberries and huckleberries, see Dad's section in this chapter.

flag showed red stripes against the blue sky. It hung from a dead tree. I wondered who had placed it there and whether they worried at all about flag protocol, given that the flag would probably get wet and tattered easily up here. Looking down, we could see Cove Lake, the billboard above our motel and tiny cars on a shoelace of interstate.

"I don't want to spend a heck of a lot of time here," said Dad. "I've

My Huckleberry Friend and Becoming a Wildland Frugivore

Black huckleberry (*Gaylusaccia baccata*).

LARRY: Warning: *Becoming a wild-land frugivore (an eater of wild fruit) requires care. Please go slow. Learn the plant well before you eat it. Don't get poisoned.*

The huckleberry looks like a blueberry but is not as popular for eating. The blueberries and huckleberries are in the heath family with the rhododendrons. You will find both of these berries along the CT, most often on sandstone derived soils. The overlook area above the Devil's Racetrack is a good place to look for them. Both are shrubs with smallish, simple, alternate leaves and edible berries.

Perhaps the only type of huckleberry along the CT is the black huckleberry (*Gaylusaccia baccata*). There are three other species of huckleberries known from elsewhere in Tennessee. The fascinating box huckleberry (*Buxella brachycera*) is often placed in its own genus (*Buxella*). It grows on thin soils over the Cumberland Plateau's sandstone. Even though thin soils over sandstone are a frequent habitat of the CT, I saw no box huckleberries as we hiked. It is sporadic. It can be seen at the overlook near the headquarters of the Big South Fork (BSFNSRRA). It forms an evergreen ground cover.

There has been little consensus on splitting up the blueberries into species. The UT Herbarium website shows 8 species for Tennessee. We will go with those eight.

You can divide them into lowbush and highbush. Think of lowbush as waist height and below and highbush as head height and above. Of course, immature highbush species are short but should not fruit at that size. The highbush species of the CT are *Vaccinium corymbosum, V. fuscatum, V. arboreum,* and *V. stamineum.* Of that list, only the first two are worth eating.

been here a lot." Exploration of new places was his goal. It was mine too, but I'd only been here once. Vistas around me inspired endless picture-taking. Soon Dad was far ahead of me.

The Racetrack's long lanes of stone reminded me of closed pocket knife blades or a stegosaurus's back. It had started out a normal wall of sandstone with layers of variable hardness, but the collision of plates turned the layers vertical (see Cumberland Mountain Interlude). Water eroded out the softer layers, forming the path where I walked with jutting quartzite sandstone

....

The lowbush species of the CT are the common *V. pallidum* and the rare on the Cumberland Plateau *V. hirsutum*. *V. hirsutum* is the hairy blueberry, a "tactile" experience for the mouth. We found it in the Laurel-Snow part of the CT.

Generally, blueberries are bluish while huckleberries are closer to black. Blueberries usually have a thin whitish coating called a *bloom*, which wipes off. Eating huckleberries is different from eating blueberries because of the taste and the larger seeds. The smaller, more numerous seeds of the blueberry are hardly noticeable while eating.

Some of you will want to learn these shrubs during the time of year when they do not have fruit. Look at the underside of the leaves with a hand lens. If there are shiny, yellow dots, then it is a huckleberry.

You may be tempted by another fruit growing with the huckleberry and the blueberry. Chokeberry is a good and a bad name for this fruit. You may choke on it, but technically it is not a berry. It is a pome. The most famous pome is the apple. Pomes have cores with the seeds surrounded by the flesh of the fruit, while berries have the seeds scattered in the flesh.

Chokeberry juice is not sold under that name, for obvious reasons. I have seen it as aronia juice in supermarkets though apparently no longer stocked. *Aronia* in italics is its scientific name.

Blackberries, raspberries and dewberries are compound berries made up of little berry compartments with their own skins. The strawberry is not a berry since the seeds are on the outside. Watch for our very tasty wild strawberry. It is occasional along the CT in somewhat disturbed areas. The strawberry-like plants in your yard are most likely a tasteless non-native plant. The yard plants have yellow flowers while the true strawberries have white flowers.

....

on either side.

I caught up with Dad. On past hikes, I'd gotten restless and strode ahead of him. Now though, I didn't want to miss out on anything that he said. Even away from the views and under a canopy as we now were, the Racetrack's glory seemed to still be influencing me, making me see the glory in every sprouting thing around my boots. Dad could help me learn more.

In this area, people had reported sightings of the skunk ape, a mysterious smelly creature. We didn't see one, but did find a skunky plant. Galax flowers growing around us caused the air to smell of skunk. Yet when I sniffed an individual flower, it had no scent.

LARRY: Perhaps the scent is created by a reaction in the air.

BEN: People sometimes collect galax for floral arrangements due to its sturdy leaves. According to Dad, so far no one has figured out how galax produces its rotten smell. Sulfur compounds seem a likely candidate.

The interstate's sound was a loop of low and high sounds, like ocean waves crashing in and out, interrupted by bird calls. The closer we got, the louder it was, even when we could not see the cars.

"You're stepping on my feet," said Dad. "Just thought you might want to know."

At Bruce Creek Falls, water flowed down a series of drops as spectacular as any natural waterfalls. It was the work neither of angels nor devils. Humans built it, as was obvious from the drill holes in the rocks on either side.

Whenever Bruce Creek flooded in the past, it eroded at the interstate's embankment from below. To protect I-75, engineers blasted the rock to make a small artificial canyon into which the stream would flow. The Cumberland Trail runs along that canyon, often following where the streambed used to be.

Devil's Racetrack and Bruce Creek Canyon had inspired me, all those years ago on our previous trip, to consider writing a book about the Cumberland Trail. To live in a world where tectonic plates collided to create a racetrack and engineers created canyons invited exploration and explanation. Before that trip, I had ridden on I-75 many times but had neither noticed the canyon below it nor ever thought that the sturdy interstate was vulnerable to the same water erosion that gave the racetrack its appearance of jagged blades. The idea that the land had stories behind it appealed to me then, and it appeals to me now as I write these words.

We climbed up a slope of loose rocks (riprap), another measure to protect the raised interstate from erosion. The traffic flowed above the slope, sometimes visible through trees and a tall fence. Large rocks that either tumbled down from the plateau top or had gotten bulldozed here to make way for the interstate were everywhere. As if to show that humans weren't the only living things that had adapted their structures to the land, a tree hugged one of the rocks with its bark.

A blackberry bush grew near our path. "See," said Dad, "these are not raspberries but blackberries. There's an inner core which stays with the berry." I shoved one in my mouth and loved the mix of sweet and sour flavors.

"Here's a concrete drainage thing from the interstate," said Dad.

"Con creek?" I asked, thinking that was what he had said.

"Yes," said Dad, amusedly. "It's a way of conning the creek."

On our previous trip, we had bushwhacked through tall grass and brambles near the interstate. We had been too far below it to see cars, but we could see a billboard meant for them. Surrounded by tall grass, shrubs and young trees, the billboard had looked out of place without the interstate visible. It was like an absurd Mayan temple rising out of the jungle, a relic of civilization in a landscape with no other visible signs of it. I do not remember what the billboard said.

Now, forest had taken over. Now-taller trees obstructed our view of the billboard. This time, we never found ourselves in high grass or thorns as before. The canopy's dark shade seemed to have blocked that kind of growth. Without words, the trees gave a more powerful message than the billboard.

"You are not in control," they said. "We will claim our ground."

We stopped for lunch in a place of limestone outcrops. I searched the low opening of a cave for salamanders by lying on my back with my head just at the edge of the cave entrance. After pointing my flashlight up, I saw the skinny red shiny body of a cave salamander sitting in a crack.

Finding that salamander made me wonder about other cracks and crevices. I pointed my light at any dark place in bark or rock, wanting to see what lived inside of it. Soon I found myself behind Dad. I kept looking though. The trail dipped down to a flat, muddy place. Both of us equally driven by obsessive curiosity, Dad and I left the trail to explore.

Beavers had gnawed and piled wood here. They'd built a dam for a pond, but much of the water had evaporated or flowed away, leaving a stream through wet grassy ground rather than a pond.

I focused in on dragonflies, my new obsession. They looked beautiful and distinct. They seemed like flying gems with their many colors. A common whitetail, with dark marks on its wings, landed on a rotting log. I snatched a lucky picture before it flew.

I stalked a thinner one with green eyes and yellow marks on the tail until it landed on a seedling, before realizing that I was sinking deeper and deeper in the mud. I yanked my leg out of several feet of it.

Other creatures had gotten their feet stuck in places along here too, judging by nearby footprints. Mine was just another footprint to join them.

Down on one knee in a drier spot, Dad examined thin green stocks of a plant in the genus *Equisetum* that he thought might be a new hybrid for Tennessee. Even if we pursued different things, we both pursued. Pursuing felt

Snake Doctors

BEN: Country people in the Deep South (mostly south of the region described in this book) often call dragonflies "Snake Doctors." The name relates to the scaly, needle-like appearance of dragonflies and to a false superstition that dragonflies take care of snakes. Some old-timers, with varying levels of fear, assume that if a dragonfly is present, a snake must be nearby. When people saw mother dragonflies dipping their tails into streams to dispense eggs, they might have imagined a snake underneath the water, receiving food or medicine.

Frogs eat dragonflies, and many snakes eat frogs, but that's hardly the same thing as the dragonflies taking care of the snakes. The best way to avoid stepping on a snake is to watch the ground, not the air. Dragonflies deserve to be thanked for the mosquitoes and other pests they eat. Still, I've heard worse superstitions, like the idea that ostriches, if threatened, will hide their heads in the sand. Anyone who's survived an ostrich kick can tell you otherwise.

Don't feel disappointed if you wanted the myths about snake doctors to be true. The facts about them can also be pretty strange:

1. Prehistoric dragonflies had wingspans of up to two feet.

2. Most dragonflies here in the U.S. spend most of their lives in the naiad stage, in which they live underwater. Some of them eat tadpoles.

3. Adult dragonflies have sex while flying, sometimes in a heart-shaped embrace, but don't let that fool you into thinking it's pleasant. The females often get quite a few punctures by the time it's over.

4. Speaking of dragonfly sex: dragonfly females usually mate with more than one partner. However, some dragonfly males are able to scrape other males' sperm out of the females.

great, even with my legs covered in mud.

Throughout the hike, Dad had pondered things he did not know and figured out things he did not at first understand. He looked at leaves with his magnifying glass to view them, just to pick out the exact species. It was an admirable curiosity. Maybe by hiking with Dad I would gain some of it.

Back on the trail, fallen trees lay everywhere. Possibly a storm had knocked them over. The Cumberland Trail Conference had warned us about these fallen trees on their website.

When we first started our hike, I'd been eager to jump off of logs for no good reason other than fun, while Dad climbed around them. Back then, Dad's aversion to jumping seemed unnecessary and fearful.

By now though, I'd seen Dad run down steep off-trail slopes and sometimes even slide on them. He'd struck up conversations with strangers easily. Neither rain, nor heat, nor mud, nor blood blisters, nor ticks, nor tickborne diseases, nor copperheads nor rattlesnakes had stopped him from exploring for plants. He was willing to sleep on the uncomfortable ground and get slapped by me while he tried to sleep. He avoided unnecessary hassles, like jumping off of logs or sitting near the edges of cliffs. When I did things like that, his eyes grew nervous, but when it came to the hassles of finding plants, he was unstoppable. "Kickass botanist" was the only way to describe Dad. I felt proud to be out with him on his quests.

So now, as we found trees in our path, I was happy to follow Dad and find routes around them.

The next day, we'd walk on more of Cumberland Mountain and see what it had to offer us.

Sources and Suggested Reading

General:
Simmons, Morgan. "Hike of the Month: Devil's Racetrack." September 4, 2009.http://www.knoxnews.com/news/gosmokies/heavenly-vew-devils-racetrack. Accessed March 3, 2015.

Galax:
Predny, Mary L. and Chamberlain, James L.*Galax (Galax urceolata): An Annotated Bibliography*. Asheville: U.S. Forest Service 2005. Accessed at http://www.sfp.forprod.vt.edu/pubs/sfpdoc9.pdf.

Amoroso, Jame. "Wild Ideas: The Odor of Galax." *Chinquapin*. 10, no. 2 (2002). Accessed at http://sabs.appstate.edu/sites/sabs.appstate.edu/files/chinquapin-issues/Chinq10-2.pdf.

Skunk Ape:
Note: As with ghosts, information about cryptids (legendary creatures) tends to be unscientific and unreliable.

Manley, Roger *Weird Tennessee: Your Travel Guide to Local Legends and Best-Kept Secrets.* New York: Sterling 2010.

Odonata:
Ackerman, Jennifer. "Dragonfly Mating Game." *National Geographic.* April 2006. Accessed September 17, 2014. http://ngm.nationalgeographic.com/2006/04/dragonfly-mating/ackerman-text/1.

Borror, Donald J., and White, Richard E. *Peterson Field Guide Series: A Field Guide to Insects America North of Mexico.* New York: Houghton Mifflin, 1998.

Sabet-Peyman, Jayson. "Introduction to the Odonata." Last updated July 16, 2000. Accessed September 17, 2014. http://www.ucmp.berkeley.edu/arthropoda/uniramia/odonatoida.html.

Zielinski, Sarah. "Fourteen Fun Facts about Dragonflies." *Smithsonian.com.* October 5, 2011. Accessed September 17, 2014. http://blogs.smithsonianmag.com/science/2011/10/14-fun-facts-about-dragonflies/.

HOT TANG

→ 27 ←

Cumberland Mountain Part 2 (Sunday, May 3)
Hike 18: Eagle Bluff to Tank Springs
5 miles.

BEN: Yesterday, we'd gotten confused and followed an old part of the trail for a while, one that builders had abandoned when they decided to start work again.

Today though, we were not going to make that mistake again. Starting at Eagle Bluff, we crisscrossed our way onto a racetrack lane and followed it. In doing that, we missed about 300 feet of blazed trail.

"I'm not worried about it," said Dad. "Are you?"

"No." I said. Maybe at one point I'd considered our hike a sham if we missed a single foot of the CT. Now I just wanted to walk and experience.

While "Devil's Racetrack" usually refers to the lanes visible from I-75, rock formations here were similar on a smaller scale.

Dad caught me stepping on his feet. It happened many times during our trek. Usually, it led to me going out in front and detaching myself from Dad. Now, my mind shifted between drifting and concentrating on the world around us. My body stayed behind Dad stepping at his pace.

The forecast warned of thunderstorms. Clouds covered the sky, but the only sign of an oncoming storm was the wind tickling the leaves. So far we had never been trapped on top of a mountain when lightning could hit us. I hoped it would stay that way.

After walking on top of the rock lane, we did a lane change and walked in the space below another, taller lane. It towered over us: a balance beam with no mat. It had ferns and birches which could trip any tormented soul who tried to race on it.

We raced along, often on narrow rock lanes, hoping to avoid the coming lightning. Thorny bushes slowed us. It was as if the bushes were saying "Yeah, you might have missed the thorns by the interstate, but you can't stop us up here." I wondered how I'd managed to leave this place the last time in shorts without looking like a bloody Morse code of pokes and scratches.

"Something of a natural guard rail here," said Dad as we walked on a raised spine of rock with a knee-high rock wall that guarded us from falling. It felt like being on the rampart of a castle or China's Great Wall. Dad was happy to avoid the usual risks of being in a high place and even enjoyed the view.

"That's the Ridge and Valley physiographic province," said Dad, pointing to an area way below us. The only stores, roads, houses and lawns we could see were in this lower region. From here, they were like small splotches of bird droppings on the giant windshield of the natural world. Hazy bumps of ridges went further and further away from us. The ridges appeared free of any houses, farms or clearings. Bird songs were louder here than any sounds of traffic.

We humans had affected this land in ways that weren't obvious, though, like killing the bison and wolves that once lived here and polluting the air. We're still on a racetrack toward destroying much of the wild world around us. Unless we can see the other lanes of life, we don't know what we might be missing in the future.

"We should be able to pick out the stores down there," said Dad, his science-sense tingling at a new mystery to solve.

Soon though, he gave up, unable to tell a Walmart roof from a Kroger. So, he went back to looking for threatened and endangered plants. Those mattered as more than a moment's interest. We wandered past a stone window, an opening in the rock lane, then off the trail, drawn by curiosity into a wet place between lanes with dense sedge clumps. The mud in them didn't suck me in, but it was sticky.

A tall lane of rock jutted from the ground to tower over us. Dad, who was hungry, hiked ahead to the shelter where we stayed during our thirsty backpacking trip years ago. I grabbed my keychain flashlight and started shining it into the cracks in the rock, like an unchecked NSA agent of the forest, eager to invade the privacy of every creature around me.

I shined my light into a crack in the rock: a spider web. Another crack: another web, thick, with a hole in the middle. A larger crack: full of tiny flying

Goats

LARRY: Feral (escaped) goats like to live in rocky areas like the top of Cumberland Mountain. They don't seem to survive indefinitely as do feral pigs.

insects. Another web, in more plain view, hosted a caught grasshopper which cast a shadow onto the orangish rocks. The rocks were a giant apartment complex with tenants who could eat guests and other tenants. The tiny life of an insect or spider contains as much drama as the life of an elk if not more.

Last time we had come here, we had lost the trail's blazes, drunk all our water and wandered around for hours trying to find the shelter.

LARRY: This is an exaggeration. We did get briefly off track on that backpack years ago. When you're thirsty, hoping for water, the time seems much longer, which is why Ben remembers it as hours.

BEN: I worried that I might lose contact with Dad, given that he was so far ahead of me. I called him on my phone and told him to expect me. "Is the trail shelter visible from the trail?" I asked.

"Yes," said Dad. Just then, I saw it up the hill from where I stood.

Without any fear of losing Dad, I headed back to the cliff to explore more.

Then Dad called me the old fashioned way by shouting "Ben!"

Being back at that shelter reminded me again of our earlier backpack in the area. We had found a small muddy stream nearby, boiled water from it to kill germs and added Tang for flavor. Hot Tang seemed like the most delicious thing that night, because of my thirst. We slept below the shelter's roof and heard the echoing sound of dogs barking, coming up from a town in the valley below.

This time, without my throat feeling dry enough to start a brush fire, being here was a different experience.

The trail ran up a ladder through a crack in the rock and then up a small boulder with easy hand and foot holds.

I climbed up the rock with my camera, my recorder and my pad of paper put away, not wanting to drop any of them. So I just enjoyed feeling contact with rock below and sky above.

Younger Ben Toon loves his questionable boiled water with Tang.

Then, after hiking along with Dad, I changed my mind. I had to get a picture. While Dad was ahead, I skibbled back to the rock with a view of the ladder-top, the racetrack's rocks jagging or roller-coasting down and the Cumberland Mountains. The pictures didn't show the vastness of the view.

I swore that I would think and experience rather than dictate or take photographs. The mountains, trees and tall rocks could be even grander without an idiotic writer walking through them, yammering to himself about how grand they were. Also, maybe avoiding taking pictures or dictating would let me hike right alongside Dad rather than lagging behind him.

Dad, once I caught up with him, still wanted pictures, though.

"Take a picture of these rock lanes," he said, as we came to a narrow pass between two of them. "The picture will really show what the racetrack area is like." I groaned and took a quick snapshot.

When I saw a lizard with orange, gray and blue scales on a tree trunk, I knew I had to break my new rule against photos again. Photos could be used to look up which kind of lizard it was. I just had to avoid confusing the flat image of the lizard from its scrambling, breathing reality.

"An annual is a plant that only lives one year, then dies," said Dad, as we walked downhill, "So there's no evolutionary sense in putting off flowering to next year. If you're a perennial, you have more of a chance to choose when to flower, but if you're dying, you make the last effort to flower, no matter what."

A Lizard of a Different Color

Eastern fence lizard (*Sceloporus undulates*)

BEN: On our rehearsal hike we saw some gray lizards that Dad immediately called "fence lizards." On this hike we saw lizards that were orangish with blue along the sides of their bellies. Neither of us could tell what they were. As it turns out, the blue sides and blue throat patch are common for eastern fence lizard males.

Both sexes love open sunny spaces, like the rocks of Devil's Racetrack. They often escape up trees or cliffs, which we saw them doing. On the Cumberland Trail, they tend to live close to such high escape routes, but further west they live out in the prairie and hide under brush. They eat insects, snails, spiders and centipedes. The ones we found were possibly getting ready to mate, which usually happens any time between March and August.

Wow, that sounded deep. I fumbled for my voice recorder, giving up on my resolution entirely.

"Sometimes, in difficult situations, a plant will flower, sensing that it's dying," Dad added. "More often it's going to hold back its energy and wait for a better time to spend its energy capital."

We continued talking about how most flowering plants have both male and female parts on an individual, allowing occasional self-fertilization. I quoted misremembered things from long-ago biology classes. Dad responded by correcting my terms. It was great to talk like this, two curious people, neither of us knowing everything, all the while descending a slope and grabbing tree trunks for support. My notions about moving beyond words and photographs could wait.

We could tell when we were near civilization by the chugging sound of a train. After passing under an in-use railroad bridge and the ruins of an older one, we found Tank Springs.

Tank Springs

BEN: Bob Fulcher, with whom I spoke at the builders' conference, had much to say about the Tank Springs area and its relation to the nearby town of LaFollette's history, particularly its rail lines.

"As you hike down to Tank Springs, you hike on the old rail track that served Harvey Lafollette and his coal cutters," said Bob. "That was the line that people used to get into LaFollette to the company stores."

While the passenger route to LaFollette is abandoned now and used for a walking trail, the old L&N Railroad, which runs above it, still gets trains. Bob Fulcher said that it was routed through the area to get the coal that the LaFollette Company was mining and manufacturing into coke.

"When you get to Tank Springs, you'll see people lining up to drink that water, because they're there every day, every night, getting water at that spring," said Bob. "There are many people who do not have good water in Campbell County, and they fill the bed of their truck with empty jugs, go there and get whatever they need to keep water in the house and fill them right there. So you should be sure and take a big drink right there and share that experience with people. There are literally thousands of people who use that water. It amazes me."

A Living Fossil?

Fraser's magnolia (*Magnolia fraseri*) and other magnolias

LARRY: All life has a single common ancestor, and DNA has been passed from generation to generation from that ancient common ancestor. If we accept these points, then each living thing has evolved over the same very long period of time. With this understanding, all living things are equally evolved.

It could be argued that the opportunity to evolve is proportional to the number of generations rather than the number of years. On this basis, surely fruit flies (generation time a few weeks) are more evolved than humans (generation time many years).

A species that appears to be similar to a fossil from long ago is called a living fossil. This suggests, somewhat misleadingly, that somehow the living fossil has evolved more slowly than other species. Evolution is often driven by a changing environment which causes selection to change. The lack of a changing environment might explain the famous fish living fossil, coelacanth. It has changed little in 400 million years. It lives deep in the ocean where perhaps the environment is more constant than elsewhere.

Our magnolias are living fossils in the sense that they share many characteristics with fossils of early flowering plants, for example, spiral arrangement of stamens (male parts). Magnolia-like plants show up in the fossil record from about 120 million years (Jones 2005) making them our early flowering plant living fossils. I have no idea why magnolias have evolved slowly.

There is an outstanding place on this section of the CT to see magnolias. As you hike from Tank Springs heading toward Eagle Bluff, look for magnolias as you start to climb the hill after leaving the streamside. There are four magnolias here, umbrella, big-leaf, Fraser's and cucumber. Another member of the magnolia family but not the magnolia genus, tulip poplar, is also here. These four are the entire CT magnolia list.

Elsewhere, I'm starting to see another magnolia, the popular southern magnolia, spreading from cultivation. We should expect it to eventually turn up along the CT. The sweetbay magnolia is another one that occasionally spreads from cultivation. The southern and sweetbay magnolias in the wild are mostly found on the coastal plain.

To recognize our CT magnolias from their leaves, look for large, simple (one blade area per leaf), alternate (leaves alone at their stem position) and entire (smooth edged) leaves. Clustering of leaves for umbrella, big-leaf and Fraser's make the leaves look whorled rather than alternate, but a close look should clear that up. Cucumber magnolia is clearly alternate.

Cucumber magnolia leaves are smaller than the other magnolias and can easily be confused with paw-paw leaves. The leaf shapes are a bit different and the buds are distinctive, but perhaps the best way to separate them is smell. Crush up a leaf. If it has a strong odor which is often described as oilcan, then it is paw-paw.

Here's my hopefully easy key for CT magnolia leaves. Start with the "1" and follow the indentation.

1. Leaves clearly alternate and not clustered............Cucumber magnolia
                                      (*Magnolia acuminata*)
1. Leaves clustered, often very large
    2. Leaf blade bases v-shaped ....Umbrella magnolia
                                  (*Magnolia tripetala*)
    2. Leaf blade bases with "ear" lobes   (cont. below)
        3. Leaves very whitened underneath (bud and twigs hairy) ....big-leaf magnolia (*Magnolia macrophylla*)
        3. Leaves not so whitened underneath (bud and twigs hairless).......Fraser's magnolia (*Magnolia fraseri*)

Of all the magnolias along the Cumberland Trail, Fraser's is the hardest to find. It is much more common in the Blue Ridge Mountains, the mountains along the North Carolina border, than on the Cumberland Plateau. Our records of Fraser's for the Plateau are few and recent. I suspect some botanists saw it but assumed it was big-leaf with unusually small leaves.

At Tank Springs, spring water falls constantly from a spigot. It had been an unbelievable relief to find that spigot last time on the thirsty tang trip. Even now, after a somewhat less thirsty walk, it was wonderful. I guzzled down the delicious water, then turned my head and loved the fresh, cool natural water splashing on my curls. It was a wordless force, a sensation. Nothing I could say into my voice recorder could do justice to it.

Our hike today felt great because it was just the two of us, without any other hikers or the interstate we followed the day before. However, even though this stretch of the CT looked wild, it had grown back from logging.

Animals introduced by humans had also influenced this land. Although we didn't see any feral goats this time, Dad told me he had seen them here before.

I drove back to the motel while Dad went shopping. I'd forgotten my room key and couldn't get into the room. So, I talked about our project to the manager's son, who appeared to be around thirteen years old and stood at the counter.

"We're writing a book about hiking," I told him. "Today we were up near the Devil's Racetrack. Have you heard of it?"

"No," he said.

"You can see it from here," I said, pointing out the window at a hazy strip of rocks going down the mountainside. He might have noticed it and just not heard of it by name.

"Have you been up there?" I asked.

"No," he said again. Well, hiking was not for everyone.

"What kinds of things are you writing about?" he asked. "Are you writing about snakes?"

"Yes," I said. "Do you like snakes?"

"No," he said. He mentioned finding a snake under the hood of a car once and being scared by it.

When I was his age, I had none of his experience of working a family business. Perhaps it was a trade-off that I knew about hiking on the Devil's Racetrack.

That evening, I sat outside, sometimes playing cell phone games, sometimes just looking up at the Racetrack, as the light grew dim. I tried to balance my technology escapism with my sense of the here and now.

Previously, when we were on the trail in the remote New River area, the only people we saw were friends who we invited to come with us or loggers who were doing their job. It's not a highly visited area.

Dad decided to have our only three-day backpack there. After all, there was no motel for us to stay in, but plenty of places to explore. It was out of order and the only time we would break one of Dad's geological divisions of the trail (see the Interludes), but that did not matter. What intrigued me was being away from all the roaring cars and once again freeing myself to wander around in the evening in a real space, not cyberspace, and also in my mind.

Sources and Suggested Reading

General:
Brill, David. *Cumberland Odyssey: A Journey in Pictures and Words Along Tennessee's Cumberland Trail and Plateau.* Johnson City, Tennessee: Mountain Trail Press, 2010.

Cumberland Trail Conference. *CTC's Guide To Hiking the Justin P. Wilson Cumberland Trail with Maps/Guides.* Accessed July 19, 2012. www.cumberlandtrail.org (accessed July 19, 2012).

Fence Lizard:
Behler, John L., and F. Wayne King. *The Audubon Society Field Guide to North American Reptiles and Amphibians.* New York: Chanticleer Press Inc., 1979.

Leache, Adam D. and Reeder, Tod W. "Molecular Systematics of the Eastern Fence Lizard (Sceloporus undulatus): A Comparison of Parsimony, Likelihood, and Bayesian Approaches." *Systemic Biology* 51 (no. 1): 44-68. 2002.
  http://bama.ua.edu/~molsyst/page2/assets/Leache2002.pdf (accessed March 16, 2015).
    The taxonomy of fence lizards may have been shuffled around a bit since 2002, but the ones in Tennessee are still considered *"undulatus."*

Magnolias:
Jones, Ronald L. *Plant Life of Kentucky: An Illustrated Guide to the Vascular Flora.* Lexington: University of Kentucky, 2005.

NAMES FOR EVERYTHING

⇥ 28 ⇤

Anderson and Cross Mountain Section
(Tuesday, Wednesday Thursday, June 5, 6, 7)
Hike 20: Bruce Gap to Norma Road
13.3 miles

⇥What Matters⇤
Tuesday, June 5

BEN: Dad's friend Alan joined us for the first part of our hike. He rivaled Dad in plant knowledge. The two could trade quips like "You're a *sanicula* kind of guy." They bantered about Latin names as though they were football teams.

We took off our backpacks. A torn-up spot near the trail had hoof prints. They looked like deer tracks, only bigger.

"So we can confirm this is an elk site," said Dad.

We had seen a billboard advertising "400 Really Cool Elk" to us on past trips to this area.

It may have just been the rarity of elk for a Tennessean of my generation, but I also found them really cool. I was eager to see one, however it might happen. If an elk knocked our tent over with her majestic many-branched antlers, causing us to careen around in our sleeping bags like fish dropped from buckets, my response would be, "Wow! Thank you, really cool elk!" I was that stoked.

We could see the woods as Daniel Boone saw them: with elk. We would not find bison or wolves, but still, we would get a sense of what the Cumberland Plateau once held.

Campbell County's Really Cool Elk.

Alan headed back. We found our campsite and lay down on the ground in the wet leaves to rest.

"I heard someone mention you taking bedding into the woods when you were little and sleeping on the ground," I said, thinking of how, in my younger days, I'd taken a sleeping bag and camping pad to the woods behind our house and slept there for a night.

"I'm not absolutely sure it happened," said Dad, pausing to sift through his memory like an archaeologist sifting through sand for artifacts, "It sounds right. I had been afraid of the dark as a kid. I was especially afraid of ghosts and things like that. My mother used to leave the light and radio on. Sleeping in the woods was a way of overcoming it."

Insects pestered me, so I had to get moving. I got up and started walking through the woods.

Two slugs with beautiful marbled patterns, one darker than the other, twisted near each other on a rock like yin and yang. Somehow I needed to be out in the forest to know how beautiful slugs were. I followed a stream where other small animals caught my attention: tiny white and transparent hellgrammites with reddish pinchers that crawled beneath rocks in the stream.

Exposed roots stuck out from trees above the stream and water fell nearby. The wet roots gleamed in red, yellow and orange like a crazy display of fireworks. Across the stream was a field with a rusty oil pump and two tall abandoned tanks.

I saw now that the forest was more than just trees of different ages, alive and dead, practicing cannibalism. It also was more than just the low-flowering azaleas with pink flowers wet from rain, the ferns and their absurd methods of sex, the rusty oil pump or the unseen bacteria that had, at our trek's beginning, made me want to waste drinking water to wash my hands. It was a world of connected elements, more complicated than anything my mind could hold. No writing of mine could ever do it justice.

All that Dad, I or any explorer can do is wiggle about like a young hellgrammite on a single rock in the universe's wide stream.

At dinnertime, I was afraid of holding the match near its head to light our stove. Instead, I held each match by the far end. They all snapped.

I pulled out a green plastic cigarette lighter. Then, I turned on the

Really Cool Elk

Manitoban Elk (*Cervus elaphus manitobensis*)

BEN: The last reported elk in Tennessee, before the current population of them, was shot in 1865. By the time people got around to bringing elk back, East Tennessee's subspecies *canadensis* was extinct. So, they went for another one, *manitobensis*, figuring that it was close enough. So far, it seems to have been. The elk have adapted to their new land well.

From 2000 to 2008, the elk rode down to Tennessee in trailers from Elk Island Refuge in Canada or from Land between the Lakes, places with closely-monitored disease-free elk. The bulls' antlers were all cut to avoid fighting and injuries on the way down.

The state chose 6,700,000 acres of land on or near the Cumberland Plateau in which the elk could roam. It was an isolated, wild area centered at the Royal Blue Wildlife Management Area, but extending far beyond it. The land included forests, in which the elk could eat bark, and strip-mine meadows, in which the elk could graze. Some of the Cumberland Trail runs through the elk area.

stove's gas. The lighter barely made any sparks, but I hoped that a spark would light the burner

"What are you doing?" asked Dad.

"Just trying to light it," I said.

"I'll get a match," said Dad.

Dad scraped the match against the box, keeping his fingers right up to the match-head. The stove lit with no more fuss.

"Where did you get that lighter from?" asked Dad, who knew I didn't smoke.

"Two hitch-hikers left it in my car by mistake," I replied, expecting Dad to lower his nearly-hairless brows in concern and give me a lecture on the dangers of taking hitch-hikers.

"I did a lot of hitchhiking myself," said Dad. "It's not as accepted now as it once was."

We ate macaroni and cheese with tuna. I walked alone after dinner. We were near the end of our trek, so as I walked, I struggled to find an important message for the end of our book.

"We are animals," I declared to my voice recorder. "We belong out here, no matter what I might have thought on other nights. There's no escaping nature. No matter how many chemicals we use, our crops still depend on

....

The state chose an area away from cities or even big farms. That way, the elk wouldn't be as much of a nuisance. Given that elk are wild animals though, they still run into trouble sometimes. They have been reported damaging fences and even eating plants at cemeteries. In one case, a bull who seemed particularly obsessed with I-75 near Caryville had to be put down for the public good. Another elk had to be tranquilized and moved after getting his antlers tangled in a well-rope.

In the summer, the male elk, called bulls, live by themselves while the adult females, called cows, live with the young elk in herds. By the fall though, the males start bugling, showing off their big antlers to each other and sometimes dueling, each bull elk trying to conquer or guard a harem of females for himself. The year-old males, or spikes, get shoved out at around this time, either by invading bulls or by their own mothers. If that seems harsh, keep in mind that elk usually live no longer than fourteen years.

By 2009, Tennessee started selling elk hunting permits by lottery. If you want a chance to get that set of antlers on your wall, go to tnelkhunt.org.

....

weather. Living off macaroni and cheese is living off the land, just like when Dad lived off the land in Kentucky."

Frogs interrupted my windbag speech before it could get any more self-important.

"Hon, hon, hon, hon" I said into the recorder, trying to imitate them. Those noises seemed to mean about as much as my attempts to say something deep about nature. As the night's first firefly flickered, I sat down, tired, at the campsite.

I did not matter. Maybe that was the lesson I'd learned, after looking outward at distant mountains, upward at branches that grew at odd angles and downward at snails, salamanders, flowers and snakes. I was a tiny, easily removed screw, in a skyscraper of a planet that included many other living things.

Yet to me, it mattered that the person sitting next to me was my father, the one who had taught me how to search for salamanders and identify plants.

"How are you feeling, Dad?" I asked.

"Fine," he said.

I asked him about the meaning behind the frog noises.

"The tree frogs will often call before it rains or whenever they feel like it. Not just during mating season."

Maybe if I shared my philosophical blathering with Dad, it would mean something.

"I was thinking about how you tried to live off of nature," I said.

"I wasn't really living off nature," said Dad. "I built my own shelter and tried to grow my own food. Really, I needed to have more of a clearing. Things wouldn't grow with light from a small opening in the forest."

"Everyone is already living off nature though," I said. "There's a law preventing us from creating matter. We're stuck with what we're given."

"Energy is at the heart of everything," said Dad.

In darkness, we talked about energy, matter and whether or not aliens would find anything unique on this planet that they couldn't find closer to home. What mattered was that we were talking. On many other nights, I'd played cell phone games in the woods or checked Facebook at the motel before going to sleep. Now, those activities felt wrong. This was our time together.

→Dog, Frog and Orchid←
Wednesday June 6

I found a spot near a dried-out stream, dug a hole in the tough ground and tried to poop. It was challenging because my body had learned from an early age to resist pooping anywhere but a toilet, or perhaps it was because I put too much effort into keeping my butt off the cold ground. I did a kind of slanted crabwalk position above the hole, shaking. An ice age hunter would have laughed at me.

For breakfast we finished off our oatmeal. Dad had forgotten to bring enough packets. We'd have to eat trail mix for breakfast the next day, meaning we had to ration it rather than eating it by the handful like we normally did.

We balanced on rocks while crossing a stream and saw the ruins of an old bridge, suggesting that a narrow-gage railroad for carrying logs had been here.

"There was nowhere for it to go from here," said Dad. "This must have been the end of the track."

I crept ahead of Dad, hoping to see an elk. The trail began to follow an old muddy road. Two deer ran across the road into a thicket. I waited for them to come back. Then came a sound like a dog running down the leafy hill.

A creature walked slowly onto a log that jutted into the road. It looked like a dog, but its tail stuck out straight back and did not curve upward like Zeke's tail. It neither begged me for food nor barked at me like a dog might. It was a coyote. It stood there until I got out my camera, then it jumped off the log and trotted away.

It seemed unlikely that the coyote would ever bring down a healthy, adult deer. Maybe the coyote was waiting for one of them to get injured.

I remembered how our dog Zeke would often sprint madly after deer. He never caught them though. He would always walk back to me, tongue out and panting like an out-of-shape kid in a middle-school gym class. Perhaps he enjoyed the chase, even if he never won. Maybe the coyote was similar or perhaps the coyote's movements had nothing to do with the deer. My lack of answers did not take away from my awe at finally seeing a wild coyote.

A tree had fallen, knocking down three other trees. Mountain laurel bushes blocked me from going around the fallen logs. I felt annoyed and confused. Dad caught up with me, but the blockade didn't grab his attention at first. He kneeled to look at an orchid. Nothing else mattered to him.

After finding our campsite, we hid our backpacks and returned to explore the same spot where the coyote had stood. Frogs hopped in and out of puddles in the trail.

"It's not a chorus frog," said Dad. "It seems like a small puddle for a green frog, but it might be one that's just transformed."

"Maybe we don't have to know the names for everything," I said.

I went the other direction by the side of a stream. Near an old rusty bucket, I turned over a rock and saw an orange salamander with a long tail. It ran away. At least I had my memory. A photo probably would have been a blurry mess anyway.

Dinner was noodle soup. The burner's flames fizzled out before the water could boil, but it didn't matter. After throwing the water into the noodle containers, the noodles softened well.

As I sat down in the evening to write about everything we'd seen that day, the task overwhelmed me. Instead, I drew the things in front of me: trees

An Orchid Encounter

Large Whorled pogonia (*Isotria verticillata*)

LARRY: While we hiked toward our second campsite of this backpack in the Wartburg Basin Mountains section of the CT, we encountered plants that looked like whorled pogonias. We have two species of whorled pogonias, small and large. The small whorled pogonia would be a Holy Grail type of find. It has a wide range in eastern North America but is rare throughout that range.

I rubbed a stem with my fingers to make sure that they were not Indian cucumber plants. Indian cucumber plants have hairs that come off the stem. There were no hairs on my fingers after rubbing. So, I hoped that these were the small whorled pogonia.

If there had been flowers, I would have instantly known which of the two species of whorled pogonia I was looking at. Without flowers, I had to look carefully at other characteristics.

The small whorled pogonia should be smaller than the large whorled pogonia, right? These plants looked small. I got my hopes up. On the small whorled pogonia, the leaves droop a bit more. I could not tell if the leaves were drooping enough.

I knew the best characteristic to separate the two was the stem color. These stems were purplish, but I couldn't remember which of the two had the purple stems.

When I got to my botany books, I found that the encountered plants were the more common large whorled. I say common, but I can remember finding the large only about 10 times in my life.

I enjoy our native orchids. Most of them are rare enough to surprise and delight when they turn up. Our most common orchid is downy rattlesnake plantain. After the thousands of times I've set my eyes on it, I still love to look at its patterned leaves.

with ripped bark and moss, small pebbles on larger rocks, water striders and fragments of moss.

I found a small rockhouse and sat below its roof. Sometimes I recorded the thoughts that came to my mind. Other times I looked out toward a rhododendron bush and tried to think in images and sensations rather than words. Sometimes, a sound, a rhododendron bush, or a pair of trees above the

---

Stanley Bentley's *Native Orchids of the Southern Appalachian Mountains* is a good place to start a study of orchids in the CT region. We have about 30 species of orchids on the Cumberland Plateau. Worldwide there are perhaps 20,000 species of orchids, most living in the tropics.

Some orchids to look for along the CT:

Pink lady slipper (*Cypripedium acaule*)
It can be seen in many places along the CT.

Yellow lady slipper (*Cypripedium parviflorum*)
I have seen it once along the CT, and I have seen it near the CT on Black Mountain. I have heard reports of it from various places in the Cumberland Mountains.

White fringeless orchid (*Platanthera integrilabia*)
It is about to be federally listed for protection. To find it, you will need to search acidic wetlands usually on the top of the Plateau. There are few wetlands right on the main CT, so you will need to wander off trail a bit. Flowers are required for identification. The flowers should be present in early August.

Southern twayblade (*Listera australis*)
Bentley doesn't have this one in his book, although his book covers the Plateau. However, I have seen it on Walden Ridge a few miles from the CT. Like many of our orchids, it is found in acidic wetlands.

Smaller spreading pogonia (*Cleistes bifaria*)
I saw this one in flower in one of the few wetland areas near the CT I visited during our CT trek. It was on the Plateau-top above Daddy's Creek.

Go to http://www.tn.gov/environment/natural-areas/natural-heritage-inventory-program.shtml to report and learn about plants protected by Tennessee.

---

stream is enough to fill me. It does not need a meaning or a name.

I closed my eyes and listened to the faint calls of birds, the low sounds of the stream and the even fainter call of a rooster.

A rooster so far away from people? I doubted my ears. Curiosity filled me, making me abandon the whole notion of moving beyond words. I wanted to identify and explain that sound, like everything else around me. Maybe I was more like Dad than I had thought.

→Surrounded by Poison Ivy←
Thursday, June 7 May 20

"This is a mountain I don't know the name of," said Dad. "We should look at a map."

The nameless mountain started out like the past two days' hikes through the woods, only steeper. Then, the trail followed a road through chaotic strip-mined country. We walked through meadows with sweeping views of pristine-looking mountains, meadows with views of clear-cuts, sharp banks, tan boulders, shallow ponds and forests of all ages jumping in to fill the gaps. Virginia pines towered in places. They are native plants but grow most often in disturbed areas.

Eat and be Eaten
Green frog (*Rana clamatans*)

BEN: We spotted this one in a shallow pool on our third day. Not all of them are very green, making the name confusing. They will jump into the water to get away from predators and will actively try to escape when captured. Their call is similar to a twanging rubber band, and they are active both night and day.

They eat crayfish, millipedes, centipedes, spiders, beetles, dragonflies, butterflies and even smaller frogs. The tadpoles will eat algae and other frogs' eggs.

In an odd coincidence, the frogs in the tadpole stage can get eaten by dragonflies in the aquatic naiad stage (see Chapter 33). Once both species are adults, the roles get reversed. Adult green frogs often eat younger green frogs too.

Other predators include bullfrogs, snakes, herons and ducks.

A Yipping Pioneer

Coyote (*Canis latrans*)

BEN: When I confused a coyote's yipping for a person talking, I was close to being right. Like human beings, coyotes are adaptable creatures that have spread far beyond their initial range. While they haven't conquered the whole planet yet, they can be found from Alaska to Panama and even the streets of Los Angeles. True omnivores, they can eat just about anything, including berries, fish, rabbits and kittens. They hunt together or as individuals depending on the prey. Originally these clever canids had a much smaller range, sticking to deserts and prairies out west.

Before coyotes, Tennessee had the timber wolf and, in a few places, the red wolf. Wolves hunt in bigger packs than coyotes and can bring down far larger animals like deer and elk.

European settlers killed many of the elk and deer. Wolves still had some big game to eat in the form of sheep, goats and small calves, but by eating these kinds of prey, wolves made farmers angry. Governments joined in the wolf-hating. For example, in Morgan County's early days, residents could get money for bringing wolf pelts to the court building, much like people receive money for aluminum cans nowadays.

As wolves died out, coyotes started moving in, with less competition from wolves. They bred with dogs and red wolves. Once deer came back, coyotes began to hunt deer in packs like the wolves once did. Coyotes would have reached the Cumberland Plateau by the time my Dad was in grade school. These days, they're everywhere.

Compared to newts and dragonflies, coyotes are poster-dogs for family values. Coyote couples stay together through the mother coyote's pregnancy and keep together after the pups are born. Pups start in a den with their mother but soon begin to run wild, joining with their parents at a meeting place to eat regurgitated food. Once they get old enough, their parents give them raw food. Then, they leave their parents to start families of their own. These are long journeys, often hundreds of miles, far more than many people travel from their parents.

While at first Dad's fear of heights had seemed absurd to me, it now seemed reasonable. He wasn't scared of views unless he was at the edge and it was a sheer drop-off. The lookouts we passed now were cliff-less, so they didn't bother him. Few fears I had were as reasonable in terms of their limitations. Maybe talking to him about his fears could help me deal with my own fears, including my fear of failure. The only thing that didn't make sense about Dad's height fears was his fear of flying in airplanes.

"Why's that a problem?" I asked. "You've got a window between yourself and the air?"

"Yeah," said Dad, "I guess that's right."

It was sort of like my irrational fear of matches having nothing, ultimately, to do with ways to avoid getting burned. Neither of us made sense all the time.

Today had been a longer hike than the previous two days. I was tired. Mosquito bites and blackberry scratches covered my arms.

We reached a trailhead by a dusty road. We waited for Carl and

Tail Wagging in Fear

Long-tailed salamander (*Eurycea longicaudata*)

BEN: I found these guys twice, both on moist land under rocks. They were near streams but not in them. For the first, I didn't have my camera. The second one escaped before I could get a good picture. Even without a picture, the long orange bodies were easy to remember. Long-tailed salamanders can grow up to 7.75 inches. They have no stripes, but their spots form z-shapes going down the tail.

Adults stay under rocks and logs during the day and hunt for worms, spiders, millipedes and insects on the forest floor at night. Both of the ones I found were probably annoyed at me taking off the roofs of their houses. They both ran away. One shook its tail while running.

Wagging its tail at the predator is part of a long-tailed salamander's scheme. Once paws, claws or jaws grab the tail, it breaks off, and the salamander runs free. A tail is no big loss compared to death for the salamander. The tail can regenerate, as I mentioned in Chapter 14 with the red salamander.

Elizabeth to pick us up. I sat down on a rock and coughed on road dust while taking notes on the hike in my yellow Rite in the Rain notebook.

After a few long minutes, Dad came over. "Maybe we should go back down to the trail, away from the road," said Dad. "We'd be out of the sun."

"But I like the sun," I said. "Can't you see I'm trying to write? I need light for that."

"You're surrounded by poison ivy," said Dad, pointing below the rock. It was true. The three-leafleted shrub grew on every side of my rock like an itchy battle formation.

"Thanks," I said, looking Dad in his detail-catching eyes. Nothing else seemed right to say.

We sat in the shade, leaning on our backpacks and chugging down the last of our water. We were out of trail mix, having finished the last of it for breakfast and snack.

At the time we hiked, the official CT lacked a trail connection between Cumberland Gap and Tank Springs, our furthest point. So, after Carl and Elizabeth dropped us off, we drove to our next stay town, the town of Cumberland Gap. Cumberland Gap was not a mere stay town, it was a Stay *Towne*.

Hence, the long tail that gives the long-tail salamander both its English and Latin name makes sense as an adaptation. The bigger the distraction from the tail, the better. Some predators might not even notice that they've only caught the tail until they've finished eating it, if even then.

For salamanders, the tail is like a backpack for built-up fat. Losing it means a salamander has to go out and find food in order to regenerate the tail and replenish its fat stores. Imagine a hiker who finds a bear grabbing him from behind. He could un-strap the backpack then run off, hoping the bear will be happy with the food in the pack. Please note that the strategy I described for a human hiker might not work because most backpacks aren't designed for that kind of quick snap-off, nor are human appendages. If humans had tails made of fat that they could break off, it might just solve our obesity crisis. Maybe it's the next stage of human evolution.

Sources and Suggested Reading

Long-Tail Salamander:
Behler, John L. and F. Wayne King. *The Audubon Society Field Guide to North American Reptiles and Amphibians.* New York: Chanticleer Press Inc., 1995.

Niemiller, Matthew et al. *The Amphibians of Tennessee.* Knoxville: University of Tennessee Press, 2011.

Mitchell, Joe and Whit Gibbons. *Salamanders of the Southeast.* Athens: University of Georgia Press, 2010.

Green Frog:
Dorcas, Mike and Gibbons, Whit. Frogs & Toads of the Southeast. Athens: University of Georgia Press, 2008.

Niemiller, Matthew et al. The Amphibians of Tennessee. Knoxville: University of Tennessee
Press, 2011.

Coyotes:
Haskell, David George. 2012. *The Forest Unseen: A Year's Watch in Nature.* New York: Viking.

National Geographic. "Coyote *Canis latrans.*" *National Geographic Animals.* http://animals.nationalgeographic.com/animals/mammals/coyote/. Accessed June 5, 2014.

National Science Foundation. "Coyotes 'Shrank' Wolves did not after Last Ice Age and Megafaunal Extinctions.
Nsf.gov. http://www.nsf.gov/news/news_summ.jsp?cntn_id=123314. Accessed June 5, 2014

Freytag, Ethyl and Glenda Kreis Ott. *A History of Morgan County Tennessee.* United States of America: Specialty
Printing Company, 1971.

Elk:
Tennessee Wildlife Resources Agency. "Elk Reintroduction Questions and Answers. *Tennessee.gov.*
http://www.tennessee.gov/twra/elkquestions.html. Accessed June 5, 2014.

Muller, Lisa et al. "Tennessee Elk Restoration Project. Last updated August 31,

2004. Web.utk.edu. http://web.utk.edu/~lmuller/AddOns/Elk04.pdf. Accessed June 5, 2014.

Tennessee Wildlife Resources Agency. "Elk Information." State.tn.us/twra. http://www.state.tn.us/twra/elkmain.html. Accessed June 5, 2014.

Rocky Mountain Elk Foundation. "Elk Facts."rmef.org. http://www.rmef.org/ElkFacts.aspx. Accessed June 5, 2014.

Orchids:
Bentley, Stanley L. *Native Orchids of the Southern Appalachian Mountains.* Chapel Hill: University of North Carolina Press, 2000.

Tennessee Department of Environment and Conservation. "Natural Heritage Inventory Program." tn.gov. http://www.tn.gov/environment/natural-areas/natural-heritage-inventory-program.shtml. Accessed February 27, 2015.
    This website has rare plant and animal lists for the state of Tennessee.

HISTORIC CUMBERLAND GAP

→ 29 ←

Cumberland Gap, Stay-Town

  We drove to Cumberland Gap, where the ridge dipped down in the dim light. Even though it was a gentle dip rather than a dramatic canyon, the shape was unmistakable.
  Generations of travelers, would have breathed sighs of relief to see that shape, eager to avoid trekking up Cumberland Mountain's tall slope. Our route, which not only took us uphill but did so repeatedly, would probably make us seem like pain-loving freaks to them.
  The pioneers who came through here faced heat, rain, rattlesnakes and copperheads just as we had, although they could add lack of medical care, starvation and hostile tribes to the list too. Some of them would consider us soft.
  We stopped at the Cumberland Gap Inn, a white building with plantation-house columns.
  "But wait," I said to Dad, "Haven't you tried to save money at every chance we've had?"
  "Just this once we won't. Just to see what it's like," he said. He walked quickly as if he had just spotted a rare orchid from a distance and wanted to put his field glass to its leaves.
  Oil paintings of Daniel Boone hung on the lobby wall, including one that appeared to show him with an inaccurate coonskin cap.
  Boone led a group of pioneers through Cumberland Gap, but he and his companions would never have even imagined a hotel this fancy in the area. The counter looked marble. Our room on the second floor had expensive counter-tops and sinks.
  Usually after coming back from a backpacking trip, I would type a blog entry. Now though, I wanted to know more about the town. We would only get

one night here in the town of Cumberland Gap. I walked on the streets alone while Dad looked at plant books.

The town felt like nothing else I had seen yet on our trip. Street signs were white with Welsh-sounding names like "Pennlyn" "Llewyn" and even "Merlyn" written in gothic font. The businesses, located in two-story buildings, all had names like the Towne Dog Candle Factory (named after a stray dog) and Nothin's Perfect, which billed itself as "a primitive place to shop." Here, primitive was a compliment.

There was no dusty general store selling vital necessities. The general store in town sold souvenirs. In spite of the town's appeal to the primitive rustic spirit, it seemed to have banished any name that seemed too hickish, like the Blistered Chicken Saloon, which we had passed near Piney River.

The town banks on an idealized old-fashioned charm which tourists can enjoy as a break from their hectic lives. Its website quotes a visitor as saying, "Cumberland Gap is kinda like walking into a Norman Rockwell Painting."

I passed the Olde Mill Inn Bed and Breakfast, with its wooden wheel and walked out to a field that was filled with booksellers, wood-carvers, soap-makers, Daughters of the American Revolution and others. It was the Genealogy Jamboree, a heritage celebration put on by the town's volunteer fire chief. He watched the festivities while standing with his collection of full-sized wagons and carriages.

Away from the main field, a no-nonsense West Virginia historian lectured a crowd on her ancestors and presumably theirs as well.

"They were buying the land from someone but whom?" she said. "A lot of it from the Indians. The Indians never owned the land; they just used it, which was what the Europeans didn't understand. For them it was empty."

She didn't care about making her forefathers and foremothers sound noble. She described the early European settlers as tax-dodgers who would move further west the minute that state governments set up counties on the frontier. "Once they got used to not paying those taxes, they saw no reason to pay them," she said. It wasn't a particularly uplifting form of manifest destiny.

Among the immigrant groups she mentioned were the Germans and the Scotts-Irish.

The people known as Scotts-Irish or Ulster-Scotts moved to the New World for many reasons, including, according to the historian, the inability of tenant farmers to pay rent on their land. I could relate.

"If I walked up near a clearing," she said, "I could tell you who cleared it. If it's German, it's cleared. If it's Scotts-Irish, they leave some limbs up so they've got firewood all the time. Still, I can drive through the counties up home

Daniel Boone, left and David Crockett, right.

Daniel Boone was a Man

"Didn't the famous Daniel Boone die at the Alamo?"- A confused commentator on notablebiographies.com.

BEN: People who were children when my Dad was a child saw Daniel Boone on TV, wearing a coonskin cap and played by Fes Parker, the same man who played Davy Crockett years earlier. So, people confused the two of them. Legends and popular media have always molded Boone's legend however they saw fit. Not long after his death, biographies of Boone described him as an action hero, swinging on vines before Tarzan made it cool.

The theme song to Fes Parker's show stated, "Daniel Boone was a man," a fact that is probably one of the best known things about him. No historian has ever proven that he was a robot, a turkey, a rhododendron or a salamander. Daniel Boone was short with a wide face. The Cherokee called him "big turtle," and the Shawnee called him "wide-mouth."

During Boone's times, land companies made illegal deals with the natives. One such company, the Transylvania Land Company, wanted a road to connect their property, and they hired Daniel Boone to do it. He

in West Virginia and tell you which counties are Scotts-Irish. The Scotts-Irish never threw away any piece of equipment they ever bought." The crowd laughed, because they knew those yards all too well, as did I. "The Germans made everything all nice and neat," the historian continued, "just like they had in Germany."

According to Dad, the Pounds family was German. I'd taken on the Scotts-Irish hoarder instinct out of a perverse combination of environmentalism and indecision, but it was not the family tradition, at least not as far as my Dad's side was concerned.

"Just throw out that trash," he would say, "It's not worth your time to be making mobiles out of it."

She talked about old wills and how they sometimes left children with nothing, with just enough to move, or with lots of property but tons of debt. Especially the ones who cohabited with Indians got in trouble.

I would have to ask my Dad about how his side of the family came to

....

cleared and marked the Wilderness Road which ran through the Cumberland Gap, expanding it from the warriors' and hunters' path it had been. By his own admission, Boone preferred negotiation with Native Americans to fighting. During his lifetime, many people considered that preference to be wrong. Still, the path he blazed meant scores of new settlers and the end of Cherokee and Shawnee dominance.

He left his family for long hunts and expeditions, making his relationship with them complicated, but ultimately a dedicated one. Daniel's wife Rebecca once thought he was dead. She conceived a daughter with Ned Boone, Daniel's brother. Daniel Boone forgave her. Years later, he would rescue that daughter from Cherokee and Shawnee warriors, proving himself a loving father to his wife's illegitimate child. Others of Boone's children were not as lucky. His son, Israel, died in the Battle of Blue Licks, a battle which Daniel wanted to avoid. Another son, James, died after being captured and tortured by the Cherokee warrior Big Jim.

Cheated out of his land in Kentucky, Boone died in Missouri in 1820. He swore that he would never go back to Kentucky again. He never did, until someone moved his ashes to Frankfort. Boone would not have approved.

....

Ohio. But now was not the time. Now it was time to go back to the Inn and sleep. Tomorrow we would end our long trek together.

After some delicious eggs and toast at Webb's Country Kitchen, it was time to hike to the end of the Cumberland Trail. The path that rose up from the town to meet the Cumberland Trail was paved and had glossy historical marker signs, a far cry from the path once trod through the Gap by herds of bison or the route of the real Daniel Boone, who by some accounts hated coonskin caps.

Scotts-Irish or Ulster Scotts?

BEN: The Scotts-Irish have a confusing history, as this historian was keen to point out. They were originally people from near the border between Scotland and England who moved to Northern Ireland. King James I, who ruled both England and Scotland, wanted to colonize Northern Ireland with Protestant settlers. It was an attempt to introduce "civility" to what he considered the "rude and barbarous" Irish. Anyone in Ireland today can tell you how well that plan worked. In the modern UK, these people are called Ulster-Scotts. In the United States, they are called Scotts-Irish-Americans.

Sources and Suggested Reading

Town of Cumberland Gap:
Town of Cumberland Gap. *Town of Cumberland Gap, TN.* http://townofcumberlandgap.com/. Accessed June 6, 2014.

On Scots-Irish:
Griffin, Patrick. *The People with No Name: Ireland's Ulster Scots, America's Scots Irish, and the Creation of a British Atlantic World, 1689-1764.* Princeton: Princeton University Press, 2001.

Montgomery, Michael. "The Linguistic History of Ulster." *BBC.com.* Last Modified November 2009. http://www.bbc.co.uk/history/british/plantation/ulsterscots/index.shtml.

Webb, James. *Born Fighting: How the Scots-Irish Shaped America.* New York: Broadway Books, 2004.

On Daniel Boone:
Encyclopedia of World Biography. "Daniel Boone Biography." http://www.notablebiographies.com/Be-Br/Boone-Daniel.html. Accessed 23 May 2014.

Ferager, John Mack. 1992. *Daniel Boone: The Life and Legend of an American Pioneer.* New York: Henry Holt and Company.

Trevathan, Kim. 2006. *Coldhearted River: A Canoe Odyssey Down the Cumberland.* Knoxville: University of Tennessee Press.

THE WILD FRONTIER

30

Hike 21: Tristate Point to Somewhere and Back Again (Friday, June 8)
Length: about 6 miles and growing

"Stand at the Cumberland Gap and watch the procession of civilization single file—the buffalo following the trail to the salt springs, the Indian, the fur trader and hunter, the cattle raiser, the pioneer farmer, and the frontier has passed by."
–Fredrick Jackson Turner, nineteenth century historian.

A sign told us about the old Warriors' Path, by which the Cherokee and Shawnee traveled through the Gap in order to fight, perhaps over hunting rights. Bison and elk had used the path as an easy way to get through the mountains. White men like Thomas Walker who named the Gap and Daniel Boone, who made the Gap famous, called the path the "Wilderness Road." While using it, they ran into warriors who had already been using the path. Once the whites had strength in numbers though, the road became theirs for cattle and stagecoaches.

Signs with old fashioned spellings told us of pioneer hardships as we climbed. Dad, however, paid more attention to the battles that plants were fighting. Exotic honeysuckles and multiflora roses had grabbed acres of soil from the native plants. Here though, the native plants had allies. Volunteers were cutting down the thick multiflora rose bushes.

Invasive plants can take once-diverse landscapes and make dull weedy clusters of privet bushes and mono-crop lawns of Nepal grass. They would eliminate the treasure hunts for the native plants that my Dad does. The land around Cumberland Gap had ceased to be a frontier for years, but now, humans had to do their best to stop it from losing its botanical uniqueness to the sameness of the invaders.

Cumberland Gap, marked as "Historic Cumberland Gap" on a

On Exotic Invaders

LARRY: Most non-native plants in our ecosystems have not yet become a problem and probably never will, but there are many which are.

The problems related to loss of diversity in our plant communities due to invasive species can be difficult to predict. The most basic principle is that rapid change to ecosystems, such as is currently occurring with invasives, is dangerous because there is little time for the system to adapt.

Bird watchers may be tempted to plant invasive species that attract certain birds. There are studies showing native birds having difficulty nesting in non-native plants. The sites below discuss effects of invasive plants on birds: http://www.inhs.uiuc.edu/inhsreports/autumn-01/nesting.html. http://www.invasive.org/101/BirdWatcher.html.

Non-natives often succeed because they lack control of their population size by insects that eat them. This lack of control allows exotics to form extremely dense populations. Paradoxically, these populations may then become highly vulnerable to attack when effective herbivores migrate in or evolve. This paradox leads to an unstable ecosystem.

Here on the Plateau, tree farmers planted large areas with pines, specifically loblolly pines for pulp. The low diversity community was created by planting rather than lack of herbivores, but it's a good example of vulnerability. Since the creation of large areas densely populated with loblollies, extreme outbreaks of southern pine bark beetle, which kills most pines of all types in the region where it breaks out, have occurred. The fact that the loblolly is just barely non-native on the plateau may not be relevant. It is naturally found just to the south. Similar outbreaks can be expected in our invasive species low-diversity communities, though they may not occur for hundreds of years.

Visit http://www.tneppc.org/invasive_plants for more information about Tennessee's invasive plants and their economic cost. It's the website for the Tennessee Exotic Pest Plant Council, which is doing important work to protect our native plant communities.

splintery wooden sign wasn't the most impressive land feature I had ever seen, at least not up close. It looked like a gravel path in a field between two forested slopes. The spot's majesty came from imagining a long history: bison and their calves, Cherokee and Shawnee sons on their first war raids, hunters far away from their childhood homes and parents, families of settlers with old men and pregnant women trying to keep step with spry youth. Escaping slaves hid in the Gap Cave, wondering if their parents or children had already reached freedom. Civil War soldiers had occupied this area too. They longed to see their families again, but hoped not to see them on the other side of the battle lines. The sunny Gap only looked peaceful because it was resting after a long and tiring career.

The Gap became famous in Britain because of a folk song, titled "Cumberland Gap." It became a number one hit single in Britain, recorded by Lonnie Donegan in 1957. Cumberland Trail Park Manager and song collector Bob Fulcher told me that it was originally written by Sam Lambdin, a left-handed East-Tennessee fiddler who fought for the Union in the Civil War.

The lyrics got changed around often. Some versions taught history lessons like "The first white man in the Cumberland Gap/Was Doctor Walker, an English Chap." Nice enough lyrics, but other versions sounded more plausible for a soldier trying to pass the time.

> *"Cumberland Gap's such a dry place,*
> *Can't get the water to wash your face."*

> *"Cumberland Gap, it ain't my home,*
> *I'm a gonna leave old Cumberland alone."*

"This is where Highway 25 was before the tunnel," said Dad, looking across the gravel road, remembering.

"Yeah, I read about that online," I said, "They blasted the tunnel into the mountain. Now the highway runs through there and skips the Gap."

"I suppose they don't say who did the endangered plant survey for the tunnel," said Dad, lifting his head up toward me. He stayed silent waiting for me to guess, until I realized he was right in front of me, the rugged, big-armed, farmer's-tanned, mustachioed fellow himself.

As it was a cleared spot, Dad found yet another black raspberry bush and we stopped to snack.

"Why do blackberry bushes have thorns?" I asked. "I've heard that they spread their seeds from animals pooping them out. So wouldn't thorns just make it harder?"

"There are no thorns on the berries. The thorns on the stems are no problem for birds," said Dad.

Nearly every book about Cumberland Gap has a painting by George C. Bingham showing Daniel Boone and his party of settlers traveling through the gap to Kentucky, trying to look important, like George Washington on the Delaware, no matter how tired they might be. One of them appears to be majestically tying his shoe. Shadows cover the land, as if to suggest that Kentucky and Tennessee were in the heart of darkness.

It had never been dark though, except to strangers. The natives, at least the ones brave enough to fight for the Gap, knew it well. I imagined George C. Bingham's painted pioneers marching across my back yard and finding it equally strange.

Detail of Bingham's picture, now in the public domain.

The late nineteenth century historian Fredrick Jackson Turner believed based on a census report that the frontier era was over. By now, I thought, it probably was. Then, I remembered Dad finding what might have been a new variety of spiderwort amid garbage, near a regrown mining area. Perhaps the wild frontier was everywhere, scurrying with salamanders under rocks, in threatened species spotted near mountain ponds, on the streets of Wartburg, Caryville, Cumberland Gap and Dayton and in my eyes as I beheld a coyote in the wild for the first time. Any new thing to see, smell, taste or feel could be a frontier to my father and me. Things that I knew well could also be frontiers, full of aspects never noticed before.

Still a place to explore.

We left the old Wilderness Road and took a path upward. Up at the Tristate Point, blue signs stood on different sides with different views. They declared each view of Kentucky, Tennessee, and Virginia to be "The Bluegrass State," "The Volunteer State," and "The Old Dominion" respectively.

This was the official endpoint for the CT. The Gap itself was not on the current CT, although it was on the Great Eastern Trail, which would continue north.

From the end of the CT we started walking back in the direction of Tank Springs. We had the familiar white blazes, leading us onto rocks high atop a ridgeline. Kentucky with its strip mines was below us to the right. Our Tennessee, with its fields, was to the left. We could tell that the trail was just now getting established here by rakes and hoes, left on a rock above a view of Cumberland Gap (the town).

Ribbons, these ones striped and pink, soon began to replace the blazes. My water was down to its last drops because I'd thought the trail would be short today. Bushes and thorns grew taller as we thrashed our way through them.

"Do you want to turn back?" asked Dad.

"No," I said, scraping through bushes and scanning for ribbons, "If we've got time we can keep exploring."

A barely perceivable trail headed down a slope, into a gap. The sun shone on the huckleberry bushes to either side of it. It had no ribbons, but it was a path that led somewhere neither of us had seen.

"Let's not go down there," said Dad, "We'd have to come back up and you're low on water."

"It looks interesting though," he added, while walking back and trying hard not to turn around. "I'd love to see the plants there."

It seemed right to leave an unfinished trail with a feeling of the journey being unfinished. It was doubly appropriate for me, whose life was still a long frontier that stretched ahead. It would have been dishonest to leave with a sense that we had seen everything. No one ever can.

I stopped to tie my boots. The laces were now frayed to the point that I needed to tie them to each other in multiple places. Then, we headed back.

A raccoon stood still. It moved only when it saw that I was staring at it, which took a few minutes. My steps had gotten far more subtle than the loud, leaf-thrashing ones I once took.

Raccoon babies get raised by their mothers. The fathers have no role. Mother raccoons even go as far as chasing adult males away from their babies.

We heard faint old-time music down in the valley and knew we were close to town and the still-continuing genealogy jamboree. I thought I recognized the tune and words of "Man of Constant Sorrow," a song probably written by Blind Dick Bernett, not George Clooney, although Bernett himself in old age forgot if he'd written the song or not. Dick Bernett was a Kentucky oil man who'd lived on this Plateau a century ago. He lived in the constant sorrow of partial blindness. I had the constant joy of being able to see, not just big things like the sky, the trees, and the deep valleys, but smaller things like lizards and flowers.

The woods of the Cumberlands could be a place of vastness and wordlessness, as I had wanted to see them. They could be a place of jumping forward without a second thought, as the frog had taught me. Yet they could also be what my Dad saw in them: a place to solve mysteries and make discoveries about small things.

On our drive back home, I treated Dad and myself to bottles of Ale-8-One, a Kentucky soft drink which tastes like something between ginger ale and 7-up. We were within its range here at the end of the CT.

"It takes me back to my days in Kentucky," said Dad, "It reminds me of the Red River Gorge."

I tried to open the bottle with my hand. I failed, so I put my mouth on it and twisted.

"Don't break your teeth," said Dad. He then opened it with his hand.

"Thanks," I said. I started to feel embarrassed, but then felt grateful instead. There was nothing wrong with getting help from Dad. I could use my own hands and teeth when he wasn't there.

After riding back to the motel in Caryville, I split up with Dad. He took his truck and I took my car back to Loudon. I drove down the interstate, past my old Walmart. It was the path I knew.

I thought about the path I did not know, the unmarked path that headed down into a gap with the huckleberries growing on either side. It headed across private unvisited lands, winding all the way to Signal Mountain. At least that's where it would go eventually. My life was even less certain.

As Daniel Boone, who had gone through Cumberland Gap centuries before me, had said, "Sometimes I feel like a leaf carried on by a stream. It may turn about and whirl and twist, but always it is carried forward."

I did not know where my life would go. Yet as the man in Dayton had said, all those nights ago, my Dad had helped me to move forward. I remembered the 1789 ballad that settlers, crossing the Plateau on the lesser-known Avery Trace, into Grassy Cove, had sung:

"You gave to me the parting hand,
And you wished me safe,
In ol' Cumberland Land."

"So I Took the Steering in my hand,
And I steered through ice and I steered through sand.
I took the steering in my hand,
And we steered our way through the Cumberland Land."

LARRY: Update 2013: The land has been acquired for that stretch of the CT between Cumberland Gap and Tank Springs. We were able to walk some of this new trail section as it is being built. We talked to the State Park Trail building crew. They are aware that if they stay with the crew long enough, they will reach Tristate Point. They have about 30 miles to go without stopping for side trails.

Sources and Suggested Reading

Invasive Plants and Bird Watching:
Center for Invasive Species and Ecosystem Health. "I am a Bird Watcher. Why Should I Care About Invasive Plants?" Invasive.org. http://www.invasive.org/101/BirdWatcher.html. Accessed June 2, 2014.

On Cumberland Gap's History, Including the Highway:
Brown, Daniel. "Cumberland Gap: A New Beginning" *Appalachian Cultural Resources Workshop Papers.* National
Park Service 1993. http://www.nps.gov/history/history/online_books/sero/appalachian/sec14.htm. Accessed 27 July 2011.

Fetterman, John. 1971. "The People of Cumberland Gap." National

Geographic, November: 591-620.

On Songs:
  I'm indebted here to park manager Bob Fulcher for my information on these songs. He performed both at a concert in Wartburg, and the two of us also attended a concert of Cumberland related songs in Chattanooga. I've gone with his conclusions about "Cumberland Gap" rather than other ones.

Guilfoil, Monessa. "Cumberland Trail Broadcast Wins National American Trails 2010 Media Awards." *WUTC.* Published March 1, 2011. Accessed March 20, 2015. http://wutcana.wordpress.com/2011/03/01/cumberland-trails-broadcast-wins-american-trails-2010-media-award/.
  This interview covers Bobby Fulcher's work in general.

On Cumberland Gap Song:
Waltz, Robert B and David G. Engle. "Cumberland Gap." *The Ballad Index.* Accessed March 20, 2015. http://www.csufresno.edu/folklore/ballads/R498.html.

Jamieson, Larry. "Lonnie Donegan-Cumberland Gap." *YouTube.* Published November 10, 2010. https://www.youtube.com/watch?v=jWA997xM9MI.
  Not a scholarly source, but shows what Lonnie Donegan's hit version of the song was like.

"Cumberland Gap." *The Mudcat Café.* Accessed March 20, 2015. http://www.mudcat.org/@displaysong.cfm?SongID=1413.
  This version has the "history lesson" lyrics.

Smith, Ralph Lee and Madeline Macneil. *Songs and Tunes of the Wilderness Road: Arrangements for the Appalachian Dulcimer.* Pacific, MO: Mel Bay Publications, 2010.
  This book has several different verses, as well as the origin story involving Sam Lambdin that Bobby Fulcher believes.

Cumberland Land Song:
Dixon, Jim, and Artful Codger. Lyr Req: Old Cumberland Land. Last Updated October 9, 2009. http://mudcat.org/thread.cfm?threadid=124667. (Accessed September 12, 2014).
  If you weren't satisfied by my brief citation earlier, here are a few more sources.

Live and Breathing. "Black Lillies - Cumberland Land (Live From Rhythm and Blooms 2011." *YouTube*. Last Modified December 26, 2011. https://www.youtube.com/watch?v=mQrluJPJfzE.
    This modern version by The Black Lillies isn't for purists, but I like it.

Palmer, Hudson Arthur. *Folksongs of Mississippi and the Background*. Chapel Hill: University of North Carolina Press, 1936.

Veal, Jenni Frankenburg. "Music of the Cumberland Mountains." *Nooga.com*. Last Updated March 10, 2013. http://nooga.com/160449/music-of-the-cumberland-mountains/.
    This gives Bobby Fulcher's account in brief of it being from the Avery Trace area. I attended the concert described here.

Wilkes, Lincoln Ellsworth and Carol A. Thilenius. *By an Oregon Pioneer Fireside*. Fairfield, Wash.: Ye Galleon Press, 1995.
    This one relates the song to the much better known pioneer destination of Oregon, although that doesn't fit the rhyme scheme.

Wolf, Charles K. "Old Cumberland Land: The Musical Legacy of the Upper Cumberland." In *Rural Life and Culture in the Upper Cumberland*, edited by Michael E. Birdwell and W. Calvin Dickenson, 274-301. Lexington: University of Kentucky Press, 2004.

On Man of Constant Sorrow:
Schlansky, Evan. "Behind the Song: Man of Constant Sorrow. http://www.americansongwriter.com/2011/06/behind-the-song-man-of-constant-sorrow/. Updated 30 June 2011. Accessed 20 March 2015.

My Source for the Quotation:
Turner, Fredrick Jackson. 1921. The Frontier in American History. New York: Henry Holt and Company.

EPILOGUE: *!

LARRY: "With an asterisk" in sports means an entry in the record books that has some limits that need footnoting. Famously, some athletes have been caught using outlawed drugs to set their records and thus need an asterisk on those records.

If there was a record book for the CT, would Ben and Larry be in it? We hiked the entire trail as it existed at the time. Assuming a CT record book, we'd get an * for skipping the road edge trail section along TN111. Also, Larry was on the drug aspirin for the entire trek. You are not impressed with our record? Oh well.

Morgan Simmons reported in the March 8, 2013 *News Sentinel* that Joanna Swanson and Bart Houck have, since our trek, through-hiked the CT as part of eventually hiking the entire Great Eastern Trail (GET). They road-walked gaps in the trail and thus did it without using a vehicle. In a photograph, it appears they were aided by trekking poles.

The Appalachian Trail does have semi-official records based on self-reporting so the Great Eastern and Cumberland Trails will surely eventually have such records too. I suspect that the transect-rare-plant survey that I did must be one of the longest ever done in a month. Interest for such records is perhaps non-existent.

The title of this chapter originally was just an asterisk, but I have added an exclamation mark meaning "Wow!" for how we feel about our adventure. It counters the negativity of the asterisk.

I am closer to Ben. I am tuned in to enjoy Ben's coming achievements and resolved to be helpful for the struggles.

I am also ready to enjoy the CT's coming achievements. We found little threat to the environment from the CT and great potential for environmental education.

I am a believer in the mental and physical benefits of hiking. Research is starting to show the benefit to people from outdoor time beyond the mere exercise. Most studies compare doing an activity like walking inside and outside.

We cut a few corners. The BLTs cut more.

The results show outside being better for mood, the immune system, blood pressure, etc.

Our trek, instead of being a last hurrah for major hiking for me, now feels like a starting point for many more hiking and nature study projects. I now have much more confidence in my physical capabilities. Astonishingly, my left knee seems to be working perfectly.

BEN: Our trek showed me that I didn't know East Tennessee nearly as well as I had thought. For me, that is the best kind of feeling. I wanted to travel the world in order to feel smaller in comparison to the grand world beyond me. Yet after standing at so many viewpoints seeing distant mountains, rivers, cattle, towns, cliffs, vultures and hawks, I felt tiny rather than small. It is good to feel tiny. It wasn't just big views that made me feel that way. I felt tiny when I was following streams over their every curve. I felt tiny when trying to wash my hands in the powerful torrents of Laurel Falls. I felt tiny when standing back from copperheads and rattlesnakes. Even the strip mined lands made me feel tiny knowing what people could do. I felt especially tiny when I saw the ribbons on that last day, showing us that the trail we hiked wasn't all the trail had to offer. If the Cumberland Trail was a sandbox, then I was tinier than a grain of sand. All this tininess was empowering.

I have a new interest in the small things, the sand. It seemed strange to me at first how my father could so often overlook the big views in favor of tiny plants growing on the sandstone. Yet once I listened to Dad's explanations about those plants, I began to see them differently. I saw them as beautiful living things, striving to survive in every possible fashion. Animals along the trail were similarly diverse and beautiful in their vast variety. I found salamanders, snakes, lizards and frogs of every specialty crawling slithering and hopping over the streams, leaves and rocks. Human history gave me tales of schemers, strugglers, sufferers and achievers, all in my own Tennessee hills.

As Dad and I started the hike, I saw us as a pair of opposites. His fear of heights clashed with my love of them. His devotion to research and practicality seemed to be the opposite of my devotion to mystery and wildness. Our small disagreements over jumping on the Snow Falls trail or how close to the edge one should sit seemed like smaller expressions of big differences in worldview.

By the end of the hike though, I saw more similarities than differences between the two of us. Salamanders, flowers, rivers and towns became more glorious the more I knew about them, not less. Half the fun of mysteries was solving them, and every answer led to even more questions. Dad's 6 AM to 10 PM schedule seemed natural, given the hours of light from the sun. Dad's carefully planned schedules were necessary to allow for the spontaneity of exploration. By the end I felt like a great noticer the way that my Dad was, even if discovering my own lost cell phone probably wasn't as important as finding rare plants.

When I first returned to Dad after my time away from home, I thought of him as someone who had sung silly songs, told fun stories, helped me learn to read and quizzed me on math problems. I hadn't thought of him as someone who had anything left to teach me. By the end of the hike though, I saw him as an explorer and investigator of the world, in the tradition of many great plant explorers like Thomas Walker's friend John Fraser, the devoted amateur John Muir and possibly King Solomon of ancient Jewish fame.

Dad was comfortable with life, yet he never stopped searching and pondering. He smiled when he found a challenge and enjoyed wildly strolling around. He had arrived where he was after a youthful wandering phase much like mine. He has my admiration as well as my love.

CPSIA information can be obtained
at www.ICGtesting.com
Printed in the USA
LVOW04s0240020316
477369LV00002B/4/P